For
Pete's Sake

and mine too!

*To Jim & Betty
in love & in friendship, always
Mary*

Mary Tucciarone

ISBN 978-1-68570-915-0 (paperback)
ISBN 979-8-89345-948-7 (hardcover)
ISBN 978-1-68570-916-7 (digital)

Copyright © 2024 by Mary Tucciarone

All rights reserved. No part of this publication may be reproduced, distributed, or transmitted in any form or by any means, including photocopying, recording, or other electronic or mechanical methods without the prior written permission of the publisher. For permission requests, solicit the publisher via the address below.

Christian Faith Publishing
832 Park Avenue
Meadville, PA 16335
www.christianfaithpublishing.com

Printed in the United States of America

This book was written in God's time, and I dedicate it to my beloved, who unknowingly reintroduced me to God the Father, his Son, and our Holy Spirit.

Let the redeemed of the Lord tell their story.

—Psalm 107:2 NIV

Words do not express thoughts very well. They always become a little different. Immediately they are expressed, a little distorted, a little foolish. And yet it also pleases me and seems right that what is of value and wisdom to one man seems nonsense to another.

—Herman Hesse, *Siddhartha*

ACKNOWLEDGMENTS

Throughout my editing experience, I realized there was an underlying thread in my journals: that it would be published. I believe Pete was the first to verbalize this more than once.

Before I specifically acknowledge and thank those who helped me get my journals to this point, I must sincerely and happily thank my dear family and friends for being patient and compassionate during the two and half years I spent loving, pining, and waiting for Pete to call me. Everyone, I'm sure, learned at least one thing and received at least one benefit from this shared experience.

I was always encouraged over the twenty years to write the book by anyone, stranger or friend, who heard my "in a nutshell" telling of our love story. More than once, it was suggested that it would make a good Hallmark channel movie. To all these people, I am grateful for the nudges I received along the way.

For Pete's Sake

To my children—Angela, Nick, and Matt—your subtle support and sense of humor was and always has been priceless. A mom wink to Angela, always pleasant, always multitasking with kindness and tenacity in the areas of love and tech support. You, your dear spouses—John, Laura, and Sara—and your children are the greatest of my gifts abiding in the deepest part of my soul.

To Gina C., you became my first real fan after I gave you a sneak peak of my manuscript. Your positive feedback was quite the catalyst.

To Annette Januzzi Wick with gratitude for your expertise, insight, and encouragement. *Grazie mille.*

To three dear ladies—my sister Sue, my cousin Julimarie, and my forever friend Kim—who were always a phone call away to listen and bear with me as I reached out for their reactions and honest responses over the years.

To Wendy Meyer, my publication specialist from Christian Faith Publishing, you showed up late in the game but became invaluable, guiding me through this "I'm an author" process. Your knowledge, patience, and sweet personality took the daunting out of my emotions as I ventured into new waters.

My dear readers,

Throughout my journals, I have cited an array of authors from various centuries, backgrounds, and religions that made an impression on my days and my heart. They, like us, have their own story.

My "soundtrack," randomly put together over the two and half years, is listed at the end of this book. It was amazing to me, the number of songs. From personal experience, if you feel like dancing, then dance!

The realization that twenty-six letters create thousand-page dictionaries is as epic as the basic seven notes of music creating melodies over the centuries.

My publishers follow the *Chicago Manual of Style* using lowercase pronouns referring to God or Jesus except in direct quotations from the Bible. Out of appreciation to Christian Faith Publishing, I respect their input and editing skills.

You are blessed.

PS. Pete always called me Maria. He said that's how "Mary" sounds with his Italian accent.

And that is Pete, in a nutshell.

Monday, January 09, 2006

I begin to "save" my journals, our love story, to disc.

I sit in our family room while my beloved is at work. He has started the 4:00–12:00 p.m. shift. My new home is with him as you will read in my words, words inspired by my love for one man that becomes love for one God, inspired by his relentless spirit.

January 8, 2002

Who is this man?

This man that I shared not even one full dance with one Saturday night—between the sound of rock 'n' roll—his hand that felt so good on my waist, and his other hand that felt so good holding mine.

The band finishes. The vagueness of meeting two of his Italian friends; we walk and talk into the cold night air.

Who is this man that puts his jacket over my shoulders? Does he know how much it means to me? Would it make a difference?

Who is this man that I easily part my lips for as he kisses me goodnight?

And, *yes*, he calls and leaves me a message. I will call him back.

Who is this man whose beautifully accented voice melts me every time he says "Marie," "Maria," "Mary"?

Who is this man that makes all my thoughts go back to and linger on him/us?

Who is this man that has undoubtedly made all my music peak with passion since that first phone call?

Who is this man that makes my heart beat faster and my breaths deeper with each word and thought?

Who is this man that makes me crave to know him better, crave to be near him, crave to touch him, crave to feel his touch?

Who is this man that asks me how my day was, asks if I slept well, and tells me to take care of myself when we say goodbye?

Who is this man that wakes me up very early in the morning without even picking up the phone?

Who is this man that told me today that I'm the one for him, and I believe him?

Who is this man that, for the past two days, has brought tears to my eyes, tears of which I cannot begin to explain, not even to myself?

This man is Pete—Peter.

The man whose phone calls I desire and look forward to every day.

I have searched my heart. It's forty-seven years old, and it has never felt like this.

Who is this man that I have shared thirty physical minutes and wonderful phone minutes with that makes me feel this way?

We need to be together. I'm sure this is mutual. I know this is mutual.

Who is this man I miss every day we are apart, when we've been together but once?

Who is this man that calls to tell me goodnight, then sleep eludes me? Sweet dreams do come until he awakens me again, and I continue my dreams into the wee hours with eyes wide open!

"Love Like You've Never Been Hurt"

Who is this man that has taken the "alone" out of my life?

How would he react? And what would his words be if he read these words? Could I handle his reaction?

Who is this man that I go out and buy new pillows for? He likes them fluffy!

I will meet him again soon! I am not afraid, somewhat nervous, and very anxious, plus incredibly happy!

Is this man for real? Will he be as sweet and kind and gentle and funny and sexy as he is on the phone with me? Will he continue to take my breath away? Or is he a figment of my heart?

and mine too!

Pete is real! All those beautiful characteristics of the man at the other end of the phone are now manifested in this big, strong man with those incredible blue eyes! Yes, he continues to take my breath away!

We dance. There are no hesitations.

It's true what they say about Italians and food—it is life, it is art. Fruit is sweeter now. Cheese is stronger now. And a dunked cookie is warm and soft and creamy now!

We shared a lot in twenty-one hours, and we shared it so well; even our hurts and pains and sadness—mine evidenced with tears. Pete's unspoken words are written on his face and in those beautiful eyes.

This is a good thing. We will take care of each other. I know why, but how? And when?

Who is this man that in just two meetings, sixteen days, and as many phone calls has me writing such words to paper? Words I didn't know were possible at this uncertain stage of my life?

Our late-night conversations are the best part of my day. The rest of my day is the "need to dos." The end of my day is mine and Pete's.

We shared a cup of tea and fudge-striped cookies in each other's kitchens. I sit at my table, the tea is hot, the lights are low, and I catch my reflection in the window and I like what I see, like how I feel.

Who is this man that has "always doing something" me sitting down to write, sitting down to "tea," sitting down to think and reflect and wonder?

Who is this man that is so very close, yet far away? Do we have to be apart for weeks? I miss him. He touches me over the phone (so very well), but I want more. Does Pete?

Who is this man that has me telling a local guy he doesn't need to call anymore?

Who is this man that I invited to come here and run my business?

Each day is good. Each day, I count my blessings. Peter has been added to my list. Amen.

This man is coming to town to be with me. I try not to make it look like I fussed too much.

I want him to feel welcome and comfortable. I want him to come back to me!

Who is this man that warms my home and my heart when he walks through the door on a late rainy night?

He's gentle and kind and playful and romantic. Everything is effortless, a kind of magnetism—it's powerful. Does this man have any idea how he makes me feel?

He serenades me in Italian with his head on my shoulder! I understand the words *evening, days, stars,* and *moon.* All the other words I don't understand are perfect!

Can people really find the person of their dreams? My dreams are blessed with the reality of Peter! Tender was the night!

I anticipate his phone calls—does he picture me on my cloud?

Who is this man with that voice that comforts and relaxes me at all the right times? That voice so sexy, so soft, so strong, so effective and intoxicating that I melt like marshmallows floating in a cup of hot cocoa, sweet and warm.

We shared feelings and emotions last night. Heartfelt words started to replace my safe phrase "I can't put my finger on it." I didn't struggle to find the words. I knew what they were. I struggled to give them a voice.

Who is this man whose own words made my words easier to speak? We seem to be on the same unwritten page. It feels like we are on this same page. I like it here.

I try not to get too many pages ahead of Peter. It would be too scary. I could get lost or lose him.

I did it. I shared some of these words with this man. The words of our first encounter. Is it safe to wear my heart on my sleeve?

Did I mention this man makes me laugh?

I almost said it tonight.

Who is this man that energizes, enlivens, and awakens me after my sixteen-hour days? How does he? And why does he do it? I think I know the answers.

It's been one week since Pete came for his first visit, and it seems like forever ago. Will there be a forever? There is so much to say, so much to do!

and mine too!

Who is this man that brought out new emotions in me today?

A sadness, an ache that we haven't been able to get together. The 130 miles between us does not keep us from getting closer to each other every day!

I long to touch his face, kiss his mouth, then rest in his arms.

Why must life get in the way of living?

Where is this man taking me?

We say goodnight. It is 3:00 a.m. I wake up. It is 4:00 a.m. The spider has not moved on my ceiling for two hours—it's 6:00 a.m. I have been lost in thought, in dreams, and in wonder. I have contemplated, I have questioned, and I have answered. I have tossed and turned and smiled and cried. I have not slept.

Our lives have become a part of each other's hearts, and I am consumed. Our lives as they are now must be lived across state lines. Time will take care of this—*I am sure of this!* All good things come from God.

Does this man believe that we are good, wonderful, perfect for each other?

Peter and I agree good things come to those who wait. Tonight, it went from "Take care of yourself" to "Take care of yourself for me."

P.S. Remember, God's time is different than ours.

It's 6:45 a.m.

Two less lonely people in the world and it's going to be fine.
Out of all the people in the world I'm so glad that you are mine.
In a world where everything was wrong,
something finally went right.
Now there's two less lonely people in the world tonight.

—*Two Less Lonely People in the World,* Air Supply,
Playlist: The Very Best of Air Supply

Thanks to page 76 of *Secrets of the Vine* (Bruce Wilkinson), I feel an abundance taking root and eagerly anticipate a sweet harvest to share and with each year, renewed strength and beauty and bounty because there will be no neglect!

Where is this man? I lie alone and create his image on the empty fluffy pillows next to me. With my finger, I can outline his silhouette from where he rests his head over his broad shoulders down his arm…over his hip…onto his thigh where I choose to lay my hand tonight as once again, I attempt to sleep.

Abundance!

Who is this man that makes the sunshine brighter? So bright! I pick up the phone to hear his voice: "Babe, it's so good to hear your voice." Wow!

His voice lifts me, yet his voice is sad. Then I hear frustration. If only I could ease his burden.

Today, he spoke such words as, "Leave our relationship as it is until we are both divorced. Talk maybe two or three times a week. Nothing sexual until both divorces are final."

My eyes shut, my heart sank, my stomach knotted. I found a place to sit and hoped my voice would not betray the tears I was fighting back.

We need the goodness of our relationship to balance out the "badness" of unfinished business with our marriages that have ended.

Does this man truly mean what he says? Is it an emotional response to his past few days?

I totally respect Peter's "nothing sexual" comment. I would never want him to do anything that he wasn't "right" about. Nobody needs any more regrets.

Please don't take these beautiful feelings that we have so effortlessly nurtured in such a short period of time and put them on the shelf or in a box.

What you and I share is alive and good. I want us to keep it in the light to blossom and grow to proportions we both thought were out of reach and let us cast a huge shadow over the badness and sadness we will never experience again.

Who is this man that says, "You know my heart, Marie." Was I being God's messenger today when I told him of asking for blessings (Jabez) that God has for him or praying for needed strength? Peter responds with he doesn't know how to pray. I reply he does because God knows what's in his heart, and my love responds, "You know my heart, Maria."

I am at a loss for words. I am overwhelmed. I pray for this man.

Does this man know how much he consumes and knows my heart? Dare I tell him? Or does he already know?

What a week. Will I lose my house? Am I losing this man? I've lost two cars. I'm going to Pittsburgh. My Nicky says to come up since so many up there love me. By name, he says himself, Angela and Laura and John and Father Ray and Peter. It is the answer I needed. I pack.

Friday and Saturday night, Peter and I are together. Our togetherness is blessed with mutual goodness, kindness, unselfishness, gentleness, passion, respect, and fun. I'm trying to choose the right words.

Who is this man that is so much to me and now my knight in shining armor (like "amore'-cool")? A no-show taxi ride has turned my mundane Monday morning into an unplanned wonderful start to my week and hopefully Peter's too! The coffee, the muffin, the passion, the market, the strolling, the sunshine-filled air, the hand-holding and all those sweet tender kisses at the bus station.

Did I mention that this man wondered why I would hide my eyes from his behind my sunglasses? Wow!

Who is this man? Is he mine?

Of course, he calls to see if I got home okay and to asks me how I felt about our public display of affection, how others saw it. I just know if I saw a middle-ageish couple sharing kisses and affections as Peter and I did, I would feel that there is hope for happiness for everyone and how sweet it is.

We choose our words carefully. It's almost like these special words are delicate pieces of a puzzle we are putting together, together. We handle them carefully, gently putting them before us, hoping for the perfect interlocking fit, hoping the finished product is the same "big picture." Will it be flawless? No, but it will be big, bright, colorful, full of life, and hopefully never completed.

Should I list some of these words? Not tonight.

Who is this man that says that he will take care of me? And I believe him. He knows I can take care of him, but does he know how much I want to? Does he know I'd effortlessly do it with my whole heart and soul? This care-giving sounds so gentle to me and makes me happy.

Why does this man bring up infatuation again? When I met Peter in the beginning, it was infatuation. How could it not be when I felt like I met the man of my dreams, a gentleman with a gentle touch, sexy eyes and mouth, a strong tender voice with that wonderful Italian accent?

I think infatuation is almost needed, like part of a good foundation.

How does he perceive me now? Still an infatuation?

This writing has made me realize I am still infatuated with Peter. I think that's a good thing, and I hope there will always be a part of my heart that stays infatuated with him and him with me, an infatuation that we will always want to know more about each other, inside and out, through the years.

Yes, infatuation is a good, living, and fresh thing.

Who is this man that continues to infatuate me as he takes my heart deeper into his? Does he know how much of my heart I have opened up to him?

My days and nights are busy and productive and tiring, and they need to be this way—for a while, I hope.

But my after-hours belong to Peter. I need more sleep, yet his voice invigorates me, and I want more:

- more of his voice.
- more of his words.
- more of his laughter.
- more of his wisdom.
- more of his questions.
- more of his teasing.

and mine too!

- more of his sweet kisses goodnight.

And when we get together, I want:

- more of his smile.
- more of his shining blue eyes.
- more of his touch.
- more of his lips.
- more of his skin.
- more of his voice, words, and laughter.
- more of what he is feeling.
- more of who he is.

Yes, this sounds selfish. I want to share:

- morning coffee with Peter and kisses.
- trips to the grocery store.
- being in the kitchen with him.
- meals and desserts with him.
- a place on the couch with him.
- TV, movies, and music with him.
- putzing around the yard with him.

I want to share:

- long, hot showers with this man.
- soft, cool sheets and fluffy pillows.

I want to share:

- all the good with the bad.
- our hearts and keep no secrets.
- wherever his footsteps take him.
- and even the air we breathe.

I want Peter to teach me. And this dear heart, is more than infatuation! A ten-year romance and one hopeless romantic:

- me, loving the way I feel now.
- me, knowing there is so much more to share and do and grow.
- me, hoping Peter feels half of what I am feeling.
- me, hoping that I make him happy and content and hopeful.

Enough for now. It's even getting "heavy duty" for me.
I miss you, love!
This man and I spoke of truly, us taking care of each other, and I believe it!
Where is this man? We talked more than forty-eight hours ago. Is he okay? Is he mad at me? Does he miss me as much as I miss him? Can he?

Hello, paper, it's been over two weeks with one week being in Phoenix.

Why have I not written, even though my thoughts and words go on? Is it because I don't feel the words will be as upbeat and wonderful and happy as all the previous pages?

It's not over, it's not negative, it's just not time. For what? I am not even sure.

Lots of changes are on the horizon, and I know that it is time, and good things take time.

Who is this man that I want to be there for when he needs me, when he wants me? Do my words push him away? This is not their intention. These words are my feelings, and it is my way to express them.

and mine too!

This man is facing changes too. One is his health. Will he let himself need me? Need me as much as possible, considering the miles?

Why do I see Peter having the same health picture as Chuck and not feel it would be a burden?

Why do I "fight off" local attention and temptation for this man? For this man has already touched my heart (the one that is on my sleeve). Does he know it? Did he mean to?

I must move. It will be okay. Scary, exciting, scary. Yet okay (vine-keeper).

Can we be each other's "silver lining?"

This man said, "Yes, but not yet."

Why will I wait?

Does this man know how wise he is?

Oh, sure, I read him inspirational words from this book and that book, and I know he listens and understands. But does he know I absorb every word he says? That his words have:

- taught me,
- comforted me,
- guided me,
- inspired me,
- exhilarated me,
- challenged me?

Have I been sent to Peter as our Lord's messenger? To touch his life? To get him to think? To have him look into his own heart?

Today, he called me "preacher." No, thank you, I'll be teacher "because teachers interact with their students" and, in turn, learn from them.

Peter had a heart catheterization today, and each time, I thought about him (ha-ha), I pressed my cheek next to his, in my heart! It's so hard for me not to pick up the phone to call him to see how he is. I want him to see that I am patient and caring, not nagging.

And when *he* called me...he sounded great. They cleared the blockage. Does this man know I would take care of him no matter what? That I would drive to him? Stay with him? Take whatever time off I needed to for as long as he needs me?

In our relationship, we have shared "inspirational" stuff, and it feels like our phone-line togetherness is becoming a religious experience.

This man is like God (in a loose sense).

- We talk almost every day.
- I know he listens to my words.
- He responds to my words.
- He makes me think.
- He gives me hope.
- He has strengthened my faith.

And what of love and need?
Yet, *I do not get to see him*, but he's always here.
I'm writing on a legal-size pad now. What does this mean?

He doesn't know if he can see me next weekend and that someday, he will explain. I'm not stupid, though he's been back together with someone he was "broken up" with when we met. "Back together," "broke up"—such teenage-like words.

I guess I can say I'm not surprised, and it's not really any of my business since we both have separate lives in separate states. But what of all we shared since we met (two and a half months)? How does it compare with his other relationship?

I cry because:
Am I mad? No, who should I be mad at?
Am I sad? About what? Just about how we don't get to see each other, and that was known before this became known.
Am I hurt? No because Peter was honest. Should he have told me sooner? I don't know.
Am I anxious and frustrated? Of course. Would me being there make the difference?
Do I feel threatened? Not really. Why not? I'm not sure, but let me try to explain.

and mine too!

Why I am not threatened?

> I know who I am.
> I know how I feel.
> I know I can make a difference.
> I know what I want.
> I know what I can live without.
> I know what I am capable of doing and doing it well.
> I know my faith is stronger than ever.

I know my heart and I know I will always follow it.

Because Peter told me I have part of his heart, is it enough? Only he knows.

Will he follow his heart? Only he knows.

Is he strong enough to follow his heart? I hope so.

And this is all the hope I need. I must be true to myself.

He said I must "decide," "choose"—I have. It was a no-brainer.

He asks why I don't "go out" or if I do, "did I meet anybody?" Why does he ask? Will that make it easier for him (less guilt, if any)?

I don't need to or want to meet anybody now. It's not important. He already has that much of me.

Maybe if he hadn't taken that much of my heart, I wouldn't be feeling this way. And what way is that? I can't put my finger on it.

I will not play games

Life is fragile enough.

Life is too short.

So Peter says we can get together Sunday before he goes to work. Why just then? What's he afraid of? Her reaction or her questions? Does he see that as her control?

I sure as hell don't want to pressure him. Our growing relationship has been good and effortless and shared, and I don't want to compromise it by "pushing" him. I don't want to push him away.

So what to do?

- Wait here quietly till he/she/they make that same mistake that "broke them up" before again?
- Not see him until I don't have to share him?
- See him, be with him, and be thankful for this small amount of time we have together? This would not be time for me to win him over because *I will not play games*. It's all about the heart.

Peter said he could call off work Sunday night. This is his call, not mine. Should he do it to make me happy? No, I want him to do it for us—just plain us.

What part of you will I get on Sunday? The leftover part or the part of you that has been touched by me like no one else has?

Mary: *I want to be different from all the rest.*
Peter: *You already are.*

Is this enough to keep my hopes afloat? Yes!
Is this what Peter wants? Is he patient enough? Or will he settle for the "instant gratification" that's in Pittsburgh?

Peter: *We can be friends, stay in touch, and see what happens.*
Mary (thinking): *I have plenty of friends I stay in touch with, thank you. You're already more than a friend, and you know it. You mean, stay in touch, see me when I come to Pittsburgh, and if it fits your schedule, we can have sex? I don't think so, especially since I only know how to make love to you.*

"See what happens."

and mine too!

Okay. I wish I could be selfish sometimes.

He talked of how we met, how we first talked on the phone and sincerely seems amazed how it happened. We both agree it has been special, different, fun, exciting, new, challenging, honest, real, and effortless from the first moment.

What a blessed package deal. How often does this happen in a person's lifetime? Let alone two people's lifetimes?

He knows I can, will, and want to take care of him. He knows all I want is for him to be happy. He knows I will put him on a pedestal (even though he is already there). Is this enough for him? Does he feel he deserves it? I know he does! And this is all I ask from him, only the pedestal doesn't have to be big.

Who is this man that I think is worth waiting for? Does he know he's made such a difference in my life? That because of him, all the gloom and doom of my married and home life that has come down around me has been made so much more tolerable, just because of the ring on my telephone and his voice and words that cross the miles?

If this man reads these words, would he feel a sense of too much responsibility?

In the book *The Rhythm of Life*, Matthew Kelly said to write down "what you want from life." I wrote mine on the inside cover—a list of nine things (except the "travel").

And none of them are physically "touchable," but they are priceless and shareable.

All these things connect with Peter. Is it asking too much? Does he see I am not a gold-digger? That we were "brought" together for more than "phone friends?" And that time will supply the other pieces to our puzzle?

Why has this man not asked about these words in so long?
Peter is a man of his word.
Who is this man that has made such a difference in my life?
My cup runneth over.
My heart is so full.
I can love again.

For Pete's Sake

Yet this love is:

a new love
an incomparable love
a mature love
a love that makes me cry tears,
and these tears taste different, there is a new sweetness,
these tears fall from my eyes so gently as my heart beats with
contentment, excitement, and anticipation
and my breath is taken away, again and again.

I sit in my chair and think and pray for so long. Sometimes I try to write my words down like this.

I look down to my bed and hope my Peter is sleeping well and sound. It seems he lost sleep over me. We are overwhelmed.

Hours go by.

"I love you, Peter"

Dare I speak these words to his face? To his eyes? To his lips? To his ears?

Dare I speak these words to his heart?

What will my Peter say?

There will be no turning back. I do not want to go back. I will take my chances.

Does this landscaper and gardener know what he has planted? Does he know how he nurtures this every day? Does he know how his sunshine keeps this blossom warm? And how his kisses, and her tears keep the blossom moist? Does he see how it has grown? Does he close his eyes and feel it grow?

How big will this blossom grow?

If you ask the blossom, she would say, "Bigger than she ever thought possible."

This touch of her gardener makes her feel:

- new and young and beautiful;

and mine too!

- and that all her petals burst with every color in the spectrum, every deep intense jewel tone, every soft and delicate pastel;
- her stem is strong and sturdy and with her many petals that reach out to embrace her gardener, an embrace to keep him warm, a soft place to find comfort and rest, and a peace to last a lifetime;
- her roots go deep, so deep. Her gardener has a special touch to create such a life in such a short period of time.

This blossom wants to keep her gardener happy and proud and please him through every season, a perennial whose colors will never fade even on the cold and gloomiest of days. She will never wither nor droop nor shed a petal as long as they share this new garden, and he tends to her daily.

All she will need is his touch, his smile, the sound of his voice, and a little music. And she will bloom happily ever after (and be true to me).

Over the past couple of years, I wondered why God would keep me from giving. I am his child, and he knows me. There's so much I have and want to give:

- my time
- my talents
- my patience
- my words
- my understanding
- my heart
- my touch
- my passions for life and all it has to give.

Sure, I lovingly gave this to my Angela, my Nick, and my Matt. I gave it to my family and friends, but why couldn't I give it to someone who truly needed and wanted it? I knew there was more. I felt these gifts God had given me were being wasted over time.

Then God sent me Peter. Now it's time.

I do not cry because I miss him. I do not cry because we cannot be together yet. Yet I cry. Do I deserve such fulfillment? For I feel so full and knowing there is so much more for us. How powerful is that?

We will complete each other every day for as long as forever will be.

Father Ray called it *"anam cara."* He saw it in me when I spoke of Peter. It means "soul friend" and if you have that, that's all you need. The other stuff (romance, sex, dancing, etc.) are all the wonderful extra layers that are like the icing on the cake—the "anam cara" is forever.

Ray is going to give me a book on it. It's about me and Pete, and he's sure Pete will let me read it to him. As my cheek touches his. This is my daily visual.

He spoke of ending the relationship with the lady this weekend. Did he? How could he not? And did I hear him say we would be able to see each other every weekend? Be still, my heart.

Who is this man that has me looking beyond the scenery of this bus ride home? I take a break from this gazing to write.

What does he see in me? And I in him?

Do we see each other's vulnerability? My heart speaks. I am an open book, and Peter reads me so well.

I do not want to take away his freedom. I want to be a part of it. Why would anyone take away something from someone they care about?

He spoke of this lady friend for a short while and then wondered why he was telling me about it. I reminded him we were friends. He nodded.

Friends. Peter referred to us as friends from the beginning, and this I found puzzling, but not anymore.

I return from gazing out the window again. It's a beautiful day…blue sky…new daybreak lighting the tops of trees…grass growing greener…a calm river, and occasionally a tree with white blossoms

and mine too!

standing by itself among the leafless trees. The blossoms white with brightness against the drab trees it is surrounded by. The blossoms looking soft and delicate compared to the harshness of the forest around it.

Are Peter and I this blossom tree in each other's lives? standing out from all the rest in each other's eyes? In each other's hearts?

Do I write a fairy tale with a happily ever after?

Do I write a love story that will never grow old?

Do I write an autobiography which is fact, but it might be read as fiction since it seems too good to be true?

I almost don't want this bus ride to end. I have peace and solitude right now, and I think of Peter.

I think of him so much that I hope God sees it as part of my praying since I know my prayer time has changed.

Good things come from God. This is good, and I am thankful. I pray others see this God-given newness in me and see me as an instrument of His peace, not as a self-serving braggart.

Good things are meant to be shared:

- Laughter.
- Grace.
- Smiles.
- Touches.
- Love.
- Deepest thought.

Not-so-good things are meant to be shared with those who truly care about us and unconditionally love us:

- tears
- sad times
- heartache
- deepest thought
- fears

Nobody has all the answers, but sharing is a good thing.

His touch soothes me.
His embrace exhilarates me.
His kiss makes me hunger for more.
His eyes tease and hold me.
His laughter is contagious.
His voice warms and comforts me.
His touch makes me crazy—all his touches (touch is good, and this is why I miss him):

- the touch of his hand.
- the touch of his lips.
- the touch of his eyes and his voice.

I try to read his eyes that tease and hold me, and I can't put my finger on it. This is what is so exciting and curious and fun and fills me with so much anticipation.

Pretty heavy-duty stuff, isn't it?

When we make a difference in someone's life or someone makes a difference in ours, the trickle-down effect is breathtaking.

How many times on all these pages have I mentioned that Peter takes my breath away?

On these pages, he is Peter. In my heart, he is Peter. Do his friends call him Pete? Those who know of me and Peter call him Pete. I believe in the beginning, I called him Pete in this journal, and I've left him messages calling him Pete. But he is Peter, more than just my friend.

Does this man know I love to dance? And that swaying in arms last night was perfect?

Last week, as we kissed in his car, he asked if I liked to have the music on! Obviously, we haven't spent enough time together!

Does this man know I love music?

I have looked at these pages for two days now, not knowing what to write.

and mine too!

He brings up the miles again. I think I'm worth the miles once in a while.

He says he's in a relationship he needs to get out of since she's a boss and pushes him around. Yet he still sees her? What's with that? Is she convenient? Am I convenient?

I can't make him feel; only he can.

I can only hope his feelings for me are the best he can give at this time.

Right now, my feelings are "whatever."

I didn't work the past two nights because of tendonitis in my foot. I don't like being alone!

So, one day, after writing the word *forever*, he calls, and the sound of his voice and the words he speaks make my day again.

Not a waking moment is this man more than a minute away from my thoughts and ever-present in my heart.

What will be the cost of such devotion?

I miss my Peter.

Today, he called. We talked, we loved, and I hope he sleeps well. Me? Once again, I cry—briefly. It's those new tears again. Not tears of sadness, pain, or despair. Tears that I can only label as overwhelming, and they are mine.

How does Peter feel? I think I will "challenge" him to write his words, how many or few as he wants—interesting idea.

With all my talking and reading to him and truthfully answering all his questions, I'm using my heart to speak more than my brain.

I think I am romancing him more than he is me. And as my thoughts continue, Peter is totally romancing me in his way. A way with fewer words, a touchless touch, and his wonderful laugh.

He calls all these pages a love story. Occasionally, I wonder if I am just writing of what I wish was real. But, oh no, it's all real—the talks, the touches, the smiles, the questions, the caring, the laughter and the giggles, the anticipation, the longing, the beating of my heart.

For Pete's Sake

I told Peter if he was in the area to stop by for dinner. He said he'd "think about it," which is a slight change from his usual "I'll try." Why does he hesitate? What makes him hesitate, especially when all else between us says yes?

If you (or me) are not true to yourself, how can we be true to anyone else?

A new feeling—respect. I give you respect.

Happiness, peace, care, comfort, calm.

Don't waste my gifts.

I only know how to love one way—unconditionally.

Does not a *good father* want his children to be happy? Why are so many denied when there is so much goodness out there? Don't let evil (negative) win this one. Let us bring hope to others.

What is this vine-keeper up to?

I can, will, and want to make your home, home again!

Who is this man truly himself around? Me? Who he is around me is the man I have given my heart to.

Mixed messages.

If I have lost him, I guess I never really had him. But I did. He told me so. When I told him he had enough of my heart, his reply was, "And you have enough of mine." I said I wanted to be different from all the rest, and this man replied, "You already are."

So? It's been five days, my heart.

I pray. I need direct answers. Am I so dense and oblivious? I need patience, and again, I read the chapter in the book, *On Caring* by Milton Mayeroff, and I wait as my heart wonders, as my heart aches, as my heart listens, as my heart cries. For what? I do not know. It is a heart full of love and so easy to be given. Surely, God would not deny a child of His to give or receive love so unconditionally.

Is it meant for this man that swept me off my feet four months ago?

How could anybody else come along and bring out in me all that Peter did? Look how my heart has spoken on these pages.

and mine too!

There is a peace we share. This is something I just realized—peace; another gift in our relationship. Does he feel it too? Yes, he does!

I miss him. Does he miss me?

Can he deny all he said to me?

Where is he, besides in my heart?

Wherever he is his business, but I want him to be thinking of me, of us, looking at real needs, the big picture. and to forego instant gratification.

Four months ago, I told people I met the man of my dreams, and I didn't know if he was the one for me, but he was the man of my dreams.

Is he the one for me? Am I the one for him? My heart says *yes!* Right or wrong, do I follow my heart? *Yes!*

I'm tired now.

Clippings from magazines were among this part of my journal:

a. A horoscope for Aries: Around the twenty-sixth, a loved one is going to try your patience and tempt your temper to blow, sending you on a Twinkie binge. Get a hold of yourself, because the air will not clear until the first, and you will regret harsh words and rash decisions. Fortunately, a supportive lover will come to your rescue and help you understand the meaning of unconditional love.

b. A horoscope for Aries for the week of April 15, 2002: Your restless spirit is often the cause of your problems, but this week, the stars are lending you a little common sense. When a sensitive personal or family situation reaches a stressful point around the eighteenth, your approach and attitude will be a major factor in determining the outcome. The Leo moon

on the twentieth urges you to express your truest feelings: make a serious commitment that will change your life.
c. And a title from an advertisement that says "Dreaming of Italy."

Okay, here it goes:

On a Tuesday, Peter calls after working a double shift, and we're having a sweet visit over the phone. He tells me he's cold (even with two blankets). My response is, "I should be there."

His is, "Yes, you should."

We warm each other with our words, the sound of each other's voice, our mutual feelings, and making love. Yes, my Peter called it making love. Does he realize what he has said? I tell my love to sleep well, and he tells me not to work too hard, and I can't wait for the phone to ring.

On Wednesday, he calls. He's just waking up as I'm falling asleep (trying to nap in between jobs). He's getting out of bed. I want to go to bed, and we laugh. We talk. Out of nowhere, he says, "I'm tired. I have to get some sleep."

Mary: I thought you said you just woke up?

Peter: I'm tired. I have to go. Bye.

What was that all about? She stopped over, no doubt.

This bothers me, obviously, as I work. I call him (Good idea? I'm not sure.). I got a quick apology when I asked him to be honest and asked him to call before he left for work if he had time—another conversation cut short.

He calls back but must leave for work—another conversation cut short.

Friday night, "bella luna." I dare to call him to share it with him. He has company. He'll call me back, but not tonight.

May 6, 2002

He asks what's for dinner—I had soup—he said that sounds like a good idea—simple pleasing conversation.

My life is sweeter when we are together. I know he feels it. Yes, we can make life sweeter, uncomplicated, peaceful, content, love—just the two of us.

Peter, where are you?
Are you OK?
This is not fair—or is it?

Then it's Wednesday again (in the margin *"Being part of his freedom"*). I've been patient and curious. I call. It is Peter, and I get "You've got the wrong number" said to me *twice*.

Why? What? I didn't deserve that, and Peter knows it. What is he afraid of? I'm assuming she was right there. If he's letting go of me, why didn't he do it there for her to hear too? What kind of hold does she have on him? If it's the kind he wants, then it's okay. If it's not the kind he wants, then I hope he has the strength to buck it (in the margin *"Blackmail?!?!"*)

I'm sure it was on the day my Peter was cold. He asked me what I would do to warm him up, and I rattled off a few things like "Take care of him," "Cook for him," "Hold him," "Give him massages," etc. It was after that I finished with I can't afford to give him everything *he wants*, but I could give him everything *"he needs,"* and he responded with, "I know."

So what is all this rejection about?

Have I cried? Of course I have, but they are still the tears of before—not sadness, not madness, no heartbreak. There is confusion and wonder, but somehow nothing negative. My heart beats positive, and patience is a new friend (*Did I mention respect?*).

How could he block out all that we shared? Do I wait? Surely because I follow my heart. Will they part again? I'm sure of it.

Just the two of us. What else will really matter?

Our children have grown up or are growing up, and their lives will be theirs, and we will always be there when they need us, but the rest of the time, just the two of us:

- taking gentle care of each other.
- keeping each other company.
- holding hands.
- lying so close to each other;

through our years, even when our parts aren't working anymore. And I think, *How can he not see it or feel it too?*

Come to me. Do not be afraid. What are you thinking?

Is he forgiven? Of course he is. Does he know?

How could I care so much?

How long do I wait? When I meet others, it will be okay, but for now, I can't get past my Peter? My problem?

I have always prayed "Thy will be done," and now for Peter, I ask God for him, specifically. Do I ask for a miracle?

I find myself literally *talking* one-on-one with my Lord, and he hears me and he answers me—he listens and has responded, "I know, I'm working on it. Of course I want you to be happy. Be patient." He cuts off my questions and lays his hand on my cheek. "I know," he repeats. It seems the "other end" will take some time, but he will take care of me. He knows what's best.

Yes, he will let me love and give and care and share my heart. I will not go to waste.

Is it for Peter?

My heart says, "How could it not be for him?"

This is the first time I remember praying for something so selfish, so specific. I make no deals or promises. I ask for Peter.

Then I fear I could lose him if he doesn't know how I am feeling. But how could he not know? Does he know I am here and it's okay?

Does he know I will wait? Has he heard my words? Will he hear them again in his heart and take a chance and call me so I can tell him again?

and mine too!

My feelings are unconditional. How did this happen?

Is he in love with me? Or is he just infatuated with all I have given him?

Dear Lord, give Peter refuge in my heart. Amen.

Peter, be strong.

Our next togetherness must be in person so I can touch his face and lips and look into his eyes and he into mine so we can see the knowing in them—the knowing so evident behind my tears.

Peter, there will be no more hurting.

To be together so he can feel how my heart beats behind my breasts that he is so fond of. Amazing how I sit and write like this. What does it mean?

Ritorno mi,—cara mia tiamo—(Dean Martin, *The Capitol Years*) written on a 4x6 Post-It Note.

Was it but two weeks ago he asked me to read my words to him?

Why does he need to hear it?

He knows I have more than words to give, so where is he?

I talk of what I can give to him. What will he give to me?

It seems he's given me enough to realize I can love again—unconditionally again.

I'll never believe he used me.

In this absence, he still takes my breath away.

I am *once* again reassured by my Lord that Peter knows. Again, I cry, for I am overwhelmed with such power from him and all the love he has for each of his children. No one is forsaken. Ask, and you shall receive.

Peter and I have been gifted to share a love. My gift has been unwrapping before my eyes.

Oh, of course, this is my gift of grace I was told about in Jabez, and it is beautiful, and it is mine. I must sit down.

Does Peter remember when I read that story to him not so long ago? And about the vine keeper. My Lord says, "yes he does."

I said this relationship was a religious experience pages ago – didn't I?

So, God, let me be His messenger. All I read to my Peter was what he/we needed to hear and share.

In humility, we are made stronger.

We need protection and guidance and unconditional love and patience. And all we need do is ask.

My Lord, I will not let you down, for you have forgiven me in all my weaknesses. Weaknesses from I which I have learned to become who I am this day and there is no turning back.

Have I made you proud today? You nod and let me rest on your chest, for I am drained knowing a new strength stirs within. Look out.

>A song plays:
>*Just one smile the pain's forgiven*
>*Just one kiss the hurts all gone*
>*Just one smile to make life worth living*
>*A little dream to build my world upon*

>I want to be his angel.
>Let me be his angel.
>"Yes," my Lord said, "soon."
>(*Do not exist with her when you can live with me.*)

Peter, we have our own miracles, a gift, just for us—no one else. We are hand-picked for each other by the Master Gardener. Together we will grow in His light.

Plus, we'll have fun!

>*May 11, 2002*

>*My dear Peter,*

>>*You took me there this morning (more than once). How do you do that? I left my tears on your*

pillow. Did you feel them? Did you taste them? Somehow, I know you felt me this morning too. It was no one else but me for only you and I together can feel this way.

Let down all your defenses my darling. I know this will take time, for they have been up for so long.

Let them down, for there will be no more hurting and pain. There will be no more doubting and no more games to play. I want you for who you are, and all you will be when we are one. How wonderful and exciting is that? All that newness to discover. You are not old. This is what you have always wanted, but you weren't sure it existed till now. That goes for me too! I had no idea such immense and deep sensations were possible, but all things are possible with God, and there is no denying that God is not part of our relationship.

Our togetherness has been blessed from the night we met.

It will all be so simple and evident, just think about it.

That's all for now. Loving you.

Maria

Written on a three-by-three Post-It Note:
You're my diamond in the rough.

And now my ever-present God has connected me with Peter. When my heart speaks, Peter's heart listens. When my heart questions, Peter's heart answers. When I share this with him, will he be able to validate this "correspondence"?

For example, Peter's heart: "I'm sorry."

My heart: "You've already been forgiven."

And I cry those overwhelming tears again, for is this not the dialogue that God has with each one of us?

With God so evidently involved in this relationship, how can this be the words of a dreamer?

Andrea asks, "How's my new relationship?

My response: "Alive, interesting, exciting, hopeful, promising."

I just realized I'm not looking for a commitment with Peter. I need not ask for one.

And my heart says we are wasting valuable time.

And my God answers we will have lots of time.

I continue reading *On Caring* by Milton Mayeroff, and I'm pretty good at it. There's much I will share of it with Peter since we will have plenty of time.

I am definitely in my life and expose myself and commit myself with my spoken and written words.

"I Believe You"

I believe you
When you say that you will reach into the sky
And steal a star so you can put it on my finger
I believe you
Baby, I believe you
I believe you
When you say that every time that we make love
Will be the first time that we've made love and every act of love
Will please you
Baby, I believe you
Blind faith makes me follow you
I'd live in a cave if you wanted to
Just ask me and I'll marry you

and mine too!

You don't have to sell me
'Cause you overwhelm me
I've made up my mind
For a lifetime
I believe you
When you swear your love will keep on
growing strong
And that forever isn't long enough to love me
Like you need to
Baby, I believe you
Baby, I believe you
Honey, I love you
Blind faith makes me follow you
I'd live in a cave if you wanted to
Just ask me and I'll marry you
You don't have to sell me
'Cause you overwhelm me
I've made up my mind
For a lifetime
I believe you
When you say you'll fill my body with your
soul
And love will grow into a freckled little girl
Who looks like we do
Baby, I believe you
Baby, I believe you
Honey, I love you

—The Carpenters, *Singles: 1969–1981*

> Anticipation
> and when we are together, forever will not be long enough
> "I've made up my mind for a lifetime…"

I wish I could explain how my heart physically reacts to all this that has been happening. My bodily heart beats deeper and louder. I actually feel it inside me. My breaths become short and shallow. I swallow harder, and when my eyes water, my mouth becomes dry (*a sense of tightening*).

What does it all mean?

I wonder (wonderful), where are you, my love?

Again, I ask myself,

Who is this man?

Is he my Peter?

"Yes, he is your Peter," my Lord and my God answers.

And I cry those overwhelming tears again.

Let us complete each other, complete each other into a beautiful oneness. This is not a job. It will happen effortlessly in our togetherness. As effortlessly as the beginning of our relationship, the effortlessness we talked about.

There may be others who can give him anything he wants, but I can give and promise to give all that is me (the open book) unconditionally. And he knows this. No deals, no exceptions, no what-ifs—just plain all of me.

I made one promise in my life twenty-five years ago, and Chuck wouldn't let me keep this promise.

Now here I find myself ready to make a new promise without having to say "I do" to Peter, whose voice I have not heard in over two weeks, and I miss him so.

> Be still my heart
> Yes, Peter, I fell in love with you
> I love you
> I am not alone
> I have not been abandoned.

and mine too!

> I become totally blown away when all that I share with
> Peter on these pages are so parallel with God
> *Wow!*
> My heart, my breaths, my tears
> And then we live, and nothing else matters

It's not that nothing else will matter, but as long as we're together, we can handle anything, face it, and do the best we can.

A dream, come true? Too good to be true?

True and good.

And so the sun is out today. It's been four days of clouds.

I want to share all the sunshine days with Peter, for they are invigorating and full of promise.

And I realize on cloudy, cold days, I want to be with him, sharing the blankets and being the warmth for each other and the brightness in each other's eyes.

I've felt some sadness, but only when I'm tired. It's nice to know it's just a passing thing.

As unconditionally as I love my Peter, so will I unconditionally accept his love.

I've just read some of the last few pages. My heart is doing that thing again. I lay my hand on the paper, run my fingers over it, and the path of the ink is so very sacred. Amen.

I pray my prayer every day, and I pray that my Peter is well.

I so need to hear his incredible laughter.

Today, I will plant my flowers!

> I see the Lord before me at all times. He is
> near me, and I will not be troubled. And so I am
> filled with gladness, and my world is full of joy.
> *And I, who am mortal, will rest assured in hope,*

> *because you will not abandon me.* (Acts 2:25–27 GNT; emphasis added)
>
> *(Me + God + Peter. This is a good thing.)*
>
> You have shown me the paths that lead to life,
> and your presence will fill me with joy.
>
> —Acts 2:28 GNT

Call me, honey, there is so much to share!
Peter? Are you ready to be overwhelmed?
"I'm getting there," he answers me again.

Yesterday morning, we went there, and neither one of us was asleep. He will remember this when we talk and share. And in each other's presence, we will be incredible.

End of May-ish.

And, today, I had another God and awe-inspiring dialogue, the kind that comes with tears. So many of my thoughts are of Peter and me and us. I know this sounds selfish, but when my feelings can be paralleled with God feelings, how wonderful is that? And it becomes reflected in my daily life, and that's what we're supposed to do: reflect God's image!

I can do this because Peter is a part of my life, and the awesome moment came today when I realized he is my taste and touch of heaven, and through us, his holy aura will reflect, bounce, and settle around all who share our Earth space! Get it?

Today: the "pedestal" revelation.

Peter said a while back, actually, when we first talked of his friend in Pittsburgh, about me being different from all the rest. "You will put me on a pedestal," he said.

God love: earthly love—my Peter.

God is always on a pedestal.

And then there is this *longing,* another parallel revelation.

and mine too!

And then there is the being "always prepared for his coming" parallel revelation.

When will this longing be fulfilled? It is God's will. Is my heart right? When my answer comes, it must be highlighted in bold print. Until then, I wait.

All these thoughts, prayers, songs, etc. and no negative vibes.

My conversations with God and Peter continue and bring me contentment.

June 5, 2002

Today, I am divorced, and I cry over loss and am sad. But I love Chuck no more, and this is sad too.

This too shall pass.

And our home?

The paths have changed, and I anticipate with adamant excitement, curiosity, and love what is ahead.

No regrets.

I am changing.

Serendipity.

For the mouth *(or the pen)* speaks what the heart is full of.

—Luke 6:45 NIV (emphasis is mine)

I am in the advent of my future.

Fruition: when? Why do I continue to ask?

Mid-June

Who is this man that takes my breath away in his absence?

Who is this man that breathes a special sense of life into my days in his absence? The daily thoughts and the conversations I have with Peter in my heart are sweet, fun, and hopeful.

Again, I ask, where is this man? When?

Of course, occasionally, there are shadows of doubt. How could there not be? Yet they pale in comparison to what my heart tells me.

June 17, 2002

Phenomenally overwhelmed. Today, I realized I fell in love with God who manifested himself in the humanness of Peter.

I am so totally humbled.

I am so evidently blessed.

Deserving I must be.

I cry "My God," and oh yes, he is my God.

My weaknesses and my humanness desire the weaknesses and humanness of Peter. And I believe.

The loss of our home seems more apparent today. I don't know how to pray right now.

Oh, yes, of course. "Thy will be done."

Meltdown. I've cried every day for a week, and now add two more days.

OR metamorphose—do all these tears wash away that coating of stuff that stunts my growth?

I choose metamorphosis—changes in me, in turn changing my world around me. I have stronger wings, wings of the Holy Spirit. Dare I learn to soar?

I have time, but impatience pounds as time ticks quietly.

Chuck stopped over to sign a paper. We talked for almost an hour. It wasn't like old times, yet we talked as easily with each other as we always had.

- He's not well. I told him to call if he needed a ride or something.
- I told him how beautiful Angela is and how hurt she is.
- I told him Matt felt abandoned, and he said he felt worse about Matt than anybody else.

and mine too!

- He mentioned one out of five of his kids acknowledged Father's Day and that it was not a good average, but he wasn't writing anybody off.
- "We all make mistakes," I mentioned. Maybe he should own up to his kids. What was his mistake? Leaving? Or how he left?
- I told him my anger was subsiding, but its roots were what he did to our children. I couldn't protect them from this loss; hell, I couldn't even prepare them for it.

How sad. I care. I guess I always will, but I will not dwell on this, and I cry. Sad things always make me cry. The sadness and the caring will find a place in my heart, and there they will stay; but as my heart has learned, it can feel passion, happiness, excitement, and anticipation again, and this is wonderful. My heart knows it can give again. It can feel and give that special love that is between woman and man, not mother and child, not daughter to parent, not sister to sibling, but man to woman and woman to man.

I learned this through Peter and all we shared in such little time. What did he learn? Does he remember saying, "I think we have a chance"? So many questions. Does he remember saying "I think you're the one for me"?

If (when) I share these words with him like I used to, he might wonder (worry) why I wrote of Chuck, but by the middle of this page, he will realize this is still his love story and that he thinks I should publish it.

Is he afraid of being hurt again? Who can blame him? He said is ex-wife hurt him, more than once, and Lena was pushing him away by her actions. I saw the hurt in his eyes, and it was fresh.

The way my heart (still) beats for him, I know I wouldn't, couldn't hurt him. The way my heart beats for him, I would and will protect him from hurt and pain, the kind doctors can't treat.

And I wait—*a domani.*

July has begun.

> You need to be patient in order to do the will
> of God and receive what he promises.
>
> —Hebrews 10:36 GNBUK

Mid-July

Who is this man? And what did he stamp my heart with?

It has left a deep impression, and the ink is so permanent that I cannot deny that it is there. There is no sign of any fading, for *each day*, my thoughts of Peter persevere and intensify his signature on my heart. And my heart grows.

Once again, I am profoundly overwhelmed by such God-parallels.

God knows my heart, and he nods and smiles.

I once told Peter that God knows his heart, and he said, "No, Marie, you know my heart." And Peter knows my heart, for I have shared so many of these words with him.

With such powerful heart "knowledge" and strength, how can we not become one? We will be stronger together than we are apart. Another God-parallel; I need to start counting.

Dare I write this? Evidently, for the hand of God helps me.

And if my earthly desire is not fulfilled? I will continue to anticipate my God-place; no, this is my God-place. I will anticipate my resurrection after my death.

Peter has "raised the bar," and we are worthy of each other.

As I continue our love story and daily pray the prayer I have written so selfishly, I look forward to writing that awe-inspiring chapter when the two lovers are brought together again, wondering if there are words that can manifest what our hearts will be sharing.

A happy ending? Oh, but of course, for I am a hopeless romantic.

Sure, the chapters after we are physically together will have ups and downs and gladness and sadness, but it will be shared by two hearts that have *never* been separated.

and mine too!

I don't know how my Peter feels, but I feel we have never been apart, not since that night he swept me off my feet like he said he would.

I think about him and us so very much. Does he know of this gentle hold he has on me?

Gentle yet inescapable:

- I can't "shake it."
- I don't know how to "shake it."
- I know I don't want to "shake it."

And so I wait.

In Peter, I will find love, comfort, and peace and warmth, refuge, and solace…and he in me.

I have a sense of walls coming down…and his pillow brings me comfort. He once told me it was part of him. Has he felt my tears like his pillow has and absorbed them?

And so often, lately, I feel his hand resting on my waist. Is it for support? Reassurance? Comfort? Hope? Desire? Yes, yes, yes, yes, and yes.

And as August approaches and autumn looms, I feel so many pieces will fit together and changes will begin, not only in the colors of the leaves.

Who is this man who is so "unforgettable?"
Who is this man that I seem to need to complete me?
Where is this man? And what is he thinking?
There's something about Thursdays.
Every love song could be ours.
Is this man not curious about the love story? Does he wonder if I still write?

Now there's that heaviness in my heart and tears in my eyes. Today neither lasts long, for someone tells my heart it will be all right.

> Ask and it will be given to you; seek and you will find; knock and it will be opened to you. For everyone asks receives, and he who seek finds, and to him who knocks it will be opened.
>
> —Matthew 7:7–8 NIV

I woke *again* at 6:00 a.m. I look forward to my daily readings and want to read more and more.

So my days begin with my books and thoughts of Peter. I greet him a good morning when he gets home from his 11:00–7:00 shift in my heart.

I am more attuned to the blessings I receive throughout each *new* day, and I am thankful. And each *new* day, I ask for the blessings that God wants us to ask for. I continue to ask for Peter and all that comes with this blessing…and "nothing is impossible with God" (Luke 17:27 ESV).

And I seek to find and feel and share more of my God each *new* day, and I do and am so blessed.

He makes me happy every day, and we are apart. How so much more will our happiness be when we are together? *Wow!*

"*Who is this man?*" (Luke 8:25 NL) is asked by the apostles when Jesus calms the stormy seas. Funny, where have I heard that question before? *Wow!*

I am pleased with my growth and the changes all these pages have made. I ask my Lord, "I'm doing good, aren't I?"

He smiles, nods, and is pleased: a smile that says, "Oh, just wait and see." And I smile back.

He and I will (are) be awesome together.

I need to work on the humility. I don't want to get too preachy or have others think I know it all, for I have just tapped the tip of the iceberg. I just want to get them excited and curious and hopeful and challenge them to basically pray.

I've been working out and eating better and reading more. I am taking better care of all aspects (physical, mental, and spiritual), and I feel good and am encouraged every day.

We're a team.

and mine too!

When I first met my Peter, there came along a song, an oldie, and oh, how I sang and danced. It made me soar and took my breath away.

"Brand New Me"

Same old coat and same old shoes
Same old me and same old blues
Then you…touched my life just by holding my hand
Now I look in the mirror and see a brand-new girl
I got a brand-new walk, a brand-new smile
Since I met you baby, I got a brand-new style
Just because of you, boy
just because of you
Same old friends, same old sins
Tell the same old jokes get the same old grins
Now the jokes sound new and the laughter does too
Every day of my life is fresh as the morning dew
Just because of you, boy
Go the same old places see the same old faces
Look at the same old sky see in a brand-new light

—Dusty Springfield, *A Brand New Me*

(I'll play it for him someday)

How many times have I mentioned Peter taking my breath away? Does he remember blowing his sweet breath to me and how I opened my mouth to take it in? That was unbelievable. There was no thought to responding to it the way I did, and it was so right and so hot and so sexy at the same time.

Of course he remembers.

Are you ready for this?

Back in May, I wrote, "When my answer comes, it must be highlighted and in bold print. Until then, I wait."

July 31 (on the cruise), reading *Grace for the Moment* (M. Lucado), and there it is: the day is titled "He's Coming Back." My breath is taken away, my heart pounds, and those overwhelming tears fall.

And if that is not enough…in "Encounter with God," the page opposite July 31, it is titled "Get Ready for Something New."

I am bursting. I want more. I share it, and I want others to want it too!

Thank you, Lord, for giving my humanness, what it needs, and I wait.

My faith continues its journey. I am stronger. I am His forevermore. Yes, I expect temptation, but temptation is wasting its time.

The *Prayer of Jabez Devotional* (Wilkinson) seems to be written for me. The words of encouragement and witness and anticipation are what I need and long to hear (read), and I want more.

I want to share them with Peter and "pump him up," and we can go there together.

(As I just wrote those last few words, I realize up until now, "go there together" meant physically.)

What a wonderful journey we will have together, heart and soul and body.

I've also realized Peter's fluffy pillow lies on the corner of my bed as a reminder of him, but no longer. Over the past few weeks, I have physically clung to it, laid next to it, or rested my head on its (his) corner (shoulder). And I smile and remember Peter saying it was a part of him. Does he remember?

Another chance to keep our home? I'll know soon. And I pray for his will to be done, for I do not know what is best for me. Is my Lord asking me to choose my home or Peter? I ask, and he says, "No."

And I ask, "Do I deserve both?"

He says, "Of course you do."

And I am humbled and feel undeserving. But as graciously and gratefully as I can, I will accept such magnificent gifts given to me by God to take care of on this finite Earth (his creation).

My friend, Rose, called me. She is the angel that started me reading the Bible ten years ago. Through these years, my on again/off again relationship with the Word has been struggling and positive. Now because of the seed she planted so long ago, I look forward to "my time" and want more. I look forward to talking with her and sharing my journey and my Peter with her.

I can't wait to tell Amanda and Kim and Bettina about my *July 31*, to share the hope with them and make them curious about God's "big plans" for them.

August 6, 2002

It is a fall morning already; an early season change?

Sometimes I wonder why I am so obsessed with Peter. Is it wrong? How selfish am I?

Obsessed with the fact that he is always on my mind, I send little prayers his way and kiss him goodnight and bid him a good sleep every morning when he gets home from work. When I was on the cruise, I thought of what it would be like doing everything with him there and sharing it all (and it was good). Sitting next to each other on the pool deck, holding hands, napping, reading, stealing kisses, those eyes, his smile, dancing, embracing:

Each other's refuge;
Each other's shelter;
Each other's paradise; and
Blissful.

In my heart and girlish mind, I imagine, dream, create, etc. our reunion. And each time I do, my heart beats in that special way that is only Peter's, and our God smiles.

I miss him.

I do not want to be "alone," and I wait.

I have never been alone nor felt forsaken, but my human aloneness can only be replaced by Peter (as I see it). And I his? I think so.

> And Jabez called on the God of Israel saying, "Oh, that you would bless me indeed, and enlarge my territory that your hand would be with me, and that you would keep me from evil, that I may not cause pain." So God granted him what he requested. (1 Chronicles 4:10 NKJV)

Jabez—expanding territory. Today, I realized how God has expanded my territory on a daily basis. Now I wake up between six and seven o'clock and have time to read and write, which I didn't have before; expanding as in giving me the opportunity to work less so the girls can get the hours they need, although they may be temporary.

Cruise afterthought

For the first time since Peter came into my life, I actually dreamt about him. He is wearing a gray suit, white shirt opened at the collar with a black tie. He looked great. Some of my cousins were around, and we were busy among small buildings, but Peter waited patiently. That's all I remember.

> Patience produces character, and character produces hope. And this hope will never disappoint us
>
> —Romans 5:4–5 NCV

and mine too!

Mid-August

God will save you from hidden traps and from deadly diseases.

—Psalm 91:3 NCV

When hope is crushed, the heart is crushed,
but a wish come true fills you with joy.

—Proverbs 13:12 GNT

Each day, my heart longs for Peter, and each day, my heart soars with thoughts of him and us. How interesting.

How could this heart be crushed when the strength of a new love fills it like never before?

Absence can make the heart grow fonder!

Does Peter realize this? When he does, will he believe it?

"Yes" is the answer, and so I wait.

So very much of my days are with thoughts of Peter and me and what lies ahead and our reunion.

How? Why? On Sunday, I asked God why can't I get him out of my heart. My answer? *"Because he belongs there!"* Who answers me? My God.

Our day for forever is closer!

What is he thinking and feeling?

August 14, 2002; Faith fulfilled

Once again, Peter was my constant companion on my drive home from Pittsburgh last night. The drive has never made me weary since I met him.

And this morning, he was with me, so with me. So much went on between us I half expected and hoped the phone would ring. I sensed my love sitting on the edge of his bed, wondering what to do about his thoughts of me and us—follow your heart…take a risk…don't be afraid.

He must know I continue to write our love story, and he must know deep in his heart it will never end and that he does deserve to be on a pedestal.

(I'm out of olive oil.)

Who is this man that makes me tremble? Yes, tremble! Does he know I fell in love with him, do love him, will always love him?

Will I tell him? Of course. Did he need to hear it months ago? Is that why he had doubts and "let me go?" I shared so much of my heart with him through my writing; surely he could read between the lines.

I thought to tell him of my love back then, but what if he wasn't ready to reciprocate? I didn't want to make him feel any pressure nor compromise what we already had going, what we already had growing. Plus, he was dealing with so much other stuff too. I myself was overwhelmed by our relationship, and as I look back, I don't think I was ready to vocalize such forever, committing words.

Yes, my Peter, I love you! A love that began from almost the moment we met; a love that has been miraculously growing with no human contact.

Miraculously, as in miracle; as in only from God's hand and heart.

And I wait.

The first volume of my journal started in Jan. 02 – a small box of note paper.
Volume 2, a large legal pad.
Now this is volume 3, the one with the lily on the cover.

This used be the journal after Chuck left. I reread the eighteen or so pages, tore them out of the binding, and then threw them out.

Now on to more hopeful, positive, and happy things.

I remember telling Peter he was a "jack of all trades," and he said, "Yes, but a master of none."

Oh, but he has mastered my heart.

Did he mean to?

and mine too!

Does he have any idea he has?

I've been reading *The Rhythm of Life* (Matthew Kelly) since spring, and I love it. And I want to share it (the book and life) with Peter.

All of us are on a journey, and I want to continue my journey walking with Peter on his. And I realize that Peter was the catalyst, the booster of my journey. Since we met, love, life, and faith have been incredible, and I want more. I want Peter. I want to share it with Peter.

We belong together. Sure, we have to work a few "earthly things" out, but we belong together.

It's all about him and me, and each day, it gets stronger and gets better. Does he sense any of this in Pittsburgh? Has he opened himself up to our gift, our miracle? Does he recall all those lovely things we said to each other?

If he feels and remembers and dreams half as much as I do than he knows, "we have a chance."

It's all about us, and maybe that's okay because if Peter is like me, we've spent so many years doing and being for other people (with no regrets, for all was done out of love), and now it's our turn. And in turn, this love that I believe will come to fruition will be a gift and a blessing to all those we love!

Can it be that we are growing closer across the miles and across this "human" silence? I say "yes," and I am in awe!

What kind of power is at work? God, of course. The Father who only wants His children to be happy, to give Him glory, and walk in faith and love!

Who is this man that makes me happy and makes me smile and makes me melt? No, he's not a figment of my imagination, for my happiness and smiles and hopes and heartbeats are undeniably real.

In the *Book of Jabez Devotional* (Bruce Wilkinson) and *Rhythm of Life* (Matthew Kelly) and the Bible itself, I keep picking up on the words *prepare* and *overwhelmed*—prepare to be overwhelmed.

My God must feel I and Peter deserve this newness in our future, for I walk with the Lord now, like never before, and I look forward to each new step with hope and love!

August 15, 2002

And I ask,

"*Who is this man?*" On some days, I ask myself, "Where is this man?" And some days, I feel disheartened and a little sad. I can't deny it, but it does not consume me or my day. So with patience, hope, faith, and sense of a new love, like no other, I wait in prayer, with open arms, and tears of joy, and a sense of peace to share with my beloved Peter.

Do you know you are my beloved?

Wow!

And sometimes, during my disheartened moments, I question what part the evil one is playing in this. Does he test my faith with my dreams? Does he want me to think my God doesn't want me to be happy, that a good Father would have given me what I wanted by now?

My answer, without a moment of hesitation, "How could the evil one be a part of such a wonderful yet untouchable 'thing?'"

He can't, for he is not capable of love in any form. Only God could create such a timeless wonder and endless love from one brief encounter, one touch, one kiss on one crisp winter night across the miles.

A timeless wonder of endless love that continues to burn deeper in anticipation of an overwhelmingness we are both preparing for.

God creates, the evil one destroys, and he can't touch this, and he knows it.

Bye-bye.

"For what God has joined..."

Look at me sitting here and writing and wanting nothing more but to share everything with Peter, to grow with him in every way, to take care of and be a haven for each other, to bring a deserving *peace* to each other.

Amanda thinks I should call Peter next time I go to Pittsburgh, and Bettina thinks I should send a note to let him know I've been thinking about him. I thought about it briefly, but my "black and white" message from July 31 said "he's coming back," and so I wait.

I—me—a brand-new me for God. The brand-new me that Peter unearthed when he swept me off my feet not so long ago.

My treadmill message:

I won't be able to do my three miles in less than forty-five minutes. The message: The journey is more important than how long it takes.

August 18, 2002

>*I'm out of olive Oil!*
>I miss you Peter.
>I often wonder what you're doing.
>I wish you a good sleep as I leave for work in the morning.
>I tell you not to work too hard when I realize it's about 10:00 p.m. on many nights.
>Do you think of me?
>Some days, you seem so close and getting closer. On the few days that come along once in a while, and your nearness is not as clear, I get sad…like now.
>Some days, I wish we could get together and get it over with. Am I waiting and wanting and wishing for us to get our chance and then to find out it won't work out? That we were not compatible? That just one of us fell in love?
>Again, my Lord comforts me as I wait.
>Me and my music. One day, Peter asked me if I liked to have the music on, and I said, "Oh, you haven't spent enough time with me yet."

"On Talking"
Kahlil Gibran

>And then a scholar said, Speak of Talking.
>And he answered, saying:

For Pete's Sake

You talk when you cease to be at peace with your thoughts;

And when you can no longer dwell in the solitude of your heart you live in your lips, and sound is a diversion and a pastime.

And in much of your talking, thinking is half murdered.

For thought is a bird of space, that in a cage of words may indeed unfold its wings but cannot fly.

There are those among who seek the talkative through fear of being alone.

The silence of aloneness reveals to their eyes their naked selves and they would escape.

And there are those who talk, and without knowledge or of forethought reveal a truth which they themselves do not understand.

And there are those who have the truth within them, but they tell it not in words.

In the bosom of such as these the spirit dwells in rhythmic silence.

When you meet your friend on the roadside or in the market place, let the spirit in you move your lips and direct your tongue.

Let the voice within your voice speak to the ear of his ear;

For his soul will keep the truth of your heart as the taste of the wince is remembered

When the colour is forgotten and the vessel is no more.

and mine too!

"Every night, I'm lying, in bed, holding you close in my dreams thinking about all the things that we said" ("The Best of My Love," The Eagles, *On the Border*).

"You'll Never Find Another Love Like Mine"

You'll never find, as long as you live
Someone who loves you tender like I do
You'll never find, no matter where you search
Someone who cares about you the way I do.
Whoa, I'm not braggin' on myself baby
But I'm the one who loves you
And there's no one else! No-oh-oh-oh-oh-oh-
oh-oh one else.
You'll never find, it will take the end of all time
Someone to understand you like I do
You'll never find the rhythm, the rhyme,
All the magic we shared, just us two.
Whoa, I'm not tryin' to make you stay, baby
But I know somehow, someday, someway
You are (you're gonna miss my lovin')
You're gonna miss my lovin' (you're gonna miss my lovin)
You're gonna miss, you're gonna miss my
lo-o-ove
Whoa, oh, oh, oh, oh (you're gonna miss my lovin)
Late in the midnight hour, baby (you're gonna miss my lovin')
When it's cold outside (you're gonna miss my lovin')
You're gonna miss, you're gonna miss mu lo-o-ove
You'll never find another love like mine
Someone who needs you like I do
You'll never see what you found in me
You'll keep searching and searching your

For Pete's Sake

<blockquote>
whole life through
Whoa, I don't wish you no bad luck, baby
But there's no ifs or buts or maybes
(You're gonna) You're gonna miss (miss my lovin')
You're gonna miss my lovin (you're gonna miss my lovin')
I know you're gonna miss my lovin' (you're gonna
miss my lovin')...

—Lou Rawls, *All Things in Time*
</blockquote>

I so look forward to my quiet times and thoughts of, with, and for Peter.

Aah, then there's Barry White's music and lyrics.

"Two Less Lonely People in the World"

<blockquote>
I was down my dreams were wearing thin
When you're lost where do you begin
My heart always seemed to drift from day to
day
looking for the love that never came my way
Then you smiled and I reached out to you
I could tell you were lonely too
One look and then it began for you and
me
The moment that we touched I knew that
there would be
[Chorus]
</blockquote>

and mine too!

Two less lonely people in the world
And it's going to be fine
Out of all the people in the world
I just can't believe you're mine
In my life when everything was wrong
Something finally went right
Now there's two less lonely people
In the world tonight.
Just to think what I might have missed
Looking back how did I exist
I dreamed, still I never thought I'd come this far
But miracles come true, I know 'cause here
we are.
[Chorus]
Tonight, I fell in love with you
And all the things I never knew
Seemed to come to me somehow
Baby, love is here and now
[Chorus]

—Air Supply, *Playlist: The Very Best of Air Supply*

"My Love"

[Chorus]
My love is warmer than the warmest
sunshine
Softer than a sigh.
My love is deeper than the deepest ocean
Wider than the sky.
My love is brighter than the brightest start
That shines every night above

For Pete's Sake

And there is nothing in this world
That can ever change my love.
Something happened to my heart the day
that I met you
Something that I never felt before
You are always on my mind no matter what I
do
And every day *it seems that I want you more*
[Chorus]
Once I thought that love was meant for
anyone else but me
Once I thought you'd never come my way
Now it only goes to show how wrong we all
can be
For now, I have to tell you everyday
[Chorus]

—Petula Clark, *The Pye Anthology*

"Strangers in the Night"

Strangers in the night exchanging glances
Wond'ring in the night *what were the
chances*
We'd be sharing love before the night (*week*) was
through.
Something in your eyes was so inviting.
Something in your smile was so exciting.
Something in my heart told me I must have you. (*I follow my heart*)
Strangers in the night
Two lonely people, we were strangers in the
night

and mine too!

>Up to the moment when we said our first
>hello, little did we know
>Love was just a glance away, a warm
>embracing dance away.
>And
>Ever since that night we've been together (*in my heart*)
>Lovers at first site, in love forever
>It turned out so right for strangers in the night
>Dooby-dooby-do

—Frank Sinatra, *Ultimate Sinatra* (emphasis is mine)

August 21, 2002, 1:50 a.m.

How much longer must I keep my love contained in a book? *Not much longer, I hear.*

It is love, I am sure of it, for it consumes me and completes me!

All these pages, all the letters, all this ink *adds* up to one possible thing: Pete + Me = love unparalleled.

If only Peter could put his hand on my heart and feel how it beats for him and only him.

If only he could put his ear near my mouth and feel and hear how soft and deep my sighs are for him and him alone.

If only he could taste and wipe away my tears that flow so freely in anticipation of him and me.

If only he could embrace me and absorb all of my innermost feelings, from my every pore, into his heart. Then I can fill it like it's never been filled before.

God has done it. Now it's Peter's turn.

Let us love every day, in every way, forevermore.

I'll try to sleep now.

For Pete's Sake

Yes, I will continue to write our love story throughout our ages, loving pages.

When our "human silence" is over, the words will be of a love connected beyond the heart.

The meshing of heart, soul, and body. Will the words be harder to find in our overwhelmingness? *It's just a matter of time.*

Just You and Me to be! (*Just be*).

"The River Is Wide"

Then fell a drop of rain to start our love
Let the river get wide, the river gets long,
now
The water runs deep as our love gets strong
Now
So, baby don't you fight and say you belong
now to me.
...no one on earth can stop a drop of rain.

—The Grass Roots, *The Best of the Grass Roots, The Millennium Collection*

In the margin, I write "And rain comes from God."

Love one another, but make not a bond of love: Let it rather be a moving sea between the shores of you souls.

— Kahlil Gibran, *The Prophet*

and mine too!

Months ago, the best part of my day was our late-night phone calls.

Since then, the best part of my day is when I sit and read and pray and write. I look forward to it and how I wish it would last all day.

"It's only been about four months."

Who is this man that has become synonymous with:

My darling.

- My beloved.
- My sweetheart.
- My love.
- My lover boy.
- My love of my life.
- My babe.
- My dear.
- My honey.
- The man of my dreams.

Way back in the first few pages, I wrote I met the man of my dreams (tall, dark, handsome, sweet, funny, sexy, gentle, Italian, etc.).

The dream became a reality.

Now I sit and marvel in the mystery of how this reality maintains itself when we have not spoken, have not touched.

The mystery is not one, for I sit and marvel at the way God is maintaining my reality so I can prepare and anticipate our union of overwhelmingness.

Tears of Joy!

My dear Peter,

Just a note, in case you were wondering about all those words, the massages, the kisses, how we were so comfortable together, the laughter, the sighs, the touches, the loving…it was just a sample of what I know we can have. For we gave it to each other so effortlessly and from our hearts.

How could something that felt so wonderful and real not endure this test of time?
I love you with all my heart!
A heart you alone have opened up again.
A heart opened only for you to fill.

Lovingly yours,
Maria Francesca

P.S. "That's some pretty heavy stuff, babe!"

Do I really hear him speak to me?
Do I really see him smile at me?
Do I really feel him touch me?
Yes, I do—into the depths of my heart and soul.
Does Peter sense all this unbelievable beautiful stuff?
Lord, please tell him it is real. It's new, so maybe he's having trouble recognizing it. So help him—quickly!
This time alone with words and writing, I love and find it harder to put my pen down each time I pick it up.
Do I expect everything to be perfect? No.
But Peter and I will be stronger together than we are apart.

and mine too!

Give your hearts, but not into each other's keeping. For only the hand of Life can contain your hearts. And stand together yet not too near together: For the pillars of the temple stand apart, And the oak tree and the cypress grow not in each other's shadow."

—Kahlil Gibran, *The Prophet*

You matter more than anything!

It's 6:30 a.m. on *August 23*, a Friday. I've been awake for two hours and ten minutes.

I read and pray and think and get angry about legal stuff and money, and I hate being angry. Too much negative energy. More reading, praying, and thinking *and* all thought flows back to my Peter, over and over again.

And then I think of my God who has so much going on with his flock, and amidst all of this, his thoughts flow back to me (and you).

I matter (you matter).

And as I shed tears, the first morning bird sang as the sky lightened the midnight blue.

And I am overwhelmed and blessed.

And I want to share it all with you know who.

"Not a love denied" (I was going to write this as a question, but someone said to me to make it a statement—God).

For my love, I am bursting, and it's all for you.

Because I could not explain these feelings to anyone else and expect them to understand. Only you can!

A love story such as this deserves more than paper and ink; it deserves to be lived!

I pray. I wait. I love.

At Mass today, the Gospel was the one where Jesus told Peter, "You are a rock, and on this rock foundation I will build my Church and not even death will overcome it" (Matthew 16:18 GNBUK).

In the margin, I write "The Lord is my rock and my salvation (from a Church song)."

Father Schmitz spoke of Peter having the keys to heaven, and naturally, I think of my Peter having the key to my heart, how he opened up a newness in my heart. Does he know how it overflows and how long it will take to close this flow?

When we are together, it will burst with not a chance of getting closed.

I have two rocks, how blessed I am.

"Non Dimenticar"

Non Dimenticar means don't forget your
heart my darling.
Don't forget to be, all you mean to me.
Non Dimenticar my love is like a star my
darling
Shining bright and clear
Just because you're here.
Please do not forget that our lips have met
And I've held tight dear
Was it dreams ago
My heart felt this glow only just tonight dear.
Non Dimenticar although you travel far my
darling.
It's my heart you own so I'll wait alone
Non Dimenticar.

—Dean Martin, *Dino: Italian Love Songs*

All I do is wait. Could waiting be sacred? (time)

and mine too!

As I lie in bed, praying, I struggle to keep Peter out of mind and mentioned to God that with Peter here beside me we would pray together every night, back and forth, with thoughts and petitions. When we're together, my prayers won't be so selfish, and I won't be so distracted.

I had dinner with Rose, my dear friend, who planted the seed twelve years ago.

I spoke of Peter. She said, "You like him" and that my eyes were twinkling and that I should call him or write him a note. "What do you have to lose?" she asked.

And on top of that, on my ride home, the song *Call Me* by Jackie DeShannon played on the radio, a confirmation of sorts (I'll get the lyrics soon).

August 26, 2002

So when I get home, I called my Peter and left him a message. It was nice to hear his voice.

And I wrote him a note and mailed it.

Both included the fact I'd be in Pittsburgh this weekend, and it would be nice to see him. I included both my phone numbers.

And I wait.

A good twenty-four hours have passed.

Eviction notice for September 6. I don't know how, what, where to take my feelings.

And I wait.

My heart skips a beat when the phone rings! How long will this go on? I still get the message "Prepare to be overwhelmed."

What if this love story becomes a fairy tale?

I will cry now.

I don't know. I just don't know!

> Trust the Lord with all your heart, and do not depend on your own understanding.
>
> —Proverbs 3:5 NLT

I have never felt this emotion before. I don't know what it is or how to label it.

Who is this man that seems more important than keeping my house? How dare he?

Prayer of Jabez Devotional (Bruce Wilkinson)–Day 6. Absolutely heart-wrenching (mine).

> Trust in the Lord and do good. Dwell in the land and feed on His faithfulness. Delight yourself in the Lord and He shall give you the desires of your heart.
>
> —Psalm 17:3–4 NKJV

In the margin, I write "I do! I do! I do!"

Today, I spoke out loud to the devil. I told him to "shut up."

I called Peter four evenings ago. Why am I not disheartened? Will I ever get the message?

Who is this man?

A season of waiting on the Lord. Could waiting be a gift? A sacred one?

Our home hangs by a thread. Did Ang lose her job? Yes, the apartment will be ready Friday. There's so much to do. No call from my lawyer. It's a long holiday weekend. When will this house be saved? What am I waiting for? Will I ever hear from my Peter? Is he mine? Was he ever mine?

I don't know what to do.

I don't know what to think.

I don't know how to pray. I'm tired of being selfish with all my thoughts and prayers.

I need to get out of this box. How? When?

So, I go to Church, and *I am lost*, never alone, yet lost. I know nothing, except that once I get past this, over this, through this, I will be more able to do my Lord's will, to be the better person I know I can be. To be *His* child and reflect Him.

I need to love and be loved. To care and be cared for.

and mine too!

Moving in three days? Not impossible. A little mind-boggling but not impossible.

Yet that message pops in and out of my life: prepare to be overwhelmed.

I guess I could be overwhelmed with negative stuff too.

After I left church, I realized I felt better, satisfied, calmer—even without obvious answers.

If Peter and I are blessed to share our love, the love I've dreamt and written and cried about, how overwhelming it will be when together, we realize how much more God loves us than we love each other. It's so much bigger than us. A love he has given all his children from all the ages and through all ages.

> The Lord is my shepherd, I shall not want.
>
> —Psalm 23:1 ESV

Does he see the changes in me? Does he see my path has changed? Is he excited, like me? Yes, yes, yes.

Will Peter matter less on my new path? I hope not, for I am so sure we could complete each other (in the earthly sense) in all our needs.

Why can I not shake these feelings, especially at a pivotal point in my life? Probably because I want him in my life. When? Where? How?

Who is this man?

God's black and white message, "He's coming back," is my hope and dream. Is it God's plan?

I am lost.

Am I lost?

> Lord, every morning you hear my voice. Every morning,
>   I tell you what I need, and I wait for your answer.
>
> —Psalm 5:3 NCV

For Pete's Sake

Who is this man that stays in my life?

"Tu Sei L Mia Vita (You Are My Life)"

Amore, when I looked in your eyes of love…
and somehow came a day I knew we'd share living
each moment for a lifetime of love.
To say la mia vita, you are, you're my life.
To live a day without you is a day without a night.
To say la mia vita, you are all I need
And now that we're together there's no wish that cannot be.
To love you was a feeling that I always knew.
And now that I have you
I'll hold you close to my heart forever.
Whenever, should I leave in the dark of night
my thoughts of our love will keep burning inside.

—Vito DiSalvo/We Three, *Con Amore*

"Il Mondo"

Stay beside me, stay beside me
Say you'll never leave me
How I love you, how I love you
How I need you—please believe me
In your arms I found my heaven,
And your lips have done their part.
Il Mondo—your love is all I need in my world

and mine too!

> Let tender kisses plead in my world
> How could I ever live without you?
> Il Mondo
> My heart belongs to you so, take it
> And promise me, you'll never break it!
> Say you stay here in my arms!
>
> —Patrizio Buanne, *The Italian*

Who is this man that manages to stay in my world?
I want nothing else. I cannot keep him out.
I would miss him so.
So I will continue to hold onto my thoughts and prayers and dreams and this pen till I can hold Peter in my arms again, for I already hold him in my heart.

"No one can perceive the power of faith unless he feels it by experience in his heart." (John Calvin).

It's September. The weather has been so beautiful, days and nights. We should (will) share days like this.
Why do Thursdays seem to be my discouraging days? Is it because of the weekends?
I get the "feeling" Peter knows I will wait. He can't get out of his head all we said to each other and all I read to him and all I wrote of.
In the margins, I write "New Feelings"
I prepare.

The hearts of the young need to be opened and energized with God's presence. They must have hope, so with my bigger heart and the Spirit working through me, I will make a difference.

Now hope does not disappoint because the love of God has been poured into our hearts by the Holy Spirit who was given to us.

—Romans 5:5 NIV

I've been totally getting the house in order, either for a move or to stay. It looks like *to stay*.

I believe I've been given this time to prepare for Peter's return and to open more hearts. For when all is in order, I can give my attention, heart, and soul to what lies ahead.

And I give thanks.

I want to go to him, sit on his lap and arms, run my fingers through his hair, and kiss his lips (that I can't forget). That's all!

Who is this man that is so much in my world yet not in my world?

Here is where he differs from my God, and so this is my daily prayer—both to share me, heart, soul, mind, and body. And me to share with them.

Surely goodness and mercy shall follow me all the days of
my life. And I will dwell in the house of the Lord forever.

—Psalm 23:6 KJV

God is goodness and mercy.
I hope Peter is well.
Does he have those moments like I do?

and mine too!

The weather is beautiful. We should be peacefully sharing this. And the grapes of summer have been sweet, and oh, how I think of Peter and abundance when I consume them; and oh, how he consumes me.

If this man that is in my heart does not return, what or who could possibly fill the emptiness that is left? God, I suppose, but what of my humanness?

How do you measure emptiness when it is the size of overwhelmingness?

You're not going to leave me empty, Lord, are you?

He answers, "No." And I wait and I long and I hunger.

Overwhelmingness awaits me and the knowing that Heaven will be so much more than we could ever imagine. I am in awe.

Completeness on heaven and earth.

We have the perfect love triangle.

Pietro, where are you?

I want to make a difference in his life as he has in mine, and oh, what an incredible, wonderful, overwhelming difference that is!

Again, I pray, "My dear Lord, please answer my prayer."

I so want these words to go from my lips to Peter's ears, not from my pen to my paper.

Is it time yet? Again, I ask.

I must give more thanks.

Does he know? I ask *again*.

Looking at the crucifix *again*.

"I can tell him" is my answer.

Does Peter long to hear my words as much as I long to say them? To give these words a voice to someone else besides me, to someone who needs them, to someone who wants them, to someone who can echo them back to me? I love you to my very core.

"Tonight I cried aloud. I sobbed. It is 1:40 a.m."

God's work done in God's way will never lack God's supply.

—Hudson Taylor

I have been given the gift of time:

Time to rest.
Time to volunteer.
Time to read.
Time to exercise.
Time to clean and purge every nook and cranny in my house.
Time for yard work.

I feel that I am preparing for a life with new direction. Today, I've realized I'll need to go back to working doubles to meet rent payments, hospitalization, equity debt, etc. But I look back over the past one and a half months and give thanks for my gift of time.

I struggle with Debbie losing her income when I go back. I consider advertising again.

"My love lifts me. 'To fall in love with God is the greatest of all romances: to seek Him, the greatest adventure, to find Him, the greatest achievement' (St. Augustine).

"To fall in love with God"—I did through Peter—"is the greatest of all romances." Remember, Peter asked what I thought of a ten-year romance? It can't be on paper, though. That last night we were together, he said he didn't want to work another ten years, and I told him, "Maybe you won't have to."

He asked, "How do you know?"

And I told him, "Things change, and things happen."

And he asked, "Like what?"

And I replied, "You never know."

Prepare to be overwhelmed.

I cry again. So when two people are in love, don't they want to make each other happy? Wouldn't they do anything for each other? I ask God, my new love, this. All I ask for is Peter, and I give him all of me to be his better child, to live to be more like his Son.

and mine too!

September 11, 2002

My Lord seemed sad and preoccupied today when we talked.

And my Lord comforts me and reminds me of "He's coming back" and asks me, "Did I say *no*?"

Why didn't he reply to my phone call or my card? I'm going back up at the end of the month, and part of me wants to pick up the phone and say, "Hi, Peter, it's Mary. You'll probably think I'm crazy, but I wanted to let you know I'd be in town again."

Is not knowing safer than "wrong number" or no return call? Yes. Do I want a yes or no? Yes. Do I take another chance? No, I follow my heart. Do I think we still have a chance? Yes. I follow my heart, inspired by God.

I know God as Father, friend, lover, and now I must learn to know him as king.

> This is my prayer for you: that your love will grow more
> and more; that you will have knowledge andunderstanding
> with your love; that you will do many good things with
> the help of Christ to bring glory and praise to God.
>
> —Philippians 1:9, 11 NKJV

Ang and John are coming home for the weekend. I have been praying and knowing that the words I speak will be those of the Spirit through me. I must be worthy.

Peter, my heart has been beating for only you. Sometimes I tremble for only you. So find your way to me, hold me so close to you, close enough to feel my heart and my trembling, close enough to hear my heart and breath. It is my humanness, and it could be for no one else but you.

And while you're holding me, please never let me go.

How did this happen?

Why did this happen?

"By the Grace of my God" is my only answer.

For Pete's Sake

Faith that is firm is patient.

—Isaiah 28:16 GNT

September 12, 2002

And when my soul goes to the Father, then He will hold me and feel my heart and my trembling and never let me go.

And so I go to continue to lead my life as the best person I know I can be and not let my Father down. How could I?

Through all these emotions of late, the presence of the "evil one" is nowhere to be found or felt—ha-ha.

If anyone ever reads all of this, my Peter included, you may think I've gone off the deep end. Don't worry because "I love it here. Come on in, the water's perfect."

How many calories does one burn sitting, reading, and writing?

Have I touched Peter's life as he has touched mine?

I don' want it to be over, Lord.

Does he know I'm still part of his freedom?

Does he care?

I shop for clothes and wonder if Peter would like me in this.

A couple of months ago, I asked God for a clear black and white message, and I got it on July 31: "He's coming back."

Lately, I feel the need for sacred assurance. I want another message. Really? Yes. No.

I'll be right back.

Chapter 31, *Screwtape Letters,* C. S. Lewis—I have lived it, *yeah!*

"You have let a soul slip through your fingers" (from Chapter 31, *The Screwtape Letters,* C. S. Lewis).

and mine too!

Last night, I was sorting through old piano music and coming across sheet music. One was titled "Blessed Assurance." I threw it out.

I just recovered it, and here are the lyrics:

"Blessed Assurance"
Fanny Crosby

Blessed Assurance Jesus is mine!
O what a foretaste of glory divine!
Heir of salvation, purchase of God,
born of his spirit, washed in his blood.
Perfect submission, perfect delight!
Visions of rapture now burst on my sight!
Angels descending bring from above,
Echoes of mercy, whispers of love.
Perfect submission, all is at rest,
I in my Savior am happy and blest
Watching and waiting, looking above,
Filled with his goodness, lost in his love.
This is my story, this is my song,
Praising my Savior all the day long.

Am I saved? Yes, I've known that most of my life since childhood.
Am I born again? I suppose, in a sense.
But today, I would call it tapped into, tapped into my heart and soul. I think it started ten years or so ago—drip, drip, drip.
Sometimes feeling dried up, then drip, drip, drip again.
Now I trace the beginning of the gentle flowing to my now overwhelming rushing, and as you might guess, it was when Peter tapped into my heart and opened and exposed it.

He exposed my heart to me, and as you know, I want to give my heart to him.

I cry again; it is almost too much.

Tears of a new emotion. If grace can be an emotion, I cry *grace!*

> *Now why wait* any longer? Get up, be baptized, and wash your sins away, trusting in him to save you.
>
> —Acts 22:16 NCV
> (emphasis mine)

> Believe me, this is not only the most important decision you'll ever make; it's the greatest decision you'll ever make. There's no higher treasure than God's gift of salvation. It's God's wonderful destiny for your life. (*The Gift for All People*, Max Lucado)

So I did five minutes ago, in the shower. It was good and very symbolic, and I'm sure each time I use it, that moment will come to mind, even for just a moment in time.

I thought also of sharing it with Peter. Did I need to? No, but I guess I felt that's what he would have liked, and maybe I felt it was my way to keep him interested. Did he do it for the same reasons?

Peter's different, and I should have been more respectful of him and myself. Someday, I will tell him this. I am sorry, my love.

Speaking of sorry, back in April, when I got "the wrong number," I forgave Peter on the spot, no hesitation, "for he doesn't mean to be doing what he did." In thinking about that today, I see a loose translation of what Christ said on the cross. Wow!

I must call my Nicky. He needs me.

My Angela was a victim of an attempted assault. She ran. As I drive to her and John, I am empowered. My faith is so strong I believe I can touch them and cast out evil in the name of my Lord. *Wow!*

and mine too!

I cry and think life is too much but soon realize I cry because God is too much! "Abba."

Three years ago today, Chuck left, and all I can say today is, "Oh well." Yet, my heart will always ache for Angela, Nick and Matt.

In heaven, I will be with my Lord every day forever. I will see him, touch him, and look into his eyes, always in his presence, never wanting to be anywhere else.

I would like a little bit of heaven here on earth in all my humanness. Soon?

Please, please, *please, please,* please, please, please. *Por favor, s'il vous plait.*

Must I give this "bit" a name?

Who is this man that I call and love? Peter.

I told that damn pillow, "I will give you peace and trust and respect and calm and laughter and kindness and gentleness and fun and unconditional love." And I heart-wrenchingly realize you have already given these to me, given in those first few months we shared.

Somehow, through these past four months, you filled my heart and soul.

And an obscure interpretation fills my heart and my eyes. "Oh, how much better it will be when we are together again."

Five pages ago, I asked for another message.

Did I really need it? "Yes. No."

Well, I got one. Randomly opening *Grace for the Moment* (Max Lucado) to October 31, the heading "Everyone Will See Him."

Then you will know the truth, and the truth will make you free.

—John 8:32 NKJV

My Matthew is coming home tomorrow.

For Pete's Sake

Oh, Peter, how I long to look up into your eyes and touch your face. Let me be your angel.

"I Could Be Happy with You"

I don't claim that I am a physic
But one look at you and I kick
Away every scruple
I learnt as a pupil
In school my dear
I'm not one to make predictions,
But I've thrown off all restrictions,
And I don't mind confessing
I think it's a blessing
That you are here.
Though I'm prepared to find I'm wrong,
I've got a funny feeling we belong together
I could be happy with you.
If you could be happy with me
I'd be contented to live anywhere
What would I care
As long as you were there?
Skies may not always be blue
But one thing is clear as can be
I know that I could be happy with you, my
Darling
If you could be happy with me.

—*The Boyfriend* Soundtrack

and mine too!

Peter knows I am waiting for him. God told him. How do I know? God told me. Grace streams down my face.

I've gone to a few movies lately, and watching a couple in love kissing makes me…miss it and want it. I close my eyes, lift my head, part my lips ever so slightly, and again, he takes my breath away.

Magic man? Miracle man? Dream man? My man?

Who is this man?

September 18, 2022

I caught the most beautiful sunrise today as my eyes opened in the direction of my bedroom window. Thank you, God. P.S. It lasted a short while. Timing is everything.

> You have not seen Christ, but still, you love him. You cannot see him now, but you believe in him.
>
> —1 Peter 1:8 NCV

This man makes me laugh out loud, thinking of a conversation we would be having. Do I make him smile too?

I'll have to ask him.

My heart will be his home always.

Today, the house will or will not be home. I worry so about my Angela, and I get a dose of what God the Father sees every day a billion times over.

So much to share.

I've been worried, confused, and even nervous—pretty much down. I want to exalt in the Lord *(hesitation)*, so I shall. I just made an important choice!

It can be nothing else but Grace, and it is a gift—*every day*.

I want *everyone* to feel it.

Did I ever write that I realized that I love Peter enough for us to have children together? It won't happen, but that sure is some love, isn't it? Well, anyway, if it were a little girl, her name would be Grace.

Again, I thank God for this gift of time. It must be tough being God.

I just finished *He Still Moves Stones* (Max Lucado). Nice book, real nice. At the end, in chapter 21, he tells us to "paint" our story for the gallery. A portrait of me before Christ flooded into my life and another portrait of me now in his aftermath.

My before would be a Normal Rockwell painting—family, peaceful, day-to-day stuff, and always a touch of something to make you smile.

My "now" picture for the gallery becomes a book, an epic, maybe, but truly a *love story* of Peter and I. A love story I never thought I would/could live—it transcends human time.

I mean, it lives and grows in our "absence."

How can this be? Dear Lord, *let it be!*

Our book is full, for there are many blank pages to be filled. People will come back from time to time to see how it's going, to read the newness, holding their breath for the reunion of Peter and Mary.

> Peter: Hey, girl (*puts hand on Mary's face*)! You're waiting.
> Mary (nods): Yes!
> Peter (hand still on Mary's face): I'm doing my best.
> Mary: I know.

Because everybody loves a happy ending!

No title on the cover yet. Just a diagram of a love triangle.

Peter, where are you?

There will never be a rut in our relationship because Peter and I are not the same people we were less than a year ago.

Then you will know the truth, and the truth will set you free.

—John 8:32 NIV

and mine too!

Dear Lord, send these words to Peter's heart. Let him hear my voice and my heart, speaking and feeling my truth. Let him hear the echo of his own words and let him be strong.

"I think you're the one for me."

"Do you think we have a chance?"

"You'll put me on a pedestal."

"You already are" (different from all the rest).

September 23, 2002

Bella luna, mi amore.

Once again, I quote John 8:32 (NIV), "Then you will know the truth, and the truth will set you free."

Peter, may the Lord show you I am your truth, if it is his will, the truth to set you free from past pain and burdens. Do you remember I told you I wanted to be part of your freedom? And you responded, "That's the idea, babe."

Meeting you set me free, and I thank you.

Free to be me.

Free to be a better me.

Free to love again, unconditionally.

How did you do that?

How and why do I continue to write such words five months later?

> Suffering produces perseverance: perseverance, character: and character, hope. And hope does not disappoint us.
>
> —Romans 5:3b–5a NASB

Amazing the lengths to which God will go to get our attention.

—Max Lucado, *A Gentle Thunder*

For Pete's Sake

I don't expect all the pieces to fit perfectly, but I want that big piece back, the piece that fits the space in my heart that Peter blew wide open and left exposed.

I am weak. I do not understand.

They both have me. I want to continue to give both more, learn more, grow more. God knows my heart. Does Peter remember mine?

What lesson am I supposed to be learning? Yes, I must want the Lord's will, and yes, I know He hears my prayer and I know it hasn't been that long. If this love doesn't exist, what will the pain and loss teach me? It seems so mean.

> In this world you will have trouble, but be brave! I have defeated the world.
>
> —John 16:33 NIV

This is not a dream. The prayer is real. The dream is real. I read every day too, looking and learning for messages and answers.

My Lord lifts me up.

Thoughts of Peter lift me up.

So why am I again having a disheartening day?

My humanness is in need, and I wait.

I am a doer, and I like results. I know, somehow, this *is not* a waste of time, but sometimes I think, what if it is?

I must be crazy. What am I holding on to? Why do I? When will I let go? How do I let go? I don't know how. I have no answers.

The Big Picture

Must not lose sight of the Big Picture
I am saved
I have been chosen
I have had a re-birth
He calls me by name
and sharing in everlasting life awaits me
I am blessed

and mine too!

I will share
I will love, but…

October 1, 2002

What a difference a few days make.

My Angela needs help, needs "saving," thinks she can take care of "it." I've planted seeds along the way, tried to be a role model, invited her home, and have unconditionally loved and forgiven. I am not God, so I have given it to Him. She will be my prodigal daughter. If she will not look to me for help, may she look to God quickly, and I pray. I didn't know how long to wait in Pittsburgh. My Nick said to "go home." I did all I could.

God said, "Go home. I'll take it from here." Between *so many tears*, I feel comfort.

So many questions! But he doesn't have to answer us and my faith is weary.

Does Satan get excited? Well, he can go to hell because I am a child of God. Ha-ha.

There goes the house *again*!

Whatever. The Lord giveth and the Lord taketh away.

I told Angela we can live anywhere, but we cannot live without love.

My beautiful Nick sat and listened and was sad. Like our Lord, he sat quietly as I poured out my aching heart, occasionally a gentle touch. It was a low, low time, more so than Chuck's leaving.

A question to sum up all my questions?
When is enough, enough?
enough giving and taking.
enough loving and hurting.
enough time and loss.
enough "tests" and feeling like a pawn.
enough strength and tears.
enough loneliness and words.

For Pete's Sake

> There is a time for every purpose under heaven.
>
> —Ecclesiastes 3:1 KJV

Nick reminded me of my strength, even as I sat there, feeling drained and angry with myself that I would question God.

> In this world, you will have many troubles, but
> be brave! I have defeated the world.
>
> —John 16:33 NIV

Matt wanted to know why I was "throwing in the towel." Huh?

My mom calls just after Nick goes to class, and this shrinking, wheezing, faithful woman, who will be seventy-five, never sounded stronger to my ears and my heart. For as a parent, she is doing God's work. Just as my dad cries with me and says we will do whatever "we" can. How God like they are.

I am overwhelmed and uplifted.

> Amazing the lengths God will go to get your attention.
>
> —Max Lucado

And I already thought he had it.

And then there is Peter, whom I've left another message for.

I left my phone on in Church and eventually shut it off there. Leaving the phone on gave me no control. What was I thinking? So I kept it shut off and gave it to God again.

Of course, all of my questions included, why Peter? Why and where is Peter? In these last thirty-six hours, I have thought of him and realize it is not time. Will there be a time for us?

What really matters is my ongoing growing relationship with God to whom I will be forever committed, knowing in my heart, that unless Peter has a true commitment to our Lord, he and I won't be able to give proper attention to each other's journey.

and mine too!

I feel I must wait. For my human questions want to receive an answer from a human.

Whatever that means. Am I so blind?

We (Peter and I) no doubt planted seeds in each other's hearts. Have his grown? Does he want more? Do his need some attention from me? I wait.

November 14, 2002

Hello, journal. I have missed this ink to paper time…this heart to written word time. The Spirit is with me! Yeah!

It has been a month, a month full of so much.

I sit in the oversized chair with a cup of coffee in an apartment. It's okay.

We moved the first weekend in October. Nick and Matt came home, and with help from Laura and Bode and Tom, we got the big stuff over and set up at the apartment. That night, we had ten kids over for pizza, ribs, and a movie. It was comforting.

The following week, I prepared for the moving sale the next weekend. With the help of my girlfriends and parents, it went well, considering people buying my hand-chosen treasurers. Leftovers went to consignment, and what was left behind is now in storage, put there by the sheriff's department. The contents must be out by November 17. It's just stuff.

"But with God all things are possible" (NKJV).

I went back to the house when the consignment truck came, and it was awful.

My last moments there, I almost cried myself to sleep on the stairs going up.

Everything was emotionally and physically hard on me. The gift of family and friends and time was just that—a priceless gift.

Where was my Angela those two weeks? She should have been here. We wanted her here. We needed her here.[1]

---

[1] It is almost twenty years later. Upon reading my words, my Angela cried to me, "I wasn't strong enough, Mom." I cried when she spoke them. I cry now as I

During the moving sale, a woman asked Carol to give me a nice bouquet of flowers and a card with a Helen Steiner Rice poem in it, and it was signed, "I see all you have been through and I weep with you. Jesus." My tears, no words attached.

I was able to share this with the girls at the moment, and we all were blessed with His presence.

Everyone tried to explain or figure it out, but to me, an angel walked through my home, did some shopping, left for the bank, and

---

type them. Two lessons: (1) share your feelings with those who love you, and (2) don't judge.

and mine too!

returned with flowers and a card from Jesus. That's my story, and I'm sticking to it.

When my sense of humor surfaced, I danced in my kitchen to "You Can't Touch This."

The card has been on my nightstand. There are times I open it and still cry.

There was a week of settling in and unpacking and then a wonderful week in Phoenix with Bettina. We "spa-ed," shopped, ate, toured, and sunned. I spent too much money—what a surprise!

I started my Italian class in September, and I love it—it's simple, fun. I wish I could spend more time at it.

Well, that's an overview. I'm back.

I miss Matthew terribly. He'll be home for a few days at Thanksgiving, but probably not the whole weekend. Nick won't be home the whole weekend either. RA stuff, but he has the week before off. Ang is having dinner with John's sister's family.

Matt is talking about staying in Chicago through the summer to take classes and work. He wants to graduate early. Because of Jessica? Maybe. He is pushing himself but seems to enjoy a challenge, like his mother.

I cried. But Nick will be home for six weeks this summer—not. That's changed too. He'll have six weeks—one at a time between clinicals. Hmmm. I cried.

Divorce has been final but have seen no distribution of funds. Back in court December 10.

Chuck's an a-hole. He knows we've moved but doesn't acknowledge it to Nick when they talk. He has not talked to Angela or Matt.

The car is falling apart bit by bit.

I'm wearing *a* contact—it's a vanity thing.

Here's something unexpected: it's awful to have people over to the apartment. I cry or cry thinking about it. I didn't foresee my reaction. I said I hate feeling this but realize it's not hate; it's that it *hurts*. It *hurts* when my parents come over. It *hurts* to have the kids be here. I don't think it will ever stop. Lessen, maybe.

I know it is a temporary home

Last night, this thought was followed by, *It's all temporary.* So I continue to try to live a better life on my road to the home my God has prepared for me.

I have to go for pre-admission testing soon for a LEEP procedure on Friday, and I pray.

Five and a half pages without mentioning my Peter. Oh, just wait.

Who is this man?
I have been able to put the man I knew for twenty-five years and married for twenty-two years in the past and out of my heart. So why not this man I got to know for only four months and haven't heard from for six?

Is it because I *loved* Chuck but fell *in love* with Peter? *Am I in love?* How? Why? When?

When I'm not thinking about what's happening at the moment, my thoughts are of Peter and my feelings and my God.

I can't think of one without the other.

If I never have Peter, I will always have God, for in Him I seek and find refuge and comfort, even with unanswered questions.

God will always come first, for he is the glue that will bring and keep our love triangle together; and I pray.

I'm not crazy or obsessive. Would I date? Do I look? Yes and yes, but Peter is the ruler by which others will be measured.

So if Jesus and Peter are best friends, shouldn't Jesus be fixing me up with Peter?

I've talked a lot of Peter, and my heart is so restless, and tonight, as so many other times, I listened to our conversations and the heart-

and mine too!

felt sentiments in my heart. I meant them. Peter meant them. What fifty-six-year-old man would say such tender words without meaning them? Why would he? He said he never told anyone the things he told me. He said, "I think you're the one for me," "You should be here, babe." And all those other words that touched my heart, a heart that still reacts with love, a breath that is still taken away, and eyes that cry in longing.

I long for his voice and laughter and touch and his lips.

Why did God bless me and leave me (in a sense) with— I have no words to finish this sentence.

"If you don't have a dream, how can your dream come true?" (South Pacific, "Happy Talk").

I say my prayer I wrote for Peter every day, sometimes with a sigh or a tear, and at times a smile.

Recently, two people assured my God wants to grant us the deepest desires of our hearts. And I looked into mine ever so deeply and then some more, and there is Peter. Nothing less or more, no bells and whistles, no pomp and fireworks—just Peter. He and I, simple togetherness, sharing in the goodness of God in all he has given us. Sunsets, grass, water, flowers, paths, warm rain, jumbo snowflakes.

I know He knows what I need more than I do. Is He pruning or disciplining? I haven't heard Him say, "No," for I have been listening and listening and waiting. My heart says, "Yes," but is it my heart or God in my heart? So that makes three of us in my heart, and it feels right.

> Trust in the Lord, and do good; Dwell in the land, and feed on His faithfulness. Delight yourself also in the Lord, and He shall give you the desires of your heart.
>
> —Psalm 37:3–4 NKJV

Frustrating, yes, oh yes, from my humanness, of course. And it feels safe too.

He is the deepest desire of my heart. I am God's child, and he knows me by name, and I matter. He is all-knowing, and I am still waiting.

I will be the answer to Peter's prayers, and he will be the answer to mine.

I continue to ask without hesitation; does God tire of it? I am sorry. Am I also stupid, naïve, and selfish? Maybe. I don't know. But since God put Peter in my heart, there he will stay until God takes him out. He has been a gift that manages to keep on giving in his absence. And what fool would turn down or give back a gift hand-picked by the Almighty himself? Not I!

I flipped through the last pages I have written, and my handwriting does not seem to betray the tears I shed as I write.

FYI: Tomorrow, I go for that cervical LEEP procedure.

I told Christine about my emotions at the apartment, and she said I'm grieving over the house now because I was running on autopilot and way too busy to grieve the loss while the big move was in progress—that's it. How long will it last? I'll let you know.

I had another parallel of such magnificence I was swept away with overwhelming emotion again.

I am dreaming, thinking, and wishing and hoping, as usual, and Peter stands down the hall from me. This is the first time we've seen each other since last spring. He waits for me as I walk slowly toward him. My heart races, my chest rises and falls with my anxious breaths, tears gently overflow from my eyes that will not blink lest he disappear; no words leak from my pouted lips, for my love, my hope, my dream stands before me, and I lift my hand and touch his face. And in that moment of this encounter, this is my reunion with Jesus, and I am home. For the face I am touching is the Lord's.

Will Peter and I be able to manifest this love gift we have been given here on earth?

Can we?

Dare we?

May we? Please answer my prayer, my Lord and my God.

and mine too!

How can I feel this way without him?

"Because I am not without him." This is the answer my hearts hears.

This is abundance, and it must be shared because it is too much (for me) and too good and too right not to be.

We would be living examples to all around us of the kindness and patience and mercy and forgiveness and love of God and his Son and this gift of the Holy Spirit, opened wide and exposed. Isn't that like being a messenger and spreading God's Word through living our lives in his image?

And later that same day, when John called, not knowing where my baby girl was and that she didn't go home with him that night, I sat down crying and crying, out loud asking God, why? I feel forsaken. Why? Are you not all merciful? I need mercy so badly. Was it not so long ago I gave Angela to God, and he said, "I'll take it from here"? What of my heart?

> For I know the thoughts I think toward you, says the Lord, thoughts of peace and not evil, to give you a future and hope.
>
> —Jeremiah 29:11 NKJV

Peter is my hope. I desire him in my future. My Lord and I on the same page?

Do I ask too much? I know I am selfish. so many crosses, but things could be much worse.

I settle down as I always eventually do. Within ten minutes, my Angela called to let me know she's okay (at Jackie's). John needs to hear from her. Eventually, they come home that night to get stuff out of storage, and Ang tells me John talked about them seeing someone and talking to them, and this is so good. And we will always pray.

Of course, it takes about a half hour after Ang's call to see that God did not forsake me nor leave me (never did), and I remember the card he sent me and realize I was not crying alone.

For Pete's Sake

So what of *all this?*

My Father is always at His work.

—John 5:17 NIV

And the angels will sing (Mary, *November 20, 2002*).
And on his Christmas card, I will write:

When God Says No

There are times when the one thing you want
is the one thing you never get…
You pray and wait.
No answer.
You pray and wait.
May I ask a very important question? What if God says no?
What if the request is delayed or even denied?
When God says no to you, how will you respond? If
God says, "I've given you my grace, and that
is enough," will you be content?
Content. That's the word. A state of heart in which you would
be at peace if God gave you nothing more than he already has.

—Max Lucado, *In the Grip of Grace*

Is it a message I seek or one from the "dark side" sent to throw we off and test my faith? If sent by God, I don't want to believe it, yet I'm not really confused. Confusing, isn't it?

"I guess I'll never know the reason why I love you like I do. It's the wonder, 'The Wonder of You,' Elvis Presley, *Playlist: The Essential Elvis Presley*."

and mine too!

This is Volume #4 (with the circles on the front).

> Meanwhile, these three remain: faith, hope, and
> love and the greatest of these is love.
>
> —1 Corinthians 13:13 GNT

It seems I cry at least once a day.

I do no not expect perfection in this life, but I expect something. Am I too bold?

All my thoughts, dreams, emotions, "dialogues," prayers, tears, impatience, weariness, elations, my gifts, my questions—will it all come together in an earthly way? Or do I live my life out here with resolution in heaven?

Well, excuse my humanness (as I was created). But what of my *deepest desire*?

I've had it with Ace, even though he is sleeping at my feet now.

Too many accidents.

I'd consider sending him to Pittsburgh or Chicago if Matt moves off campus. People will say, "Oh, you'll miss him." Well, I'd get used to it.

Hell, I got over:

- Ang leaving for college.
- Nick leaving for college.
- My husband just plain leaving.
- Matt leaving for college.
- Having to leave our home behind.

So Ace can join the list.

I haven't (can't) added Peter to this list (Yet? Ever?). I miss the time and *all* we shared almost every night and those special weekends for four months.

And what of my humanness, this heart?

> Because we have this hope, we are very bold.
>
> —2 Corinthians 3:12 NIV

Potential big problem at work tonight. Girls locked keys in one office with four more to get done. Well, through a short series of phone calls and some good thinking on Tracy's and Deb's part, all but one got done.

And once again, in a short time, I hear, "If God is present to help with the small things, imagine how He will tend to the big things (a loose translation of something I read)."

And my spirits are lifted through the Spirit.

It's times like these that show how we should always be listening and looking for God in our lives.

My Nicky comes home tonight!

My baby comes home Tuesday night, and we'll get to know Jessica. I hear she is "awesome."

My heart aches to have them close.

Ang and John will be back the Friday after Thanksgiving.

Feeling financially drained and burdened. Lawyers still dragging and talking and not caring. I hate Chuck for not caring *at all*.

Funny thing, more than a few people over the past couple of weeks have told me how "good, great" I look, adding "It's in your eyes. Your twinkle's back, alive." I guess there's something they see that I don't quite feel all the time.

They say, "The eyes are the window to the soul," so this is a good and hopeful thing. They (my eyes) don't seem to betray the tears I cry, and this is good too.

The Lord is my rock and my salvation.

He gives me comfort and strength.

Ah, another Peter parallel. The obvious is Peter: rock. Through him, opening my heart, I am unmeasurably closer to my God, my salvation. And when we were together and miraculously for six months, he brings me comfort, and with his strength, he lifts me up.

and mine too!

Just turned TV on. Channel surfing stops on a show (EWTN) *Life on the Rock* coffee shop.

> Guard your heart above all else, for it
> determines the course of your life.
>
> —Proverbs 4:23 NIV

There will always be crosses to carry, but never alone.

> Behold, I am the Lord, the God of all flesh.
> Is there anything too hard for me?
>
> —Jeremiah 32:27 ESV

Had a restless heart a couple of days ago. Spoke aloud, "Something is missing" for my humanness's sake. It is Peter.

By the next day, I ask aloud, "Is it Peter?" Why does it have to be him? Why does it have to be anybody? I love God. I want to know him more and please him and never be without him. And so goes the paralleling—again.

If it would be someone else, does he know how to open out my heart like Peter did? And sweep me off my feet like he did? And stir a hungry passion like he did? Yes, God knows.

> Not even the worlds of the dead can keep the Lord from knowing
> what is there; how then can we hide our thoughts from God?
>
> —Proverbs 15:11 GNT

Does Peter have any inclination of what he did to me? Is he curious? Does he think about me?

It is such a longing, and I worry that it occupies so much of me that I'm missing "the boat" or the real message. Yet, I'm always listening.

I touched his heart and can love him like he now needs to be loved, for I am "different from all the rest." For I am God's child, and he knows me by name.

I've never heard "let go"—or am I missing it or blocking it out? And for all the times I ask myself these questions or write them down, my heart says, "No, I'm not."

I have been gifted. This is our love story, not just mine.

> Therefore do not be like them. For your Father knows
> the things you have need of before you ask Him.
>
> —Matthew 6:8 NKJV

Bishop Sheen wrote of "companionship for the heart."

Who is this man that has been keeping my heart company for almost a year? Why does it not feel like a waste of anything? Am I so alone that I cling to thoughts of Peter?

I don't know why.

I don't know how.

I want to know when.

I want to know if at all.

I don't feel trapped, but I feel I'm not doing God's work like I could be. But I must be where I am at for some reason or another.

> The longing cannot be stilled by our own
> power, but with the aid of another.
>
> —Bishop Fulton Sheen

I have given us to God, so why do I go on and on? And on and on? And on and on?

As I lie in bed, I remember you; all night long I think of you.

—Psalm 63:6 GNT

and mine too!

Where would I be without all this "stuff?"

Wednesday before Thanksgiving, I cry. I can't find my roaster. I am homesick. Thanksgiving Day, I cried, cooking the giblets without Angela being here.

Dinner was very nice. I am thankful.

Father Ray called, and we had a wonderful talk. How blessed I am to have such a busy person, with his own health problems and other stuff, to think of me and take the time to call me, knowing full well he'd be doing a lot of listening. His words reassured me.

We must suffer to "see God." We truly love those in who we have seen the "best of."

Every dream is a manifestation of our spiritual state.

—Carl Jung

That is why I feel the way I do about Peter. I saw the best in him, and he probably doesn't even know it.

"Did Peter see the best of me?"

And he will always have a soft sweet place to rest in my heart, and it hurts. Ray told me to "pick up" this pain and hand it to God, and he will put it down. And in this "picking up," we lift up, and the hurt will turn into an uplifted spirit. Did that make any sense?

Then Ray spoke of swimming and keeping our heads above water, where most people like to be. I have to go to a different place, suspended underwater, *waiting* underwater, and somehow, it's okay. There will be a time when I'm above the water, but when life should pull me under again, I'll be okay. My Lord will sustain me. Ray said some people are afraid to get into the water.

"Human impatience never promotes the work of God. If the Lord has promised something, he does not look for our help in keeping His promises.'" (from *Encounters with God*, January 1, 2003).

When I suffer for anything, I will try to remember how Jesus suffered so ultimately. So, to be Christlike, I will offer my suffering to God, for His glory awaits.

Has this been my farewell to Peter? *No way.* It's just an important perspective of all he has done and been and is to me. The love story continues…

After I got off the phone with Ray, I wished I could make him feel better. I also thought of a Max Lucado book, *In the Grip of Grace*, for there I was!

We pray for deliverance from our "thorns," but if God answers "no." His grace is available to help us persevere, and in his wisdom, this also brings him glory.

My legacy for eternity depends on my being Christlike and "running the race, fighting the good fight."

> Keep Christ first in our thoughts and actions.
> Press ahead toward God's goal for our lives.
> Let the past go.
>
> —B. Wilkinson, *The Prayer of Jabez Devotional*

I am frustrated where I am. I need to get out of "this box" I call selfishness.

"It's all about me."

Another week has gone by, and Peter has not receded in my heart. Why can't I let him go? Is it because it feels safe?

> When a believing person prays, great things happen.
>
> —James 5:16 NCV

Am I afraid if I let go, I'll weaken or lose my relationship with my God? Remember, God *used* Peter as his catalyst for this outpouring of newfound love. Our love triangle will be broken.

and mine too!

I know it comes down to God and me. But our (my) triangle felt so right.

Was there or is there a chance I could be used as a catalyst for Peter? He asked me if I thought we had a chance.

And I get mad at myself.

And the card from Jesus says he "cries with me."

Is He not tired of crying? I am.

Is this not getting old? I feel stifled.

Has Satan taken my Peter and *used* him as a wrench in my life, slowing me on my journey? My stupid heart says no.

If he has, "In the name of my Lord, be gone, Satan!"

How dare he use any child of God!

Why does Peter seem to be the missing piece? And why do I feel if he comes back into my life, all will be better? Probably, it was so better for those nearly five months. Perfect? Never, but ever so uplifting and hopeful and loving and tender. Why does it seem nothing else matters? For if he comes back into my life, all will be tolerable, for he will be my *grace*.

(After much hesitation, searching for the right word, I chose *grace*.)

Why can't I let go?

I should be doing more of what God has planned for me, not writing and crying.

Dear Lord, please accept all this "stuff" as my prayer.

When can *we* stop crying over this?

I think it was this morning, early. I let Peter go. It is done.

I didn't cry but I am crying now, again for myself—how dare I?

I should be praying for my Nicky with his upcoming finals and newly broken leg.

I should be praying for Mary Pat, just diagnosed with lymphoma.

I should be praying for Father Ray and Julie's surgery on Monday.

Is this disciplining? Pruning? Dare I ask for a break? My life is a bowl of cherries compared to others.

Why do we beat ourselves up for answers when we won't get them? Or if we do, what are the chances we'll understand them?

> If He chooses to remove some particular created thing, it cannot matter very much—for He himself remains.
> —Bishop Sheen, *Lift Up Your Heart*

So now what?

Yeah, how about *some* financial relief?

Yeah, how about a clean bill of health?

Yeah, how about taking away this loneliness?

I've seen you in the little things every day. How about something bigger?

Why do I even ask? It has been written that our answers aren't yours, and "we know not how to pray."

Enlarge my territory…more working hours?

I thought I had so much to give, especially nurturing love, caring, and giving. And the one who *I* wanted and needed is still in Pittsburgh.

Did I not tell you I would take care of him here on Earth?

If not that, *what?*

Am I so blind? Deaf? Stupid? Selfish?

Is this a cleansing? All these tears.

The only thing for sure is you'll always be with me. Your card told me so. And this will sustain me through all this sadness and dark times.

Do I ask for too much?

If you created us with such a capacity for loving and giving, humans with the need to survive and the desires of the flesh, why not put the two together in harmony to make manifest that love triangle I experienced and even penned a prayer of? Oh, this is probably another stupid question.

Is this earthly love story over? What a sad ending.

The earthly eternal love story goes on, a guaranteed glorious ending.

Then why am I crying so? What about now?

and mine too!

I really thought and felt Peter and I were "different" together. But what the hell do I know?

Why are some men such a-holes? Cheaters? Liars? Self-serving?

Why are we so different?

Where are all those men that write all those love songs?

No money, lawyers that don't care—some men.

What's with friendship? No one goes out of their way to get together. Something I did? Do? Things have changed!

I do not want to become a cynical old bitch. I'll try to keep things to myself; more humility—that's a virtue I need more of.

I'm going to play Dr. Mario now.

> Love may be defined as mutual self-giving and self-outpouring which ends in self-recovery.
>
> —Bishop Fulton Sheen, "Hymn of the Conquered"

It's been two days since I wrote those last five pages with my troubled hand and mind and heart.

I did not let Peter go. I don't know how to let Peter go. I do not want to let Peter go.

Who is this man?

If I do, am I afraid my grasp of God will loosen? Nah.

If I do, will I miss the safety and comfort of my thoughts of him and us?

This is truly amazing.

Is it my comfort zone?

It feels right, all this stuff, for I am sure it doesn't feel *not* right.

> My grace is all you need for my power is greatest when you are weak.
>
> —2 Corinthians 12:8 GNT

Who is this man that lifts my spirits and creates hope and brings a smile to my face and turns me on and continues to be the deepest desire in my selfish heart?
Of course, I want to be right.

Pleasure is of the body, joy is of the mind and heart.

—Bishop Fulton Sheen

I can wholeheartedly say all I shared with and without Peter has brought me both from beginning to end.
Lucky me!

Nothing has really happened until it has been described.

—Virginia Woolf

O tidings of comfort and joy.

—"God Rest Ye Merry, Gentlemen"

God brings me comfort every day of my life. In knowing and loving Peter, I experience joy—oh, joy, a gift given to me by my Lord who brings me comfort. Please let me know this joy again. Please.
Oh, joy of joys.
Tonight, I wait for a call from friends to go out, a temporary pleasure. It does not come. Am I surprised? No.
Am I disappointed? Yes.

and mine too!

Oh, the lessons in living.
Will I get over it? Of course.

> A good person out of the good treasure of
> his heart brings forth what is good.
>
> —Luke 6:45 NASB

We Surrender So Slowly

We surrender so slowly.
Rationing pieces of us bit by bit.
Believing we know our own heart.
Holding that last precious item,
unaware that our grip is a myth:
our rigid certainty is not secure.
To slice the myth in half,
is to see Christ in the middle:
balancing what is before and what is beyond.
Christ in the center, without compromise.
We surrender slowly
to the narrow path.

—Angela Belcastro

It's been over a week since I've been here. The holidays were great. Sue, Jim, and the kids and my kids and Dad and Mom—thank you, Great One!

Matt was only home a week. I was sad. Nick was awesome, broken leg and all.

Angela was home with John for two days. In them, I see two beautiful hearts and pray daily that they face what needs to be faced and bloom.

> "Do not envy sinners, but always respect the Lord. Then you will have hope for the future and your wishes will come true."
>
> —Proverbs 23:17–18 NCV

I picked up Nick in Pittsburgh before Christmas and had a great weekend. Met Rick at a bar, lots of fun and talking. He speaks of divine intervention and meeting positive people in his life. Of course, this hits a nice note with me. I take his number and tell him I might call when I get into town again. Next thing I know, he's standing next to me, pushing his leg up against mine. *Aaargh!* Mixed messages. I'll let you know what I do with his number.

Met Paul at a dinner party on the twenty-ninth. Ron called it "dynamics." Bettina called it "chemistry." Whatever. It was a fun laugh-filled wonderful evening. I sat next to Paul during dinner, and it was all around a good, fun, comfortable exchange between us.

> You removed my clothes of sadness and dressed me with joy.
>
> —Psalm 30:11 NIRV

Have my thoughts been caught up in this? Of course because that's me:

- The dreamer.
- The hopeless romantic.
- The passionate lover.
- The lover of passion.

I try to hold this in check. My last experience has or continues. I never had a day without Peter. How did "Soon we can see each other every weekend" become "Wrong number" in a matter of a couple of weeks?

Where is this man? Do I still touch him in any way? Where are the answers? What happened to "He's coming back"? "Everyone will see him"?

and mine too!

Am I so blind? So stupid? So *selfish?* So delusional? asks the dreamer, the hopeless romantic, the passionate lover.

Thank you for your grace, Lord, which accepts me as I am and transforms me into what I will be.

Between all the lines and pages and letters runs a common thread, a strong thread of endless length and a touch of glitter. A gift—grace, I'm sure—that gently and firmly holds my angst, my questions, my frustrations, my hopes and joys, my tears, my repetition together.

It is *my faith*, my trust in God, the presence of *the* Spirit. It protects and strengthens and supports. It is an endless spool so it does not comprehend time like I do, but I begin to understand that it is mine. It is irreplaceable and priceless.

My God, I thank you and hope I will not let you down because the final "big picture" is you and me. Continue to guide my choices and let my words bring peace and happiness to all who pass through my life.

Make me an instrument…

> Pleasure is of the body: joy is of the mind and heart. You can quickly tire of pleasures, but you never tire of joy.
>
> —Bishop Fulton Sheen

Some words I've read along the way have been making more sense lately. Like, "The longer you continue the journey, the harder it becomes. The path becomes narrower."

What was my preoccupation with needing and wanting a man in my life? I know the answer.

This is the second night in a row I've been awake at 3:55 a.m.—not sleeping at all. It reminds me of the nights my Peter would call and keep me awake after we hung up the phone.

We can reflect that even trials like these are nothing but the blessings of God's good discipline from which we can benefit.

—*Encounter with God,* June 5, 2003

Why are true lovers denied to love while the a-holes continue to be a-holes? Feeling like a pawn.

January 5, 2003, 1:15 a.m.

I know nothing.
I have never been so confused.
I feel like I have stepped/fainted backward into a horrible state of uncertainty about everything.
Do I pay homage to myself by claiming to be the glue of my family?
I'm tired of it being about me.
I know not how to pray anymore.
I am blind to the answers I seek.
I don't know how to read or where to look.
In the margin, I write "Satan must be enjoying this."
I thought I knew the deepest desires of my heart; I know nothing.
I am deaf too.
Words run together. They are repetitive and jumbled.
I am lost and tired and alone in my confusion, but the heart that is aching for a burst of anything also knows her shepherd is near, probably still crying with me.
The Lord is my shepherd. There is nothing that I want. So here I lay, Lord, before you. Take me and do what you want, for I know nothing. I doubt everything. I can make no decisions.

My grace is sufficient for you, for power
is made perfect in weakness.

—2 Corinthians 12:9 NIV

and mine too!

At the end of each day, you know I give thanks and realize I am nothing *without you*, and you will not forsake me.

Yet I am tired.

You are all I need, and you have me forever.

Then why do I feel so drained? So you can fill me?

Ready. I doubt myself, all the things I thought were answers. Lord, you are so much to me. Please be my interpreter through all this. Okay?

> I do not want to be a person who is "always learning and never able to come to the knowledge of the truth."
>
> —2 Timothy 3:7 NIV

The effects of Chuck leaving still linger. Words with my sons, creating a distance—I'm afraid. I will try to keep my mouth shut and will remember to pray to his Spirit for the right words.

Please, Lord, let this strengthen us, not divide us. Amen.

I am reassured, just two days later by Matt. He says that we'll be fine. He acknowledges this tension and agrees we will be stronger and okay. Thank you, Lord.

And my birthday card from Nick shows me that we will *always* be there for each other through it all, good and bad, no matter what. Thank you, Lord.

> Turn to me when I warn you. I will generously pour out my spirit for you. I will make my words known to you.
>
> —Proverbs 1:23 GW

I've been meaning to write about this for quite a while. It is peculiar.

> My God—my dog.
> I take him out 4-6 times a day
> on a leash

> he follows me—shouldn't he be leading me?
> I get impatient with him, especially when I'm cold
> he wants to be friends with every person and dog he meets
> he has an accident, I'm not quick to forgive.
> when I'm mad at him he still lays in my lap,
> close to me and forgives my anger
> he is constant in my life
> always happy to see me. Peculiar, isn't it?

I am forty-eight years old. My spirit breathes like that of anything new and vital and growing and learning and reaching and questioning.

Just like that brand-new me that Peter brought out. I am excited. I love.

Thanks *again*, Lord.

Picked up another great book, *The Power of the Praying Woman* by Stormie Omartian.

I mentally flex my muscles. Watch out.

Somewhere in these pages, I know I will read the Bible and *never tire of it again*. I'm afraid I'll miss something.

I think of Peter every day. Stories of rekindled love in *Simple Magazine* made me cry today.

What part did free will play in our parting?

Talked to Ang briefly today and John for over an hour. I find myself exhilarated to bring God into their life's struggles. John calls me his angel and the strongest person he ever met. I am humbled, and all is with the grace of God.

He wants to help my Angela, and I want him to take care of him too.

He reminds me of me not so long ago of feeling others needing God's help more than he does. So with the continued prayer to God to let me be "his voice" and a newfound patience (because I've been there), I give all I have to be anybody's angel in the name of our Lord, Jesus Christ.

Who is this man whose voice I still hear?

Is it real or just me trying to fill my own need?

He asks if I still think of him, then he asks when, and I answer when I eat a grape or an olive, when I have a cup of coffee, any Italian song, every night, and every morning next to that damn pillow. As each thought comes to heart and mind, I shed tears.

If God was so not involved in this, I'm almost sure I would be over him.

What does it mean? What's wrong with me?

I have asked God to guide me to a life that is simpler, and priorities are where they should be. It seems to be taking shape since I feel more at peace.

Peter fits somewhere.

Peter fits somewhere?

The deepest desire of my heart.

The deepest desire of my heart?

Who is this man that still brings a smile to my face?

And God is good.

His good work is changing me to be more like his Son. I look forward, with wonder, at how it has come to be and knowing all my words cannot capture the glory of it all. May others see and long for it and make a commitment to it, for it is ever-giving.

January 14, 2003

> The blessings of the Lord makes one rich,
> and He adds no sorrow to it.
>
> —Proverbs 10:22 NKJV

Once again, I write of that very special blessing of mine, Peter—so many words and pages expressing the riches I've been filled with by having him touch my life and heart and soul (I am overwhelmed once again with my God/Peter parallel).

And neither has added sorrow; only both bring me joy and comfort and hope (of course, I am crying). "He's mine!" I cry aloud.

For Pete's Sake

Over this page, I drew a shining crucifix with a heart over the bottom of this cross.

Who is this man? He is like me, a child of God. Loved and tended by the Vine-keeper. Pursued by the Shepherd. Forgiven by the Redeemer.

I went to daily Mass for about a month in September. About my house, I had to give it to God. I was at a loss.

On a Monday in September, I gave Angela to God. I was at a loss. I threw in Nick and Matt (John too).

A few years ago, I believe I gave my marriage to God. I was at a loss.

Not very long ago, I gave Peter to God—and us. I was at a loss on what to think, how to pray, etc.

I have learned in this giving of all that is precious to me I was free—or maybe *emptied* is the correct word. Now there is room to be filled with all that I need to be more.

> If you abide in me, and my words abide in you, you will ask what you deserve, and it shall be done for you. By this my Father is glorified, that you bear much fruit.
>
> —John 15:7–8 NKJV

Christlike, I am anxious.

This Bible passage has been popping up lately in different books I've been reading.

> In this you greatly rejoice, though now for a little while, if need be, you have been grieved by various trials, that the genuineness of your faith, *being* much more precious than the gold that perishes, though it is tested by fire, may be found to praise, honor, and glory at the revelation of Jesus Christ, whom having not seen you love. Though now you do not see *Him*, yet believing you rejoice with joy inexpressible and full of glory.
>
> —1 Peter 1:6–8 NKJV

and mine too!

I am on my fourth read through of *Secrets of the Vine* by Bruce Wilkinson—phenomenal!

I keep my eyes on the prize not the pain.

—St. Paul

Mmmmm.
I trust you
I need you (more than ever)
I want to know you better
I confide in you
I cry to you
I love to be with you
I pray to you
I love who I am when I'm with you
I confess to you
I question you
I listen to you
I listen for you
I've given all that is precious to me to you
I'm counting on you
I don't hate you
I more than like you
Do I love you? I must.
But this is a different kind of love—as different—
unexplainable because it's not of this Earth and time.

Why do you think it's important to God that patience be growing in us? It's because God's timing is not our, timing. He is always doing more than we see or know, so we have to trust Him on how

For Pete's Sake

long He takes to bring things to pass. God perfects and refines us before He brings us into all He has for us, and that takes time.

—Stormie Omartian, *The Power of a Praying Woman*

I don't understand.
I want to do the right thing.
Last night, my Lord and I spent two hours in prayer and pen, and it was great. I love these times and look forward to them every day.
Like with my Peter, I want more.
Dare I ask for a miracle? Do I deserve it? I can wait. But these negatives have been going on and on and on. Relief is fleeting. Do I ask too much? Do I miss the answers for what I ask?
My Lord is so here, and then again, he's not. But I know he's never apart from my jumbled soul and crying with me lately, again.

Why does God wait till the money is gone? Why does he wait until the sickness has lingered? Why does he choose to wait until the other side of the grave to answer the prayers for healing? I don't know. I only know his timing is always right. I can only say he will do what is best… Though you hear nothing, he is speaking. Though you see nothing, he is acting. With God there are no accidents. Every incident is intended to bring us closer to him.

—Max Lucado, *A Gentle Thunder*

Why is Peter so crucial?
Such a key player to me?
Do I hear his voice
in my heart?

and mine too!

<blockquote style="text-align:center">
Do I want him in my life?
What does all this mean? My God.
And sometimes I hear "It will be so much better."
And hope burns,
and love burns,
and faith is alive and well,
but the humanness is weary—so here I am Lord…
protect my children
keep my parents from suffering and pain
may all who know me continue their journeys knowing
You better. May they receive your strength and grow in
that all that is good and forever comes from you!
</blockquote>

God will always give what is right to his people who cry to him night and day; and he will not be slow to answer them.

—Luke 18:7 NCV

Mrs. Galloway said I looked as if I had been crying. I hadn't since the night before. Have I become so transparent?

And There Is No Turning Back (a possible title of my book).

I hired Gregg for night crew. He trained this week. He stopped by for keys and before he left our eyes met, and he gave me a beautiful smile. I closed the door and thought, *Wow!* His features said, "Everything is going to be okay." Was it my Lord or an angel? It was heaven sent, for sure, and it was for me. I give thanks. And I am in awe.

> The Lord has set apart from Himself him who is godly; the Lord will hear when I call to Him.
>
> —Psalm 4:3 NKJV

> Ask Him to take away the dreams in our heart that are not of Him and bring to pass the ones that are.
>
> —Stormie Omartian, "Surrender Your Dreams," *Power of a Praying Woman*

She continues to write:

> Even if the dreams you have in your heart are from God, you will still have to surrender them. That's because God wants you clinging to *Him* and not to your dreams. He doesn't want you trying to make them happen. He wants you to trust *Him* and He'll make them happen.

In the margin, I write "This is an answer, a message for me. Thank you, Lord, Amen!"

I said this how many pages ago? Did I give Peter/us to God? How many prayers ago did I ask God to take Peter out of my heart because I couldn't do it on my own?

> Now, faith is in the substance of things hoped for, the evidence of things not seen.
>
> —Hebrews 11:1 KJV

and mine too!

>Faith grows
>Hope grows
>Trust grows
>Things bloom in Spring
>Well, God stood in the doorway today!
>I thanked Him.
>I told Him I loved Him.
>He was relaxed and pleased. An efficient vine keeper is He.
>He knows my heart.
>I shed tears as He nodded.

Of course, I mentioned Peter, and shedding turned to crying. My Father knows.

I have been through the season of disciplining. Lord, feel free to discipline me so I stray from you no more.

My season of pruning is fading into my season of abiding.

I expect times of trials to continue, but now that I abide in the Lord, he will see me through with ever-present strength and love. Now I am not afraid to ask.

I've spent a lot of time alone, and it's okay for the learning and the need to read his Word, and the words of his modern-day disciples have been fruitful. Thank you for my gift of time, Lord.

Sometimes I feel I need to be "out there" doing his work, but I'm pretty certain this is where I'm supposed to be right now—quiet, passive, searching, finding, etc.

This is what God had been waiting for when my ink and pages are of him and not that of Peter. Nice job Lord. And we smile!

Yet, speaking of Peter, a song this morning on my to work by The Stylistics, *You Make Me Feel Brand New.*

For God blessed me with you.

Who is this man that has continued to keep alive the newness and who could take my breath away with the sound of his voice?

That newness that brings hope and promise, only by the grace of God.

We are abiding.

> His goal is not to get you what you want,
> it is to get you what you need.
>
> —Max Lucado, *A Gentle Thunder*

> But because Jesus lives forever, he has a permanent priesthood. Therefore he is able to save completely those who come to God through him, because he always lives to intercede for them.
>
> —Hebrews 7:24–25 NIV

Wow, Jesus prays for us.

Quite a while ago, I told Peter, "I can't give you everything you want, but I can give you everything you need." *Wow!*

He answered, "I know."

Is this where free will came (comes) in?

In the name of my Lord, Jesus Christ: Satan, be gone.

I am so drawn to guiding John now.

Why not Angela or the boys? Interesting.

I haven't cried in a couple of nights. Part of me thinks something is wrong if I don't.

I thought of Peter today, as usual, but not as intensely.

Am I missing the answers or message from God? I ask for the discernment and wisdom they talk about in the Bible. I should be following the heart of my Lord, not my own. *Oops.* I've told many others to follow their hearts, especially my kids. I'll try to rectify this.

But once again, Peter has no negative vibes.

His presence in my heart doesn't seem to hold me back. Blah…blah…blah.

Answer, please!

"How can love not love?"

and mine too!

I wrote this prayer *back in May* and keep it in *Grace for the Moment* (Lucado) and am compelled to rewrite on these pages:

> *Please let Peter be the strong man he wants to be. Strong enough to humble himself and ask for his gift of grace so that he may be filled with a peace so long overdue in his life. Let him feel like a child of God who can go to his Father for anything.*
>
> *Let him see that I am his gift for the rest of his years and my years on earth till we get to heaven. Here on earth, we will live reflecting love and, thanks to our everlasting Father, an example to all whose lives we touch and those who touch us.*
>
> *And for those we loved once, a prayer that their lives will be good and they will find our Lord on a daily basis and not feel forsaken.*
>
> *In the name of my Lord, Jesus Christ: Satan, be gone.*
>
> *And all is right.*
>
> *Peace on Earth.*

And a few months later, I added "My dear Lord, please tell Peter not to be afraid."

And just before 2002 ended, I added "Thank you for my gift of Peter, for he brought me closer to You, for only you are forever."

Yes—*my own* words. The first part came out of my heart while I was on the treadmill. It was so overwhelming I hopped off, grabbed a Post-It pad and pen by the phone, sat down, and just started writing, sweat giving way to tears.

I have prayed it every day, save a few days when I thought it was time to put it aside because there was no answer or sign of one. That's what I thought. So it is my daily prayer (that's why it is with that book), for I just wrote that my faith, hope, and trust grows.

Who said miracles happen in a moment?

What is time (but my gift) when God is involved?

Is this Peter thing something I've created to fill a void? Take up time? To fill my loneliness? Or has it been a timeless gift, my Lord?

My heart is beating rather rapidly right now. I haven't had that for such a long time.

God never promises us an easy time. Just a safe arrival.

—David Watson, 1933–1984

Had coffee with Sheila and spoke of many things and a lot of how Peter opened my heart and how God has been ever so present since we met. I was lifted up speaking of God's work and my hopes, etc.

But as the day went, on I hear "Your love keeps lifting me."

How inspiring. Then, *Swearin' to God* by Frankie Valli. And I cry.

Then *Someday We'll Be Together* by Diana Ross. And I really cry.

As the day goes on, my heart sinks a little. Are these tears in vain? Why is this all so profound? How come I cannot name all these tears?

For I am confident of this very thing, that He who have began a good work among you will complete it by the day of Jesus Christ.

—Philippians 1:6 NASB

Does Satan bring this on to test my faith and make me question my God's will?

Oh, I forgot to mention at Mass the gospel spoke of when Andrew brought his brother, Simon, to meet Jesus, and Jesus said, "From now on, your name shall be Peter." Because he will never be the same, so his name must change too! My beloved.

I'm not a dramatic person, but all this sounds so.

I will cry tonight, again, alone. This water and salt is not good for my complexion.

and mine too!

>Peter, where did you go?
>Are you well?
>Do you think of me?
>And I follow my heart, for God knows it well.
>What else is there to do?

Wait for the Lord: be strong and take heart and wait for the Lord.

—Psalm 27:14 NIV

January 20, 2003

>Feeling forlorn today.
>My life is advent—preparing.
>My life is anticipation of *the* goodness of the Lord.
>My life is waiting for the next encounter "with God," for that *deepest desire of my heart* to be graced upon me and manifested before my eyes.
>Do I make a fool of myself?
>Am I clueless?
>I need blessed reassurance, and it must be obvious.
>Am I too selfish?
>My Angela will be twenty-four tomorrow!
>I talked to my birthday girl, and she sounds wonderful. I pray for her every day in thanks and in hope.
>Oh, and at Mass, Father said to go out and be an Andrew and bring our brothers and sisters to meet Jesus!
>I'm going to Pittsburgh this weekend and "warned" her I'm bringing books.
>Paul called tonight, and we talked for two hours—enjoyable and insightful. Great weekend with my kids in Pittsburgh.
>Paul came over. We rented a movie. He stayed late. Aargh! Confusion, deception—is the evil one working him too? Temptation. Justification. And I know that I know and I pray, "Thank you that

you hear my cries and will save me from any weakness that could lead me away from all you have for me."

> My Lord "drew me out of many waters" and
> "delivered me from my strong enemy."
>
> —Psalm 18:16–17 KJV

Lord, I know You are "not the author of confusion but of peace."

—1 Corinthians 14:33 KJV

Do I ask for the impossible?
No. Everything is possible with God!
Blessed assurance. And this I have.
Should I have told him I loved him?
But he got a glimmer of all that was in my heart and saw that he was there in every sentence, between every comma, hyphen, and period; every verb, noun, and adjective. I'm sure he loved it there (drew a heart)! Was it too much for him? Did he think he didn't deserve it? Does he wonder if he still has a chance?

> He who is in you is greater than he who is in the world.
>
> —1 John 4:4 ESV

A conviction that he can and a hope that he will.

—Max Lucado, He Still Moves Stones

And the name Peter I hear and feel.
My path narrows, and I have come upon another climb.

and mine too!

Where Paul and I go, anyone can go. I want to be *different from all the rest*. And Peter has already told me, "You already are, babe."

Who is this man?

I didn't lead Paul on and I don't plan to.

I thought a new relationship with mutual companionship and conversation and some physical attention was what I needed/wanted. As I wrote before, Peter raised the proverbial bar.

A friend said that Paul calling me was an answer from God. I'm not so sure. Do I give it a chance? What is immorality?

Did I not teach carpe diem?

I want no regrets.

He's still in my heart. I couldn't get him out of my heart, so I prayed to my Lord to get him out of my heart since I couldn't do it myself, and as of today (*January 28, 2003*), this man I call Peter has his place in my heart, for he has burned a perpetual, beautiful, and living phenomenon in my heart that was never noticed nor touched till that late Monday night (*January 8, 2002*). Look and read how this has sustained me and brought me comfort, peace, and hope for all that is good to come.

He brightens my days and nights?

For the past few hours, so many thoughts, and my heart was literally pounding, the pounding only Peter could "trigger."

I pray that the God of peace will give you every good
thing you need so you can do what he wants.

—Hebrews 13:20 ERV

For Pete's Sake

My heart beats for all that is good, for nothing bad has come from that spot of Peter's, that he left on my heart.

> Follow my heart? Yes.
> Follow God's heart? Yes, yes.
> For my heart now wants to follow God's
> for I dwell in His goodness,
> for I dwell in the shelter of His love.

Confused again, but in a matter of a few hours when I wrote the last few pages, Paul stopped over, and all was peaceful and unthreatening and uncompromising.

And, once again, God is active in my life. Prayers answered and hope given in many subtle ways. Once again, I am gifted, and once again, I am thankful! His kindness is infinite.

> "He himself bore our sins" in his body on the cross,
> so that we might die to sins and live for righteousness,
> "by his wounds you have been Healed."
>
> —1 Peter 2:24 NIV

Got a clean bill of health. *Cured* was the word used by the gynecologist. Tonight, I read of Jesus the *Healer* in *The Power of a Praying Woman* (Stormie Omartian). Cool.

Feeling a tug-of-war of sorts with me and God versus Satan (temptation), just in a sense that I'm not focused as I have been.

and mine too!

One day later, more focused and craving more of everything that God has waiting for me. I love the blessings. I hope I don't miss any.

Was out with "the girls" for dinner, and we talked about a lot of things. I gave Ellen her *Grace for the Moment* (Max Lucado) birthday gift. She was looking forward to it since that's what I gave all "the girls" this past year. Then it began, the "I'm too tired to read. It puts me to sleep." One page a day? Whatever! Oh well, a seed planted anyway.

This year, I think I'll be giving *The Power of a Praying Woman* (Stormie Omartian). I'm almost finished with it and am looking forward to rereading it already.

He is ever-present.

I want to excite people and pump them up about all that could be by letting God in.

> If we are not faithful, he will still be faithful,
> because he cannot be false to himself.
>
> —2 Timothy 2:13 ERV

I love to feel joy and am grateful.

Let me write of Paul for a while.

Nice, pleasant, good-looking, comfortable to be in the company of.

Our first "date" held more than a goodnight kiss. We had fun, but somewhere along the line, I didn't want to ruin a potentially good relationship the way it happened to me thirty years ago (before Chuck).

Well, the next night, he came over for a while, and we sat and talked about stuff, especially our divorces. He kept his arm around me as I held his hand in the big chair. Then he kissed me goodnight. He didn't call till Saturday, and I don't know how to "read" this.

Paul came over Saturday with the gang, and we had a fun night. Of course, we always do. So he held my hands and stole a half a dozen kisses, and we said, "Goodnight." It was so sweet.

What does it mean? Does he see what I meant about risking a potentially good relationship? Or is he just, I don't know—I have the gift of time, and I am grateful.

Just found out Chuck got married (number three). Can only laugh/chuckle and shake my head. It's sad and pathetic. No tears. No anger. I feel sorry for my kids. It must be hard for them to know their father has "lost it." If he would search for faith and call to God for help, then *we could all* find comfort in that.

Must study Italian.

> Great is He who is in you than he who is in the world.
>
> —1 John 4:4 NASB

God is "at work" in our relationship. Duh!

I think it, feel it; or am I "making it up" because it is what I want?

Does God want it? I pray for his will to be done, but my humanness!

It seems I misread my love triangle with Peter. Am I now misreading the beginning of this new relationship with Paul? Again? If it's even a relationship.

Do I dare hope? Am I prepared for another earthly disappointment? How many human hearts will affect mine? Can I be anything but a hopeless romantic?

I don't want to "rush into" anything, for time has been my gift.

But my prayer will be:

> Thy will be done—Lord
> Please help me to be humble—Lord
> Let Paul see your light in me—Lord

and mine too!

Let him realize that you will be first, and because of you, I am able to give love unconditionally and care selflessly and commit with a true heart, if it's your will.

Do I love him? No, not yet.

Is it possible? Of course, for I am a loving person, and with God, all things are possible.

I just don't want to be part of pain—giving or receiving—at least not for a while. I'm tired of crying in my lack of confidence in seeing your answers to my prayer(s). Give me what it takes to be part of your everlasting goodness.

Remember, Lord, my deepest desire is to continue my journey to you and with you simultaneously sharing with a man chosen by you, named by you, created by you, and given to me by you to love and care for and to be loved and cared for by him. I know he's out there, for you know my need. Or am I wrong about that too?

Well, anyway, with all my love and faith that is yours more than ever before, I thank you. With love and an anxious heart, Mary Frances.

What's my new name?

The ways in which a lover seeks his Beloved are long
and dangerous: they are populated by meditation,
sighs, and tears, and illuminated by love.

—Old Sufi Saying

For Pete's Sake

I volunteered to be the corresponding secretary for the ISDA (Italian Sons & Daughters of America). I included Proverb 10:22. My territory is expanding with each newsletter I send out. Amen.

I know the thoughts I think toward you, says the Lord, thoughts of peace and not of evil, to give you a future and a hope. Then you will call on Me and go and pray to Me, and I will listen to you. And you will seek me and find me with all you heart.

—Jeremiah 29:11–13 NKJV

Even in my loneliness, I give you thanks, my Lord and my God. Love, *Mary*.

Having the right words is no substitute for experiencing the light and love to which our words can only point.

—John Kirvan, *God Hunger*

In all your ways acknowledge Him, And He shall direct your paths.

—Proverbs 3:6 NKJV

Why are the weekends the hardest?
Started a new book, *Everyday Grace* by Marianne Williamson. *Woweee!* Right from the beginning. It's for me and about me—amazing! Seems I have a magic wand—my focused thought, my intentions, my principles. It was a birthday gift from Jim and Jackie.

I have been in prayer and meditation for three hours now. Guess what?
Guess who?

and mine too!

Who is this man?

My Peter. My beloved. Oh, how I cry tears of overwhelmingness in the wonder of it all.

This man who has survived and nestled and grown in my heart and only by the sheer presence of the *Lord who is alive and well.*

Does he wonder if I still write? Our love story will be finished when God himself closes my book and writes "The End" with his own hand.

I went to Church Alive International with the Natolas. They invited me. I called them and went today. Quite an experience—awesome music, speaking "in tongues," laying on of hands, giving witness. I loved the sharing of the "hand of the Lord" being so present and the sound of faith, hope, and humility.

The reverend spoke of miracles, and I realized any miracle is a great miracle—size doesn't matter.

I also "heard," "He's coming back" and "Others will see him." And when my "others will see him" and I say, "'This is Peter," they will know deep in their hearts that I say, "This is Jesus, he is alive, well, and real and walks among us."

They will see a miracle. They will see the power of faith and be given the gift of hope, and they will want "some." And my territory will be expanded, and through the power of the Holy Spirit, they will let me plant seeds of God and let me nourish them—nourish them personally or through my silent prayers.

Whatever it takes.

Where there is great love, there are always miracles.

—Willa Cather

So how can one day I be so pumped up and sure again about Peter and I, and then a couple of days later not be so hell-bent on it?

It was so strong on Sunday.

Elizabeth had God's hand at work in her life so obviously the other night, except she didn't see it. I pray that she will. It's a great thing.

So much reading and especially to share with John. I'm not sure why. God works for me. That I am sure of.

Paul and I went out. It's like old-fashioned dating—sweet, fun, and uncompromising. And I smile, like it, and look forward to his phone call. Thank you, Lord.

Peter is my joy.

I can have the joy of God without him, but I can only have the joy of him with God.

He lifted me and still lifts me, for my heart still hears his voice and laughter. His precious words have stood the test of time in my memory and mind and always in my heart.

As I shed tears of gratitude, my heart races.

Susan Hatta always asks about Peter, and I tell her of our relationship that burns in my heart. I told her of last Sunday when he was so evident *all* day long, and she casually said, "Oh, he must be thinking about you." And I told her how my writing shifted to God and Peter, and she responded, "Oh, this is love."

> Trust in the Lord with all your heart, And lean not on your own understanding; In all your ways acknowledge Him, And He shall direct your paths.
>
> —Proverbs 3:5–6 NKJV

And once again, both these "guys" gift me, and I long to "see" them, "touch" them, to look into the eyes of unconditional love and expose myself through my eyes.

So long ago, I wrote of a heart message that I "heard:" "Prepare to be overwhelmed." I "heard" it again.

A friend of Mom's looked at my star chart; seems Capricorns have had it tough, but all will be incredible, things will fall into

and mine too!

place, and everything I didn't do before will be part of it, no worries. I was curious about the forecast, but I knew that God would answer the deepest desires of my heart, and it would all be better than I expected.

I asked Susan, "What do I do in the meantime?"

And she said, "Be Mary."

Jesus returned from His Resurrection as a *Gardener*.

—Max Lucado, "Sacred Delight," *The Applause of Heaven* (emphasis is mine)

Mom and Dad renewed their wedding vows today—how wonderful. An obvious and active love. The kids and I have been blessed to have them as role models. They have allowed us to reach higher in all we do.

It's time for us to take our own wands now and transform a few pumpkins of our own.

—Marianne Williamson, *Everyday Grace*

February 20, 2003

What a night of reading. I cry and cry. Father Ray called them the tears of the Saints. I am not a saint, but I try to continue to grow more Christlike. Anyway, I cannot name an emotion to describe them. Maybe *overwhelming revelation*.

Is it the presence of God?

It is the presence of God.

I am not worthy, but I will not let him down.

I want everyone to feel this way, to take the step and with new curiosity begin their own journey. I want them to nurture the seeds that have been planted by me or anybody else so they may experience their flower that will burst open with *joy!*

For *I know* they will hunger for more and more and pass it on and on, and our Lord's will, will be done. *Amen.*

> You have begun to live the good life, in which you being made new and are becoming like the one who made you. This new life brings you the knowledge of God.
>
> —Colossians 3:10 NCV

Are my tears representing my blessings?

Blessings have fallen on me like tears from my eyes!

Yes, that is it!

My Lord is pleased. He nods.

A miracle sits in an oversized chair, writing with a single pen in a wire-bound book.

I am the handiwork of God, created in his image. Let me reflect; let me shine. I can, for the Spirit is with me. God gave him to me. He probably gave it to me a long time ago. Well, we've got to make up for lost time.

Where does Peter fit in all this?

Well, I thought about him a lot today.

I still think I'm the one for him.

I sometimes wish there would be closure, *but I would miss him so.*

Oh *wow.* Oh the tears. What an incredibly powerful comparison. And my Lord nods again. I'm getting it.

I don't miss him now. I want to be with him and all the "stuff" that goes with it.

Because of our love triangle, Peter is alive as God and I are. God sustains individually, and together, we will be awesome.

What a *love story.*

and mine too!

Where does Paul fit in all this? I talked with him tonight, enjoyable as usual, and I look forward to seeing him.

> For whatever things were written before were written
> for our learning, that we through the patience and
> comfort of the Scriptures might have hope.
>
> —Romans 15:4 NKJV

Another day goes by, and:

- every love song is our love song.
- every tear is part of him, each full of hope.
- he has my heart, no doubt.

I did it again—*my God/Peter* parallel.
Who is this man? My God everywhere for evermore.
Who is this man? My Peter of this earth.
I need them both forever
I want them both forever
I have them both forever.
How could I ever let them go?
Peter, darling, take a chance. A year ago, you laid beside me and asked if I thought we had a chance. I said, "Yes," and you agreed.
Do you hear the song of my heart?
Come closer and listen!
So last night, Paul and I went out to dinner. I got dressed up, straightened up the apartment, hoping for some selfish shallow reason he'd come up afterward. No. He dropped me off at the door again.
This is no reflection on him. It is God protecting me from something I would regret, something that is more sacred to him than obviously to me. In my human weakness, I long for attention and affection and all that gentle stuff. And so I wait…for Peter? Yes, for I get no other answer.

Jesus stands in the doorway, leaning on the hinges. I trust him more than myself. I love him more than myself. All my hope is in him than in my own earthly hopes.

Never envy evil people, but always respect the Lord. This will give you something to hope for that will not disappoint you.

—Proverbs 23:17–18 ERV

A year ago, for four irreplaceable months, the best part of my day, every day, was when Peter and I were together.

Since then, the best part of my day is my time in prayer (as selfish as it may be), reading and writing in the presence of God.

Yet another Christ/Peter parallel.

So many blessings.

So many tears.

And then I turn a page from *Grace for the Moment* (Max Lucado) and read another blessing. It is titled "God's Help Is Near."

Faith means being sure of the things we hope for and knowing that something is real even if we do not see it.

—Hebrews 11:1 NCV

Oh magnify the Lord with me, and let us exalt His name together.

—Psalms 34:3 ESV

and mine too!

Tears. And I pick up *Praying God's Will for Your Life* by Stormie Omartian and read:

> You have to trust that God has your best interests in mind and be willing to do what He asks of you, even if you don't understand why at the time.
>
> Must place our desires and dreams in the hands of God so that He might free us from those that are not His will.
>
> Often the desires of *your* heart *are* the desires of *His* heart, but they still must be achieved His way, not yours, and you must know that it is He who is accomplishing them in you, not you achieving them yourself. *God wants us to stop holding on to our dreams and start holding on to Him so He can enable us to soar above ourselves and our own limitations."* (emphasis added)

Whenever we let go of what we long for, God will bring it back to us in another dimension.

In the margin, I write "I see a love triangle here."
More blessings.
More tears.
This morning, I wake up to a voice mail from Angela (she left it at 12:37 a.m.). She said she was thinking about me and that she loves me. Of course, she was choking back tears between her words.

Dear Lord, keep our children safe. I'll be there on Friday to speak your words from our hearts to theirs. Amen.

Here's a fact I don't think I've admitted to on paper: so many times when the phone rings, I hope and say, "Maybe" or "What if?" Did I mention he takes my breath away?

On my journey to be like Jesus, Peter is the icing on my cake.

For Pete's Sake

> You will learn your spirit is bigger than your
> circumstances, as soon as you put your spirit first.
> A restored sense of self will attract whatever abundance we need.
> *Claim your good, for it is on the way.*
>
> —Marianne Williamson, *Everyday Grace*

> It is my business to look into the very face of God until I ache with bliss… Now I like the Lord's presence so much that when for a half hour or so He slips out of my mind—as He does many times a day—I feel though I had deserted Him, and as though I had lost something very precious in my life.
>
> —Frank Laubach

What a personal parallel for me and God and Peter.

February 22, 2003

Last Saturday at Mass, it was to celebrate St. Peter, the Holy Chair. FYI.

February 25, 2003

Today I read:

> Let unbelievers hear the passion in your voice or see the sincerity in your face, and they may be changed. Peter was.
>
> —Max Lucado, *Just Like Jesus*

Next day, kind of crappy, giving up my hours to let the girls work. No money, but I enjoy the free time. Same thing tomorrow. A check bounced on the Corp., and Dell is calling about my credit card. What the hell did I spend all that money on? Why these hassles? I should have felt a little ahead. Now what?

and mine too!

Is it God getting my attention and more discipline? Or Is it Satan trying to rattle my cage? Is God asking me to let this problem be turned over to Him? I realized I've given Him so much of my life but not yet the financial part. I created these problems with my "seizing the day" attitude, yet I am a "victim" in some respect too.

Well, Lord, here goes—my financial ups and downs have been frustrating and ongoing. It upsets me and worries me. My heart is heavy today because of it. So, from my heart, I lay this before you too! Guide me to make the right choices at the right time. Let your messages be obvious, Lord, for I am unsure of myself and my feelings.

You're all I have.

You're all I need. Amen.

Tears may flow in the night, but joy comes in the morning.

—Psalm 30:5 GNT

Unbelievable the blessings a message can bring. Yesterday, I wrote of financial stuff, and today, I read "Because we can't separate money from our lives, God must be made Lord over our finances and we must obey Him" (S. Omartian, *Praying Gods Will in Your Life*).

She also wrote, "Giving is a step of obedience that brings life, health, healing and abundance."

Something is better than nothing, and in an instant, I realize this is *so not* true. I am better off with "*nothing*" because this *thing* becomes Peter, and he stands alone and he becomes Jesus, and I nod and smile, and oh the pieces fit so well.

Thank you, Lord of my life (*February 28, 2003*).

Depend on the Lord; trust Him, and He will take care of you.

—Psalm 37:5 NCV

Today, I realize that my thoughts of Peter are my gifts. I am gifted *every day*. They are a delight and comfort to open over and over again.

It's okay to cry, and my Lord has told me, more than once, "Yes, it's okay to dream."

Thank you! Amen!

Going back to this past weekend in Pittsburgh, lots of laughs. Saw comedian John Pinette with the kids. The point: late, late night conversation with John and John H.—interesting, insightful, challenging, disheartening. As I looked back again and again, the devil or evil forces (call them what you may) were at work. Relationships were being undermined. The challenges threw clouds of doubt on all that is always uplifting.

All three of us were pawns for the power of evil. I know I was and am almost sure John and John were speaking from their hearts. Yet this "force" seemed hurtful, critical, and accusing as our conversation progressed. When we seemed to be reaching out, seeking approval and some compassion, the "other two" put up a verbal wall of "I'm okay, you're not."

This is one of those situations that, although felt regretful, I realized in living, we learn. So I will guard my heart, and with the help of the Spirit, guard the hearts of those I love. Amen.

I want the tall quiet man.

Above all else, guard your heart, for it is the wellspring of life.

—Proverbs 4:23 NIV

Yet God's compassion is with us at every step, not seeking to judge but to heal, that we might learn from life and then proceed differently.

—Marianne Williamson, *Everyday Grace*

and mine too!

He wants us to have a hope-filled heart…just like Jesus.

—Max Lucado, *Just Like Jesus*

Hello, book, it's been at least a week. I've thought of writing and what to write about but obviously didn't do it.

Added a new book to my "library:" *God Hunger/Discovering the Mystic in All of Us* by John Kirvan. *Fabulous! Beautiful!* Incredibly timely for me.

This road that narrows before me has me challenged, frustrated, and full of anticipation. Not only does it narrow, but it darkens. Faith and trust and my sense of humor are my companions. I will not abandon *my* path, for my God will not abandon me. Each step, I look for him; in each encounter and conversation, I want him manifested in all around me. This keeps me going. I started this Friday evening alone, not liking it all. I came up with plans and options and listened to the "voice" of my Lord standing in my doorway, "Stay and read." I did. I feel better now.

Dr. Phil has been talking to people, especially women who are afraid to be alone, and I've been listening. We need to like ourselves and like being alone with ourselves. I don't think this is my problem.

When I look back on the times that I'm sad being by myself, I realize it was okay; it was more like a gift, quiet time to read and learn and grow.

I just want to share with a man, a child of God, share all that is good and support each other like no other human can.

Am I afraid of being a "failure" to the eyes of the world? Not anymore. Yet I worry that *my* daily thoughts on the subject are holding me back from my "real purpose."

I feel stupid, like I'm missing the message, the plan.

Oh, that's God's plan now, and that's fine with me. The Bible tells me so, and that is way better than anything I can come up with.

God has been so beautifully patient with me. Now I will return the favor.

I feel better now.

Angela saw Peter a few days ago. Small talk, like "How's your Mom?" etc. It looks like he was one of those people that comes into your life and leaves a mark, etc.

Did I hang on to all the moments and words we shared ever so tenderly and close because it was so magical? I never felt better being so uplifted by every iota of our relationship. Is that why it's so hard to let go and file it away?

Was I so blind? Have I wasted all these days and prayed for the wrong thing (again and again)? I am hoping my reservoir of hopes and dreams is not too depleted.

Yet, Peter is so there. Why do I hear *him* say, "You know my heart, babe"?

"You're already different from the rest."

"You'll put me on a pedestal."

Am I so blind? Can't I take a hint?

God must finish this love story.

I can't.

I don't know how.

I don't want to.

What am I afraid of?

What's wrong with a happy ending?

Hell, maybe it's as happy an ending as it's going to be.

I am in God's hands. Be gentle with my heart.

> I trust and I go on trusting, in spite of all disconcerting appearances, my best and deepest longings.
>
> —Evelyn Underhill

and mine too!

How have I put a twenty-five-year relationship and twenty-two-year marriage behind me as over and done, yet cannot close that part of my heart that I shared with Peter for only four months?

Saw Chuck in court today. He gave a small smile, and I softened. I saw my husband. It makes me sad. He put no value on what we had done together.

I have not written for almost two weeks. Oh, but my heart and soul are in *good* hands. My emotions soar daily. I've been listening to books on tape as I walk for one hour, wherever. The newest one is *Enchanted Love* by Marianne Williamson.

She wrote of my heart. Her words and prayers are synonyms of mine that I have written on these many pages of *my love story.*

I walk and I cry, for *Peter is my beloved and I will wait.* For if you heard my heart, my prayers, my talks with our Lord and God, or God through Jesus, you would agree. And just maybe you would understand. And I pray that your life would be so full and uplifting and hopeful.

Who is this man?

He is Peter. I pray for him daily. I miss him daily. Someday, he will ask me, "What have you been doing without me?"

I will answer, "My love, I have never been a day without you."

Since day one, he has been the best part of my day.

I am in love with this man.

It can be nothing else.

I cannot live without this love.

This love sustains me.

I do not know where I'd be without it.

My Lord, open my lover's heart like he opened mine.

Open his ears so he will hear again the words I spoke so tenderly to him, and hear the words I read to him from my penning of our love story.

Let him speak aloud again all the words he spoke to me that melted my heart and made me dance and lifted me ever so high.

Let him pick up the phone with the slightest hesitation and a faithful heart, knowing that I will be at the other end and it will be like no time has passed.

My Lord, how can there be anyone else for my heart? You have gifted me with your strength – that supports the love triangle only you could give birth to—bring your children together and ooh, the *Applause of Heaven* (Max Lucado).

Ooh, the light that will shine from this union, your signature will be all over it.

Ooh the blessings for so many, the *God Hunger* (Kirvan) that will be birthed, ever growing, ever giving, everlasting.

Why do all these tears I'm *now* shedding do what they do? I can't describe it. I only know I feel, want, and know it's a good thing or a sign, and I do not mind it.

In fact, if I did not cry in this special way, I would worry and be afraid too.

Be strong, my love.

All will be new and sweet and peaceful. You deserve it. You deserve the pedestal. It is long overdue in your life, and God has chosen me to be your angel on earth. How blessed am I? I will not let you down nor hurt you nor push you away.

I will hold you, stay with you, fulfill you—it will be effortless and unconditional. How do I know this? Because that's how it has been since that first night you called me.

I love you, Peter.

Somewhere in your heart, you know this.

I will continue my prayer, the one I wrote back in May.

I get the feeling heaven is holding its breath, knowing, but having to wait for our earthly "moment."

Hurry, my darling, for there is so much to tell you. Yet, somehow, I believe we will be able to be still and quiet and know, just know, that *he* is and *he* has joined us together. And what God has joined no man can bring asunder.

Do you ever think of me? Deeply?

Have you ever sensed me thinking of you?

Is there a sort of telepathy going on between us?

and mine too!

Sometimes I think I wait on a shore for you while you're out on your rough seas. How arrogant; maybe it is you waiting for me to come ashore from my storms.

Please, Lord, bring a quick end to our troubled waters. No one can calm a storm like you.

I know we will have rough seas when we are together, but we will be together, sharing, for we will be stronger together than apart, and it will be something!

Must I go another summer without my love?

I *hear* "no." Is it your "no," Lord?

My favorite place to be and thing to do is to be alone in prayer and meditation with my Peter, my heart, my books—in my chair and on my walks. Everything I hear and read, I look for answers, insights, and affirmations of Peter and him and me. Like my *God Hunger* (Kirvan), I have a hunger for Peter. I will never have my fill of either, but—

My Lord, you manifested yourself to me through Peter. Love, like nothing I could imagine, exploded.

Today, I ever so humbly ask you to manifest, to bless, to be a miracle (I don't know how to say it) and join our hearts and bodies together again—till death do us part.

I know you want your children to be happy. This would be beyond happy, but together, we three of us, we can handle it. Amen.

The above prayer began seven pages ago and was written *April 2, 2003*. Goodnight.

And the angels will sing.

Oh, sweet angel that watches over my beloved, whisper my name into his ear. Let him hear music and laughter and quiet and gentle.

Then whisper my name again and again and again. Softly, yet strong enough to enter his heart, to the place there reserved for the three of us that he's not sure exists yet.

Tell him it's time to take *that* chance!

I went to Pittsburgh this past weekend. Does Peter sense my presence? He kept me company once again as I drove there and back.

Sometimes my emotions are so there I wonder if he "feels" me. It. Us. We three.

Feelings so strong and tears never-ending, I wonder how he could not sense something. And, Lord, give him the strength and courage to go in search of that something, the courage to search himself, forgive himself and others; the courage to face his fears.

Love is the opposite of fear.

Help him face his fear and look beyond it.

And *if it is your will*—please, I ask you again—let me be there waiting lovingly, unconditionally, for your son that you may be manifest through me as you manifested yourself to me through Peter (for this I am forever grateful).

This must be your will, for I am here waiting lovingly, unconditionally, waiting for your son.

Who is this man?

Love.

My Lord, I have gone through so many changes, all shapes and sizes, with your love and guidance of Spirit. I wouldn't and couldn't change a thing. I love where I'm at and will continue my journey for you will always be.

There's more to do, and you are the journey, not the end of it. Be patient with both Peter and I. Join us soon. We will share and contribute in our own way to each other's journey.

Those who see us together will see you and "want a piece of the action." The trickle-down effect will be explosive! Love: what the world needs now!

Can/May Peter and I *together* be on a mission in your name? The possibilities are endless, and I am only human.

What do you see, Lord?

and mine too!

Goodnight, my love.

April 10, 2003

Happy birthday, darling!
As these pages know, I've wondered "why God sent me the man of my dreams and then took him away." And God still tells me "I didn't."
He didn't. Peter is not away, just in the physical for now. He is so here, this pen is alive, the ink continues to flow, but not as fast as all my emotions have flowed over the year. The words of my heart are timeless for us, and they dance with every beat of my heart. Some days, the words drop on these pages as easily as tears drop from my cheeks. And then there are the words that pause between the next as I catch my breath—the breath that Peter still takes away.
My love, do you have any idea?
Oh, that feeling has come back again. Frustration? I don't know. I'm afraid I'm "wasting my time" and selfishly praying. Am I wrong? I want to do things right for my Lord. Is my "obsession" an obstacle? Oh, dear Lord, if it is, please remove it. It will hurt, and I will be lonely and alone, but please keep me on your path, keep my heart safe and ready to give and to share with another heart you've chosen for me. Is it Peter? I hear "yes" three times, but is it my yes or yours? Help me to discern. Help me to see your will, and it will be done. Amen.

I sent Peter his birthday card four days after. Why did I hesitate? What do I expect? I have no idea.
Driving on I-90 out to Vermillion this past weekend, once again just thinking about us, I realized I could just keep going, thought after thought, exit after exit to the ends of the Earth. I believe so, for here my soul, my heart, and my mind are content and safe and hopeful and alive. Please, Lord, send me my passenger, and together, we will be your copilots. I love you both, and I know you know.
I know I am preparing and being prepared in so many ways so subtly. Carry on, even at your pace, not mine, for I am yours. Amen.

Goodnight!

A fun frantic Easter in Chicago with everyone!

Took a walk on campus and wondered why and where my thoughts of Peter have been. *Waning* would be the word. At the end of the walk, God said, "I even want your thoughts of him."

Even my thoughts? What would I be left with? I'm human.

I'd be left with God—okay.

And all my hope would be in him—okay.

I've realized this, and what more could I want?

I am a hopeless romantic and dreamer—I've always been. I thought God loved us as we are. There's always room for improvement, and *I think* I've come a long way and, like most of my life, have not had too many regrets.

What will be left of me, the brand-new me, the me I told Chuck I liked, and he said he didn't?

I've thought of giving my thought(s) away like God asked. I thought they were included in the package of my heart that I already gave to him. Maybe I'm holding back. Well, come and get it, Lord, for I do not want to keep anything from you that you desire.

I'm reminded of a quote that goes something like "God can't do anything for you that he can't do through you." It means a lot, but I'm having trouble grasping it. Is this my problem?

I'm hanging again. Questions. Oh yes, answers. Maybe never. Maybe I'm missing them or misinterpreting them. I just don't know.

The reader must think I'm obsessive.

The writer doesn't think so, for she has been touched and moved in a direction she never expected. The door was blown open on the ever-opening path, so bright and encouraging, just as it narrows and gets spotted by shadows.

I walk it not alone, for God is everywhere with me.

I left this door open for my love to follow me, to find me, to join me, to stay by my side. Daily, I pray for his courage and strength for the day he takes a chance. And I cannot help but look back and hope and wonder and dream for such that moment.

and mine too!

As I did my daily readings, I wondered if I could parallel myself with God the same way I've been doing it with Peter for so long.

A gift. Thank you, Lord. Amen.

Thy will be done. Goodnight.

Another day and gifts to my eyes…the Bradford Pear trees not yet in full bloom, but with the perfect blue cloudless sky above them, they were glorious side by side on so many tree lawns.

I ended my walk gazing at two weeping willows in yellowish green blossom next to the glistening and rippling pond with the soft yellow haze of a 6:30 sun behind them. One tree is much larger, and its willows gently reach to the smaller one. And on the drive home, two old and grand magnolia trees in full bloom.

One treat after another, and I remember saying to God, "I'm sure, I want to share all this with someone."

And He said, "Share it with me."

And I did. Peter was there, too, and neither one seemed to mind. For this soul still sees and feels the love triangle.

Forgive me, Lord, if there's too much Peter. I want to do your will, and if all good things come from you, how could I possibly let go? If I must, show me how. Amen.

I stopped.
I gazed.
I caught my breath.
I sighed…at the beauty of God's creation,
at the sight of my beloved, God's creation.

—April 23, 2003

This is Volume #5, the one with polka dots

Two wonderful things happened today.

1. On my walk at Westlake Rec. Ct., *three* swans paddled across the pond (drew a triangle) toward *me, together,* and stopped at the bank of the shore, watching me watch them. Really.
2. Shopped and had dinner with Julimarie and how *uplifting* to talk with her of God and the Lord and mysteries and hope and faith and children and love and Mark and Chuck and Peter and marriage and divorce and innocence and growth.

Thank you, my Lord, again.
Amen.

And, today, I cried as I responded to my dream as if it had come true—arms raised, tears being shed, walking in the spring grass among the pin oaks, singing the praises of a loving God.
Imagine crying real tears as I dream of my dream coming true.

For He who is mighty has done great things for me.

—*The Magnificat*

Also, in this day, I "preached" to Greg via Debbie that God will be made present to them both about the "work situation." And if this is fulfilled, they will become more and more aware of his love and his work so alive today. Amen.
"It is he that is at work."

and mine too!

> For if you do not overcome this need to
> understand, it will undermine your quest.
>
> —*The Cloud of Unknowing*,
> Fourteenth Century

Wow, why still so much of Peter?
Why still, is all of him the best part of my day?
Why does it feel good?
Why does it bring me comfort and security?
For in him, I am home! Yes, home!
Home as in the closest I know of heaven! Yes, heaven!
And our Lord calls us home to heaven, and my Lord lets me call him Peter on Earth.

And there are no words, but oh so many tears.

I was going to go to work today, but in Church today, God said, "Don't, and I'll give you a miracle."

I am sure the realization of the above paragraphs is that miracle. I am in awe, overwhelmed, and oh so graced.

> I cannot capture you with my words, but only with my hope.
>
> —John Kirvan, *Silent Hope*

I will love, honor, and cherish you both through all my days and into my eternity.

How can I not?

Does he know, Lord? Does he have an inkling? Is it too much? Does he know he's still on that pedestal? Is he not ready? Am I not ready? With you, with us, join us soon in all our weakness and disrepair. For with you, we will continue to repair and prepare for all you have planned for us together.

For Pete's Sake

Way back, I realized God manifested himself to me through the humanness of Peter. How phenomenally this still continues. I must deserve this most beautiful gift or it wouldn't be so alive.

If we do not understand each other in speech, we
can make ourselves understood by love.

—Ramon Lull

Lord of my heart
Lord of my soul
Lord of my life
Bless and bring me my beloved.
For he too, in his humanness
is the human lord of my heart,
is the human lord of my soul,
is the human lord in my life.

Are you ready, my Lord? Are you waiting for the green light from your Father, my God?

Oh, the wonder of it all.

Does he know I will care and love his heart?

Does he know I will care and love his soul?

Does he know I will care and love his life?

"Will" as in future? I do care and love now as in the present and regret not one second of it!

and mine too!

> What does not satisfy when we find it, was
> not the thing we were desiring.
>
> —C. S. Lewis

How can there be words, my Lord, when we join again? Will he understand my tears and speechlessness?

How can this not be a creation of heaven?

I have told people, "Oh, how the angels will sing!"

This weekend, I spoke of my love with friends the hopes, the dreams, and most of all, the presence of God. Speaking with most certainty that it was okay with God and that in a way, I was planting seeds—seeds of faith and hope and patience, all with the help of the Spirit, planting a seed or starting a fire. They were interested and want to know what happens and hoped for a happy ending.

Happy ending will also be a jubilant beginning. Oh, to be so blessed!

> Like a fool, the Lover went through the city singing of his
> Beloved, and men would ask him if he had gone mad.
>
> —Ramon Lull

And when I introduce my beloved, "This is Peter.," with tears in my eyes, I hope they will hear and see "this is God." For God will once again manifest himself through my Peter and I.

And love will grow and hope will grow and faith will grow. And there will be more peace and more happiness and more striving for what is good and truly real.

And Peter and I will be His disciples and live our lives reflecting all that is good in all the goodness God has bestowed on us.

For Pete's Sake

What God has joined together no man can bring asunder!

> How, Lord can I expect
> others to understand
> when I hardly understand myself?
> This madness
> is sanity.
> This darkness
> is light.
> This absence
> is presence.
> This emptiness
> is fulfillment.
> I feel like a fool.
> But only sometimes.
>
> —John Kirvan, *God Hunger*

I loved Chuck unconditionally and was totally devoted to him. But this love that I didn't know I had in my heart has been in a deep, quiet, safe reservoir for Peter and I. It is obvious to me.

Dear Lord, if I've got this all wrong, please bail me out soon. I don't want to be on the wrong path.

Nope, can't be wrong; it feels too right.

I'm babbling in ink.

Goodnight.

> Jesus' plan is a reason for joy!
>
> —Max Lucado, *The Applause of Heaven*

and mine too!

And, today, I read from *Enchanted Love*, "Of Space Captains and Angels…" by Marianne Williamson:

> "You prayed for him of course."
> "Oh, yes. With all my heart."
> "Well. Job well done. Sorry if your heart was a little bruised on this mission."
> The angel was trained for love, she was disciplined in love, but her tears still flowed.
> As the angel turned around to weep her superior called her back. I say one thing… Do remember you'll see him again someday.
> "Will I really, Master? Will I really?"
> "Of course, you will. You must cling to your own faith at times like these. How else can you convince them of theirs, if you don't?"

Amen! Amen! And Hallelujah!
I am not crying, but my eyes twinkle, and ooh, how I am smiling.
Thank you, Lord, for gifting me in such obvious ways.
I dance with my heart and eyes and arms.
I feel like an angel afloat being so close to heaven, so close to love.
Did Peter call me his angel once?
Oh yes, to be sure.

> God always has the final say.
>
> —Marianne Williamson, *Illuminata*

What are you doing, sweetie? Do you have any idea what's going on? Do you feel an undercurrent? Tremors? Do you have a sense of anticipation?

I finished reading that chapter called "Of Space Captains and Angels" three times, and oh my God—yes, my God told me or my angel told me or my heart told me—I ripped out those pages from another copy of the book and attached a note that said, "*Dear Peter. After reading this over and over and over again, I could not not send it to you. Boldly, bravely, and always. M.*"

Sealed it, stamped it, and it will be gone in the morning mail. My heart is racing, my breaths deep. I am crying now. This is powerful, unbelievable. There is no fear, no negative sensations at all.

How long will I be an angel with one wing? How could the matching wing belong to anybody but Peter?

Peter, please understand.

> Do not conform yourselves to the standards of the world,
> but let God transform you inwardly by a complete change
> of your mind. Then you will be able to know the will of
> God – what is good and pleasing to him and is perfect.
>
> —Romans 12:2 GNB

> Do we then nullify the law by this faith? Not
> at all! Rather we uphold the law.
>
> —Romans 3:31 NIV

"I Believe You"

I believe in you
When you say you'll reach into the sky

and mine too!

And steal a star so you can put it on my
finger
I believe you
Baby I believe you.
I believe you, when you say every time we make
love
Will be like the first time we make love
And every act of love will please you.
Baby I believe you.
Blind faith makes me follow you
I'd live in a cave if you'd wanted to
Just ask me and I'll marry you
You don't have to sell me
'Cause you overwhelm me
I've made up my mind for a lifetime.
I believe you.
When you swear that your love will keep on
Growin' strong
And that forever isn't long enough to love me
like you need to
Baby I believe you.
Baby I believe you.
Honey I love you.
Blind Faith makes me follow you.

—The Carpenters, *Singles* 1969–
1981 (emphasis is mine)

For Pete's Sake

Humble yourselves, therefore, under God's mighty hand, that he may lift you up in *due time*.

—1 Peter 5:6 NIV (emphasis added)

"Let It Be Me"

I bless the day I found you
I want to stay around you
And so I beg you, let it be me.
Don't take this heaven from one
If you must cling to someone
Now and forever, let it be me.
Each time we meet, love
I find complete love
Without your sweet love, what would life be?
So never leave me lonely
Tell me you love me only
And that you'll always let it be me.

—Petula Clark, *I Couldn't Live Without Your Love: Hits, Classics, and More*

The Lord will always lead you.

—Isaiah 58:11 CSB

and mine too!

    Did I mention that I have not seen the three swans since last week?

Happy Heart

There's a certain sound that always follows me
around.
When you're close to me, you will hear it.
It's the sound that lovers finally will discover
When there is no other for their love.
(chorus)
It's my happy heart you'll hear, singing loud and
singing clear
And it's all because you're near me—my love.
Take my happy heart away; make me love
you, make my day
In your arms I want to stay, Oh my love.
Feeling more and more, like I've never felt
before
You've changed my life so completely
Music fills my soul now; I've lost all control
now
I'm not half, I am whole now with your love
(chorus)
Don't you hear my happy heart?

—Petula Clark, *I Couldn't Live Without
Your Love: Hits, Classics, and More*

> I go on desiring you, because I already have you.
> It will be enough for now, for this night.
>
> —John Kirvan, *Silent Hope*

Today, on my walk, two cardinals, male and female, together on the bush, together in flight.

Today, Peter should have received the story.

My blind faith, silent hope, and living love continues to sustain me. Thank you, Lord, for such wonderful gifts—gifts full of your grace.

Heard a love song, *The Wonder of You* sung by Elvis. A man singing to a woman, yes, but definitely me singing to my Lord. Amen.

My Nicky graduates tomorrow night. I thought with another year and half, this would be a nice night. Oh, no, it will be a wonderful night. He is a joy, a gift, and I am honored God chose me to be his mom. I hope I never let either of you down.

And Angela and Matt, if you ever read this, I feel the same. I wish you all *true* happiness always.

Dear Lord, Do continue your saving of all of me.
I will assume Peter responds to the work you are doing in him.
But may I ask that you bring us together through this process?
Mary

> Sometimes the way God answers our prayers is not by changing what is around us, but by changing us so that we can cope.
>
> —R. T. Kendall, *When God Shows Up*

So much to share, so many tears shed in just one evening.

Bocelli, "A Night in Tuscany," is on DVD.

We had a wonderful commencement weekend. The Mass was awesome, the commencement memorable, and our after party and luncheon the next day was beautiful.

We ate at Georgetown Inn on Mt. Washington where the three rivers meet. It was sunny and in the high sixties. Father Ray was able

and mine too!

to join us. What an incredible guy. He is totally himself, and we find we are, too, when we are around him. Lance joined us, and it is always good to be with him.

Chuck was present, but that's all. Once again, he did not acknowledge me or my mom. He spoke to my dad, but only because he approached Chuck. And, once again, he did not thank me for anything nor offer a penny.

> The only beloved who can always be counted on is God. The
> ultimate partner is a divine one, an experience of ourselves
> that is totally supportive and forgiving. Until we know this, we
> keep seeking sustenance from men that they cannot give us
>
> —Marianne Williamson, *A Woman's Worth*

On the other hand, he looks awful. His health is awful. I'm truly sorry he's at such a terrible place. It's sad. But once again, I ask, "How dare he?" Fortunately, my frustrations take a back seat to my compassion for his life. You give nothing, you get nothing.

Saw *X-Men 2* with Father Ray and the "kids." The character Nightcrawler spoke of the Archangel Gabriel etching all the sins on his body and, in one scene, he prayed the "Our Father." How powerful! The Word reaching everyone who sees it, even if subtlety. Praise the Lord!

> Keep knocking at the door and Joy will
> look out the window to let you in.
>
> —Rumi, *A Ruby*

Peter seemed to be on the back burner for a couple of days, which happens once in a while. This rattles me slightly, but never lasts. For one day later, my beloved consumes my day.

This can only come from God, and he does not take Peter from me. He accepts my longing.

I wait for that miracle day, but today, I realized that all of what my heart unfolds and holds is in itself a miracle. Mine. Ours.

There is no one else.

One day, God will again be present on earth, manifest in his son, Peter. And I will be his Mary, his Martha, his Magdalene, his Zacchaeus, his Lazarus, his Thomas, his John, his Peter (rock), his angel.

When he holds me, it will be my taste of heaven, lying in the arms of God. He will know the sound of peace in the beating of my heart.

Be still, my love, and know that I am yours!

God loves every person as though there were no one else to love.

—St. Augustine

Last week, I realized that in one of our conversations, Peter asked if I would "keep" him. I said, "No." I wouldn't want to be kept, so why would I want to keep anybody?

Well, my darling you are being "kept" in my heart. Do you have any idea? It's a safe place. Remember when you agreed that I can give you everything *you need*?

Today, on my walk, two bunnies hopped across the path not far from me, one behind the other, obviously to the same destination. A gift, you bet, for me.

Still haven't seen the three swans.

> For we do not know how we ought to pray: the Spirit himself pleads with God for us in groans that words cannot express. And God, who sees into our hearts, know what the

and mine too!

thought of the Spirit is: because the Spirit pleads with God
on behalf of His people and in accordance with His will.

—Romans 8:26–27 GNT

Yes. Amen. Yes.
Cried all the way to and from Italian class. Needed Kleenex. Is it longing? Is it loving? Is it of this Earth? Is it of this time? Grace has made my faith so strong. Grace is a gift of God, and may my life reflect my love and thanks. Amen.
P.S. Thanks for that glorious sunset too!
Lyrics have been hitting me in the heart and soul, so I'm going to pen some of them, for me.

For it was by hope that we were saved; but if we see what we hope for, then it is not really hope. For who hopes for something he sees? But if we hope for what we do not see, we wait for it with patience.

—Romans 8:24–25 GNT

Dear God, Please protect and nourish my beloved. Surround
him with your power and grace. Make clear the road that
you would have him walk, easy the goals You accomplish
in his life, and soft the pillow he rests on. Use me to
provide for him an ever more wonderful life. Amen.

—Marianne Williamson, *Enchanted Love*

So rest in me, and I will rest in you. The
rest is in the hands of God.

—Marianne Williamson, *Enchanted Love*

For Pete's Sake

God is the only partner we need. The human at our side is a partner we desire. A clear difference between the two puts our inner world in balance, and then and only then, can love rule all things.

—Marianne Williamson, *Enchanted Love*

I draw a triangle with a cross at the peak, an M in the lower left angle, and a P in the lower right angle. We're our own little church.

Peter, did you not see tomorrow in my eyes?
Did you not hear tomorrow in my words?
Did you not feel tomorrow when I touched your cheek?
Do you think of me? Often?
Do you wonder?
You know I wait, don't you?
Do you find it comforting?
Do you have any idea how comforting it will
be when you and I are together?
Do you know it will last forever?

Lord, how could my heart be for anyone else? You are above all else and always will be. Then there's Peter, your son, my man (man-ifest). You did this. No one could conceive it, plan it, or know where to begin. It is so beautiful and feels eternal already.

Continue to care for our hearts till soon, our three hearts will be such a glorious life source and light source for all to see.

In faith. In hope. In gladness.
In love, Mary.
Amen.

and mine too!

It is no longer winter but the spring of our emotional cycle, and love, quite literally is in the air.

—Marianne Williamson

"Viene su, viene su"

Come along through the years with me
Can't you see how I adore you?
And how long I've waited for you?
Viene su, viene su
Won't you say you love me too?

—Dean Martin, *Italian Love Songs*

"Show & Tell"

These are the eyes
That never knew how to smile till you came
into my life
And these are the arms
That long to lock you inside every day and
every night.
And this is the soul of which you've
taken control
I'm tryin' to show love is right? (emphasis added)
Show and tell
Just a game I play

For Pete's Sake

When I wanna to say *I love you* (emphasis added)
So show and tell me
That you feel the same way too.
Say you do, baby
These are the hands
That can't help reaching for you if you're
anywhere in sight.
And these are the lips
That can't help calling your name in the
middle of the night.
So, show me and tell me…

—Al Wilson, *Show and Tell:
The Best of Al Wilson*

But by God's grace I am what I am, and the grace
that He gave me was not without effect.

—1 Corinthians 15:10 GNT

"Just to See Her"

Just to see him.
Just to touch him.
Just to hold him in my arms again one more
time.
If I could feel his warm embrace
See his smiling face

and mine too!

Can't find anyone to take his place
I've got to see him again.
I would do anything.
I would go anywhere
There's nothing I wouldn't do
Just to see him again
I can't hide it, no.
I can't fight it, no.
It's so hard to live without the love he gave
to me
Doesn't he know it
I tried hard not to show it.
Can't I make him realize that he really
needs me again.
I would do anything
I would go anywhere
There's nothing I wouldn't do
Just to see him again
He brightened up my every day
Made me feel so good in every way
If I could have him back to stay
I've got to see him again.

—Smokey Robinson, *My World*
(The Definitive Collection)

I changed the she to he and the her to him.

The serious business of heaven which he fully expected to be joy.

—C. S. Lewis

For Pete's Sake

The command after all was Take; eat: not Take, understand.

—C. S. Lewis

What is doing anything and going anywhere? To me, it's remaining and growing in the Lord and doing his will until…

"You'll Be in My Heart"

Come stop your crying
It will be alright
Just take my hand
Hold it tight
I will protect you
From all around you
I will be there
Don't you cry
For one so small,
You seem so strong
My arms will hold you
Keep you safe and warm
This bond between us
Can't be broken
I will be there
Don't you cry
[chorus]
'Cause you'll be in my heart
Yes, you'll be in my heart
From this day on
Now and forever more
You'll be in my heart
No matter what they say

and mine too!

You'll be in my heart, always
[chorus]
Why can't they understand
The way we feel?
They just don't trust
What they can't explain
I know we're different but,
Deep inside us
We're not that different at all
[chorus]
Don't listen to them
'Cause what do they know?
We need each other
To have and to hold.
They'll see in time
I know
When destiny calls you
You must be strong.
I may not be with you
But you've got to hold on.
They'll see in time
I know.
We'll show them *together* (emphasis added)
[chorus]
You'll be in my heart.
Believe me, you'll be in my heart.
Now and forever more.
Always and always.
Just look over your shoulder.

—Phil Collins, *Tarzan* (Original
Motion Picture Soundtrack)

For Pete's Sake

> The trial you are going through at the moment
> may be God's hint that He's there after all.
>
> —R. T. Kendall, When God Shows Up

> The Goddess… She is not held back by what happened to us in the past. She is conceived in consciousness, born in love and nurtured by higher thinking. She is integrity and value, created and sustained by the hard work of personal growth and the discipline of a life actively *in hope.* (emphasis added)
>
> —Marianne Williamson, *A Woman's Worth*

My advent continues.

I have written for a year without sharing my words with my beloved. I continue to write as the second year amazingly begins. Yet, I realize and know that time is irrelevant in this "being," this relationship.

I can truly say I do not miss Peter.
I long for him.
We made love last night.
I read to him afterward.

And my crying continues. My tears that I cannot label. The tears that reassure me. The tears that make me question so much when I do shed them. Tears that definitely nourish my emotions, just as the rain nourishes all that grows and keeps them alive.

> Intimacy comes from trusting the Universe (God-mine) to provide what you need, when you need it, and in the manner that is most appropriate for you.
>
> —G. Zukav, *Heart of the Soul*

and mine too!

Tears, salty, yet life-giving.

Lately, these tears follow a thought of a conversation with Peter that makes me smile, that melts my lips and opens my eyes as they overflow. There is a beautiful silent rhythm to this phenomenon.

Who is this man?

Will I only love him from afar? Forever?

That seems so cruel, and my Father is not cruel. Satan is cruel, and only he would try to twist me with such thoughts. So, in my Father's name, begone, evil one, and leave my beloved alone—forever!

Curl up and crawl away, scum. You are weak and puny and jealous. You don't stand a chance. You are out of time. Go to hell. Amen.

Our tears might turn into balms with which we heal each other and comfort each other, after so many years of getting it all so wrong.

—Marianne Williamson, *Enchanted Love*

Mmm...

Who is this man? My question over and over again.

"But who do you say that I am?" Jesus questions.

—Mark 8:29 NIV

Interesting, to be sure.

Sometimes I wonder how far-fetched my thoughts, hopes, and dreams are, and then I read or hear or see something that affirms what my heart feels, and I smile and feel empowered.

But there are also days when I question my discernment at what I read, hear, or see. Yet, the best of all and most of all is that I believe they are messages from God to keep me growing in faith, hope, and love. I hunger for more. It feels wonderful. I am not alone.

Love is a miracle. It's a God job.

—Marianne Williamson, *Enchanted Love*

I hunger to know God and myself better, and I hunger for the forever when God will once again and for always manifest himself to me and my world through my Peter. Amen.

I believe Peter is being healed like I am, surrendering like I am, growing like I am. Again, I ask my Lord. Let us join and be a strength to each other and comfort and encouragement on this path of growth. I know that the path does not end (I would not want it to), but am I asking for too much? Heal us enough, and then hook us up as we continue, the three of us forever. Amen.

Hi, my weaknesses see your weaknesses. Want to dance and grow strong together?

—Marianne Williamson, *Enchanted Love*

It's not Peter.
Is it not Peter?
I couldn't have "made this all up."
"I didn't say that," God just said to me. "I just want to make you think."

and mine too!

Oh the presence of God in my life is unmistakable and constant. I receive many gifts, and they bring me comfort and awe. Are they to "tide me over" till it's time for me to be joined with my beloved?

Oh, the wonder and power and exhilaration of my new faith and hope!

Passion is the unfolding of joy.

—G. Zukav, *Heart of the Soul*

Who knows the mind of the Lord? Who is able to give him advice?

—Romans 11:34 GNT

Dear Peter,

You will not fall down today because my love is here for you. You will not be emotionally homeless because my love is here for you. You will not be lonely today because my love is here for you. I see you in the arms of God and I know that we are together.

Love you forever,
M.

The above was from *Enchanted Love* by Marianne Williamson. This book is like a volume to *my* personal journals. We have written the same words, more or less. But she is so much more eloquent than me. Her words have affirmed and manifested so much of my priceless emotions unearthed in my love for Peter. An enchanted romance with the physically absent Peter? Absolutely.

She also writes:

> We will meet who we are supposed to meet, as the meeting itself is ordained by God. But what we do in a relationship is entirely up to us. Enchanted love, under the direction of God's spirit, is both a path and an example of divine illumination.
>
> All who meet, according to the principles of miracles, will one day meet again until their relationship becomes holy… What is chosen *by us* now will seem to be chosen *for us* later. The love we give is the love that will be returned to us, a thousand times over, in ways we cannot imagine, so great is the probable light. (emphasis added)

Possibility is the secret heart of time. In its deeper heart, time is transfiguration. *Fear changes into courage, emptiness becomes plentitude, and distance becomes intimacy.* (emphasis added)

—J. O'Donohue, *Anam Cara*

I'm sure Peter will let me read this to him.

Do not conform yourselves to the standards of the world, but let God transform you inwardly by a complete change of your mind. Then you will be able to know the will of God what is good and pleasing to Him and is perfect.

—Romans 12:2 GNT

and mine too!

CD player not working. I miss my music playing in the background.

Later on this day, thoughts, dreams (while awake) of our physical reunion. With them comes audible sighs from the overwhelmingness of the moment, the dream. It's happened a couple of times before. But again? Wow!

Overwhelmed to such a point by a thought? By a dream? Wow!

As in the Bible, when they speak of a woman in labor, is our new love near to being born? Am I stretching this dream too far? Again?

And with it came the predictable tears.

Thank you. Amen.

For I know the plans I have for you declares the Lord, plans to prosper you and not harm you, plans to give you hope and a future.

—Jeremiah 29:11 NIV

Now and Forever

Now and forever you are part of me
And the memory cuts like a knife
Didn't we find the ecstasy
Didn't we share the daylight
When you walked into my life.
Now and forever I'll remember
All the promises unbroken
And think about all the words between us
That never needed to be spoken.
We had a moment
Just one moment
That will last beyond the dream

For Pete's Sake

Beyond the lifetime
We are the lucky ones
Some people never get to do
Oh we got to do
Now and forever I will always think of you.
Didn't we come together
Didn't we live together
Didn't we cry together
Didn't we play together
Didn't we love together
And together we lit up our world
I miss the tears
I miss the laughter
I miss the day we met
And all that followed after
Sometimes I wish I could always be with you
The way we used to do, oh
Now and forever I will always think of you
Now and forever I will always be with you.

—Carole King, from the movie *A League of
Their Own*, *The Living Room Tour* (Live)

This is from a tape titled *The Luminous Mind Workshop* by Marianne Williamson.

A Course in Miracles says love waits not on time, but on welcome. We can come to a place in our hearts where we are ready for something and the psychological conditions of the situation might not be such that it is yet time to do this or that. But we still get, within our hearts, the benefit of the movement we have made within our hearts even if it is not yet time to take an outer action... So if you move forward in terms of your understanding and awareness then the Spirit within you will guide you.

Maybe it will be that it's time to breakthrough, write a letter, make a phone call, something... Maybe it won't be time. But I know that if you can make the breakthrough in your awareness, the benefit will come into your heart.

Oh yes!
And I think...*God chose Peter* to "represent" him in my heart.
I choose him, too, for countless, yes, countless reasons. Why do I feel so sure? I feel sure enough because God is the glue. I am overwhelmed and actually *giddy* today. So many times, while on my walks, I just want to dance!

> One definition of spirituality then; the ability to close the gap between the time of the Lord's appearance and our being aware that it is the Lord.
>
> —R. T. Kendall, *When God Shows Up*

> Let your hope keep you joyful, be patient in your troubles, and pray at all times.
>
> —Romans 12:12 GNT

Can I arrogantly pen "Peter will choose me"? The presence of God will show him the way and the how! Amen.

I met this guy walking the other day. I'll write about the encounter when I'm not so tired.

No sign of the swans.

My drawings of our love triangle...

Phil Collins wrote a song, *Two Hearts.* I count three! Amen.

For Pete's Sake

As the roots are allowed to grow, so goes the uprooting.

—Matthew Fox, *Prayer: A Radical Response to Life*

Now listening to *Abundance* by Marianne Williamson. Side A is incredible. I'll write from that too. But not tonight. Goodnight, and thanks again!

Do I ask too much?

Meanwhile, these three remain: faith, hope and love and the greatest of these is love.

—1 Corinthians 13:13 GNT
(emphasis added)

May 28, 2003

Each tear is a gift.Each tear is a prayer.
Real love is radical!

To try to create ourselves instead of revealing ourselves,
is to come from such a lack of self-esteem that it
would be hard to keep a man interested anyway.
On the days when I feel love and compassion and forgiveness
in my life, I am happier and more attractive to other people.
Those feelings are the mystical keys to beauty and happiness.

—Marianne Williamson, *A Woman's Worth*

and mine too!

> Because we have this hope we are very bold.
>
> —2 Corinthians 3:12 GNT

God is here to stay. Amen.
I want Peter here to stay. Amen.
The three of us. Amen.
Oh glorious love!

Guess what? There were never three white swans at the rec center pond. That was my response when I inquired about them with the rec center staff. My gift, another miracle/sign. So there!

Who is this man?
Who is this gentleman?
Where is this gentleman?

Every thought, every memory, every word and action we shared was gentle.

I desire more.

> Most men have no idea of the lengths to which a woman will go for love or the depths of our despair when we feel it cut off.
>
> —Marianne Williamson, *A Woman's Worth*

Oh, the tears I shed yesterday. *Overcome* as I walked more than once, and each time, it was with the overwhelming presence of God and his knowledge that these tears are necessary—a part of something huge.

Brought to tears as I worked (six offices). Were they cleansing me?

And so many times in between with so many love songs on the radio: *You'll Never Find Another Love Like Mine* by Lou Rawls, twice; *You are My Special Angel* (The Vogues) plays now.

Did anyone hear my gentle sobs and whimpers? Besides my Lord, of course. And when the peak of overwhelmingness hit, my breath is taken away for a split second, yet taken away nonetheless.

> The spirit of man is the lamp of the Lord,
> Searching all the inner depths of his heart.
>
> —Proverbs 20:27 NKJV

My breath, alive with the Spirit, taken away by the same man who took my breath away not so long ago. Only God could sustain such a love as this because it is a love he created.

Peter, my beloved! What are you doing? How could you be doing anything but thinking of *us*?

June 8, 2003

There is no wall, sweetheart.

If you still feel it/see it, I will continue my prayers for you daily, for there is no one put on this Earth for you, except me. Please let me manifest the love of God to you as you did for me. It's beautiful and timeless and pure and innocent and giving and forgiving and true and powerful, and it's ours to give to each other and then others around us.

God does not need translators to understand the words of our soul.

—John Kirvan, *Raw Faith*

and mine too!

I love you, Peter Tucciaroni. I will wait forever for you.

I realized this a week or so ago. I don't need to date another or want a phone call from another. It is you. I will be true to you. I am yours, and somewhere deep inside, you know this. And you are mine, and deep inside, you know this too.

Let it go, baby—the truth will set you free!

My girlfriend said she wishes she could be like me because "Mary waits for no man." She said this regarding Paul. She is wrong, for Mary waits for Peter.

I just say what I want to God and he never fails to understand.

—St. Therese of Lisieux

Something else amazing, and I don't think I've penned it either, making love is not what it's about. It's not necessary. This love, our love (or is it just my love? "No" is the answer I get), goes beyond the needs and wants of mortal men and women. So when we are united, the art of lovemaking will be the icing on the cake for Peter and Mary.

And we will be blessed again! *Wow.*

And if it's not Peter? Well, the Bible says what God has planned for us is better than we can dream of (or something like that).

And I realize it might not be of this Earth. This is very hard to manage in my heart. The rest of my life waiting for heaven? Father, thy will be done.

As this day passes into night
hear the silent yearning of my soul.
I have no other language.

For Pete's Sake

> I need no other.
> For I do not know
> what I want to say,
> or even what I truly want
> My soul is tongue-tied,
> but more eloquent than I know.
> Hear me.
>
> —John Kirvan, *Raw Faith*

Walking and listening to a tape on the *Celestine Prophecy* (James Redfield), a section on coincidences and how they are messages, signs, stepping stones. The more we become aware of them, it becomes clearer that it is an integral part of our individual life. The more we see/hear them, the more we look for/watch for them.

I switch to FM radio as my walk becomes my "spirit" time, and I hear, instantly, these lyrics by The Beatles:

The Long and Winding Road

> Many times, I've been alone,
> And many times, I've cried.
> Anyway, you'll never know
> The many ways I've tried.
> And still they bring me back
> to the long, winding road.
> You left me standing here,
> a long, long time ago, oh, oh.
> Don't leave me waiting here.
> Lead me to your door.
> (The 1st verse I didn't hear, but looked it up…)
> The long and winding road
> that leads to your door
> will never disappear,

and mine too!

> I've seen this road before, oh, oh
> It always leads me here,
> Lead me to your door.
>
> —*The Beatles 1967–1970*

> The normal thing is this simplicity, the fact that we have seen and tasted that the Lord is good. We need to thank God for that.
>
> —Thomas Merton, *The Springs of Contemplation*

So this night, *June 11, 2003*, I "hear" say goodbye, and I "hear" it again in the morning. *June 12, 2003*, I "hear" say goodbye again. Each time, my response is, "What? No, no, no. What is this all about?"

> Make room for love and it always comes. Make a nest for love, and it always settles. Make a home for the beloved, and he will find his way there.
>
> —Marianne Williamson, *A Woman's Worth*

I don't want to say goodbye to Peter, to us, to writing our love story. But somehow, I know it will be okay. Somehow is the grace of God and knowing he will always be.

I get choked up but haven't really cried yet. I know I am comforted.

I pondered this "goodbye" off and on during the day. Maybe it's the goodbye I need to really say, to *really* give it to God. I thought I had, but maybe he wants my every thought even before I think.

I don't understand. More discipline?

I always thought God wouldn't be so cruel as to not make this manifest.

I didn't know I could be so wrong!

> Don't you know that your body is the temple of the Holy
> Spirit, who lives in you and who was given to you by
> God? You do not belong to yourselves but to God.
>
> —1 Corinthians 6:19 GNT

I thought following my heart was good and right, especially since I've met God and Son and Spirit in such a new and beautiful way—alive in this heart.

Was I told "goodbye" because Peter's use of his free will was not to choose the spaceship, the angel, me? Doesn't he get another chance?

He told me he thought we had a chance.

I don't get it. But it will be okay. Some Bible quote, "Man cannot begin to comprehend all that God has planned for us." Okay. Now what? When?

I'm getting it, but why can't I get it while this love affair continues?

> I am your servant; give me understanding
> so that I may know your decrees
>
> —Psalm 119:125 CSB

I asked God aloud, "What has this past year been all about then?"

He answered, "You'll see."

and mine too!

More hope.
More patience.
More tears—here they come.
Do I really know it's God I hear? Yes, I've been able to separate his words from mine and have been more confident doing this as time goes on. Plus, I know the positive, fearless, and hopeful stuff are of heaven. That's what this journey has been. Nothing negative. I do know negative.
A test of faith?
Well, my Lord, I know you've never left me, ever. Please know I will never leave you, ever. Help me to see and do your will. Keep me humble. I am yours.
Let me love.
Amen.
Who were the swans for?
Was the goodbye for Peter?
What of the love songs?
Was it ever a triangle? Yes.
Have I been delusional?
What of these pages?
What more?
What's next?
Peter, you have been loved, you know. I think and am almost sure in the way you've needed and wanted and deserved. Let me rewrite that in the present tense.
Peter, you are loved, you know, in the way you need, want, and deserve. There, that's better.
I am aware!

> The most I can do is to open my heart and leave it open, so that you can show yourself it is your turn. As it always is. As for me, let me stand clear. Let me get out of your way.
>
> —John Kirvan, God Hunger

How could I have been so wrong? So misled? By whom? Certainly not by Peter. By myself? Maybe some. By the devil? He's not that talented. By God? But why? I followed my heart, and when I found God there, how could my heart be wrong?

I can't get mad or spiteful or bitter or sarcastic or cynical because I want God's will in every aspect of my life. I love him, and *I know* he loves me.

Was it Peter's free will that did the choosing in not choosing *true love?*

I prayed for him in so many ways. Didn't he ever see me as his angel?

> If I write a book, a novella, a love story, I would title it *The Perfect Love Triangle.*
>
> —Mary Magazzine-Hudak, *June 15, 2003*

Did I not pray that he should not be afraid? And for his strength? And that his burdens be lifted? What message did I miss? When was it sent?

Pages of love spanning almost fourteen months. Was it always one sided? Why would God keep me there for so long? I asked him to take Peter out of my heart months ago since I couldn't do it myself. When Peter continued to grow in my heart, I thought that was where he was supposed to be till we were reunited. What does it mean?

Walk with Him long enough and you come to know His heart.

> —Max Lucado, *The Great House of God*

Why do I bother? Have I been so selfish? What do I do? (*My handwriting becomes very intense.*)

What do I write of? What was the goodbye for? Who was the goodbye for?

What of the deepest desires of *my* heart, my humanness?

and mine too!

Yes, I'm on the right track, though.
Now I'm sad.
Why should I be treated any differently? How many lonely souls are out there waiting?

> I believe that with all my heart, when we are walking in the light, what is withheld from us is really a blessing that one day we'll appreciate more fully.
>
> —R.T. Kendall, *When God Shows Up*

I thought I had what it takes for Peter and I and that Peter had what it takes for us and that he was working on it too.

"Taking care of our shit.," as he said.

Will he ever know how I felt and feel? He loved our love story.

> I am the Lord, the God of every person on Earth, nothing is impossible for me.
>
> —Jeremiah 32:27 NCV

Dear Peter,

Take care of yourself. If you ever need anything, unconditionally call me. I have loved, darling. You!

And if God sends the spaceship again, I hope he assigns me to be your angel. You have raised the bar, you silly man. Do not deny yourself. Punish yourself no longer.

Don't work too hard.

Did both you and God forget about me?

You both know my heart.

I'm confused and sad.

I thought this was it—our love, a light to each other. A light to the world. The trickle-down effect would have been sweet.

Was I too self-centered? Did I not give in the ways I should? Not enough humility? Tell me, God, I want to do it right and make you happy and proud. What does this prove?

Please be clearer with your answers and messages. I don't mean to be so ignorant and arrogant.

(More intense handwriting.)

I think this started out as a letter to Peter, and now it's to both of you. Isn't that how most of this started?

"You were taught to be made new in your hearts, to become a new person…Made to be like God—made to be truly good and holy."

—Ephesians 4:23–24 NCV

It started on that day I realized (or thought I did) that God manifested himself through Peter so I would fall in love with God. And after all this time and all these pages, you two are interchangeable and in sync and inseparable (yes and no).

What does it mean?

I'm going back to read those two sections of *Enchanted Love* by Marianne Wiliamson now. If I don't come back tonight, it is because I've cried myself to sleep.

Excuse me for being human.

and mine too!

> As this night closes in
> let me not be saddened
> by the fire I never see,
> by the voice I never hear.
> It is enough to know that it is there.
> That you are there.
>
> —John Kirvan, *Silent Hope*

> Our spiritual journey will not grind to a halt at
> every evidence that we are still human.
>
> —John Kirvan, *Raw Faith*

Well, another day.

Who/What was the goodbye for?

Not Peter. He is so alive and well in my heart. I thought I could, but I guess not. Maybe it won't happen overnight. Lord, if it is your will, I need your help. It's not a choice. I was somehow okay with the goodbye, but he won't leave my thoughts, won't leave my dreams, won't leave my heart.

Does he know he's being so well taken care of yet?

So if it's not a long goodbye, it is meant for something/someone else.

> The fact is, the more you write, record and accumulate,
> the more power you give to your vision.
>
> —Suzanne Falter-Barns, *How Much Joy Can You Stand?*

Today, Father's Day, I had a beautiful walk/run. No headphones today. Just me and my thoughts or lack of. Temperature: seventy-four degrees; sunshine, clear blue sky; and the most beautiful of clouds. So light and wispy, yet the sun lost none of its power to penetrate them. We called them horsetail clouds in grade school science. Today, they became angels everywhere. Feathery wingspans of peace and hope in flight. They were sent to me, and I sent them to Pittsburgh to remind Peter that I am his angel. It seemed like the thing to do. I am his everything. Why do I feel so strongly about this? Is it too arrogant? No.

In my efforts to be less selfish, I asked that these angels in the sky would be visible to others in hope and peace and love.

Wait patiently on the will of the Lord with courtesy and humility.

—Anonymous, *The Cloud of Unknowing*

The following is from chapter 5 of *A Woman's Worth* by Marianne Williamson:

> We usually know a lover is on the way well before he gets here. A woman in touch with herself can sense the coming of things.
> We can feel a love approaching and when we are in touch with the *Goddess*, we prepare ourselves in advance. How do we do that?
> We are about to give birth to a new creative force. The highest preparation is strengthening of our calm, a focusing of our clarity on who we are and what our values are. The core values— are those of love, forgiveness, and the desire to serve God. We serve him to the extent that we have thoughts of purity. Purity means that we do not manipulate, or seduce or pre-program or project hidden agendas onto anyone or anything.

and mine too!

The Goddess is in her highest glory when she is in love. Our highest work is to remember how important it is for the world, for our spirits, for the relationship itself—that we learn to be a *friend* to the beloved and a *spiritual companion* to our beloved and provide a sense of home to those we love the most. (emphasis added)

Once we meet him, we'd better have our spiritual chops down, because the attraction—will tempt us to forget the truth if it's not a solid part of us already. If it is, then there is no higher high than that of passionate love. Our *bodies* don't just feel as though they melt, *they do melt*, and our *spirits* don't feel as though they merge. *They do merge.*

How important it is to know that he is as tender as we are and just as lost and just as scared. Until we know this, we miss the point.

We are meant to be the healing of the wound (relief from pain); and if we allow it, our love will heal us both.

Remember the eyes of the one who loved you, and don't forget the mark on your soul. Carry it always, the badge of a woman who has opened her heart and allowed it to hurt, for herself and for him. She has gone crazy for love and been ridiculous for love and grown neurotic for love and wasted her time for love. But she has grown from the heartaches and endured until the sun shone, and finally she has seen the sky.

This is the journey of every woman who has loved a man. May we all find sustenance in knowing there's a remarkable prize waiting for us as we approach the truth. We are so full of miracles for all who come to us with pure and open hearts. We are so full of love for those who approach with tender souls. We are so full of beauty for those who believe it's there.

And men are such a gorgeous lot, the boys who made the climb from the arrogantly weak to the humbly strong. The initiate into the ways of love is like a letter from God telling us that he's here. The initiate, both man and woman, have seen a dark night and another day. There is no substitute for the fires that purify us; whatever they were, they served a purpose. And now we will know how to love and be loved, and never again will we lose our way.

Women in love are closer to enlightenment. For angels and lovers, everything sparkles. Most men have no idea of lengths to which women will go for love or the depths of despair when we feel it cut off.

The only beloved that can be always counted on is God. The ultimate partner is a divine one, an experience of ourselves that is totally supportive and forgiving. Until we know this, we keep seeking sustenance from men that they cannot give us. The source of our salvation, deliverance, and meaning is within us. It is the love we give as much as it is the love we get. The passion we must need to feed is our relationship with God. This is ultimately our relationship to ourselves.

It is work. Personal growth, recovery, religious practice, spiritual renewal—these are the keys to our return to sanity and peace.

Our role in a relationship is to bring peace, by receiving it from God and allowing him to spread his peace through us to all humankind.

Love is very serious business. It takes a powerful heart to invoke it clearly and prepare for its coming.

and mine too!

No one remains outside the gate - only the devil is there, and he can reach us no more.

The love in our hearts is the power that matters.

—Marianne Williamson, *A Woman's Worth*

The steps of a good man (woman, *mine*) are ordered by the Lord.

—Psalm 37:23 NKJV

Memo to self: next time, photocopy the pages, and use a highlighter.

Once again, Marianne Williamson has taken so many words from my journals and put them into shape.

So if what she says is acceptable and God-inspired, I am on the mark, the good path, and the devil is further and further from me. And Peter is my beloved.

Who is this man?
He is my beloved
I can love him forever
I will wait forever.
His name is Peter.

The wicked have set snares for me, but from your precepts I do not stray. Your decrees are my heritage forever; *They are the joy of my heart*. My heart is set on fulfilling your laws; they are my reward forever.

—Psalm 119:110–112 NAB
(emphasis added)

So if we have longings for a better world, longings for eternal life, it's likely we're designed "for another world." We're made for better things! So, we need to keep the fire of hope burning, moving toward that eternal realm Jesus prepared for us.

—G. Reed, *C. S. Lewis Explores Vice and Virtue*

It is a shock when you realize the value your own inner secrets hold for others.

—Suzanne Falter-Barnes, *How Much Joy Can You Stand?*

And what of the unconditional beloved? God! I now know this. I myself penned it. So much of this is in that small prayer I wrote for Peter and I way back in *May 2002*, the prayer I read every day.
Wow!
Believe it or not, my life is not only fulfilled with God, Peter, and my spiritual growth. My journey has been beautifully blessed since I realized I was really on one.

I'll just have to get used to it… To your way of doing things, To your expectations, not mine.

—John Kirvan, *Raw Faith*

and mine too!

Oh, to write of my graced children, my adored parents, my gentle friends and my providing business. Oh, the pages that would be multiplied. So:

Dear Lord of mine,

My thanks multiplied for each day of my life would not fulfill what I truly feel. Only you can feel what I feel—for there are no words.

I have been blessed. May your blessings, and mine, that I am able to give through your grace be bestowed daily on my children, my family, friends, my girls, and my business, on all I meet daily in all the world for peace. I love you. May I never let you down again.

Thank you for your forgiveness and patience and letting me bring all of me to the foot of your cross. You didn't have to. Aah, but such a love that we are all so deserving of in your eyes.

I know through Peter. Remember him, Lord? That beautiful man you manifested yourself in for my humanness. A love on earth that I know is just a hint of what you feel for all your children.

I'll write the next part, even though you know (everything). My tears fall as I raise my eyes and cry aloud, "I want to fly with him! I want to fly with him! I know I can fly with him.!"

I give you my heart and my life as long as it is your will. In this, I find innermost contentment and peace, truly.

Here on earth, you know my desire: to give my heart and life to Peter as long as it is your will.

Let the angels sing. Amen.

Mary

For Pete's Sake

You gave me life and showed me your unfailing love. My life was preserved by your care.

—Job 10:12 NLT

I forgot to mention that in the angel clouds today, there was a rainbow in one of them.

Law is the form love takes when we are away from it.

—Tillich

Hello

I've been alone with you inside my mind
And in my dreams, I've kissed your lips a
thousand time.
I sometimes see you pass outside my door.
Hello, is it me you're looking for?
I can see it in your eyes.
I can see it your smile.
You're all I ever wanted, my arms
are opened wide.
'Cause you know just what to say
And you know just what to do
And I want to tell you so much, I love you.
I long to see the sunlight in your hair
And tell you time and time again how much I

and mine too!

care.
Sometimes I feel my heart will overflow.
Hello, I've just got to let you know
'Cause I wonder where you are
And I wonder what you do.
Are you somewhere feeling lonely, or is
someone loving you?
Tell me how to win your heart
For I haven't got a clue.
But let me start by saying I love you
Hello
Is it me you're looking for?

—Lionel Richie, *Can't Slow Down*

Remember the eyes…and don't forget the mark on your soul. Carry it always, the badge of a woman who has opened her heart and allowed it to be hurt, for herself and for him. She has gone crazy for love, and been ridiculous for love and grown neurotic for love and wasted her time for love. But she has grown from the heartaches and endured until the sun shone, and finally she has seen the sky.

Pray for your loved one often.

Dear God, bring him happiness and peace. We want him present so we can touch his spirit from a closer place. We touch his eyes so we take joy in the fact that he really exists. We want him to be happy so miracles can happen around him.

See him as you want him to be: in such deep peace, full of every feeling that would make him melt. If we carefully imagine one human being, completely happy, then we can begin to imagine heaven.

And that is why we learn to love: to care so completely for one other person that our hearts break open wide and we learn to love them

For Pete's Sake

all. That's the meaning of love and that's the purpose of love, that one person might signify our love for God and all humankind. It's a place where love is holy and the earth itself is reconceived.

—Marianne Williamson, *A Woman's Worth*

Once again, Marianne Williamson puts all my pages neatly and emotionally into these paragraphs.

Has God let Peter stay in my heart so I won't be alone, waiting ever so patiently for what I don't know? No words right now.

So—
Since this is so me, and Peter is the individual
who signifies my love for God—
will he ever be...
mine?
with me?
by me?
in love with me?
my forever?
my destiny?
ready to take our chance?
will he ever...
know how I feel?
know how I pray for him every day?
know how I think of him every day?
know he deserves a taste of heaven on earth?

"For Pete's Sake" just popped into my head.

and mine too!

I am very much afflicted, Lord; Give me life in accord with your word. Accept my freely offered praise, Lord, teach me your decrees. My life is always at risk, but I do not forget your teaching.

—Psalm 119:107–109 NAB

You have not seen Christ, but still you love Him. You cannot see Him now, but you believe in Him.

—1 Peter 1:8 ICB

Your soul knows the geography of your destiny. Your soul alone has a map of your future, therefore you can trust this indirect, oblique side of yourself... Yet the signature of this unique journey is inscribed deeply in each soul.

—J. O'Donohue, *Anam Cara*

June 27, 2003

Is the "Say goodbye" working?

I think of Peter every day, but it feels like it is becoming a memory. Not as alive and vital. I feel sad...somehow a little guilty, confused.

Peter, my dear Peter. I thought it would be you! God knows I thought it would be you!

And if and when it is you, I will know what to do. The Spirit who opened our hearts to each other will do it once again, and then we will know that forever will be just fine.

> Do not be troubled but trust in the Lord. If you pray and
> hope in the Lord and do what you can for yourself, God
> will bring about in your soul all that you desire.
>
> —Teresa of Avila

July 5, 2003

> Search me, God, and know my heart; test
> me and know my anxious thoughts!
>
> —Psalm 139:23 NIV

So much for following my heart. How could my heart be so wrong? I loved him with all my heart!

Who? It was Peter. Or was it the Peter I created in my heart and soul? Am I so shallow? So fickle?

But God was with us. For it endured time as God has lifted and healed. Like God does, it was gentle and sincere and passionate, like our Lord.

I don't get it. I hate this.

I feel lost and let down. Is this disciplining or pruning?

I know we will never have all the answers. I know I have the love of God, and he has mine and all my trust and hope. So why am I crying my heart out?

I loved who I was and where I was with Peter in my heart. He was my beloved.

How long will I move as I am now? Slower, busier, confused.

I must be incredibly weak to feel I need a human to create a miracle.

How long ago did Peter figure this out? Did he ever? Did he choose the easy way? Did he not know the harder path would be the right path?

> But I am sure that God keeps no one waiting unless
> He sees that it is good for him to wait.

and mine too!

When you get into your room you will find the long wait has done some kind of good which you would not have had otherwise.

—C. S. Lewis, *On Faith*

I feel I, all of me, have grown and learned so much in the past few years, but now I am more confused. God's will is my bottom line desire.

I feel like, what of my simple *human* heart? This heart who will always live to be like Christ, it's the humanness that is sad and right now is clouding the joy and the grace. The God-ness of my heart reassures in a "gray" kind of way as if it is mourning with me.

I'm not so naïve to think that life will be a bowl of cherries with such a love, but such a love would make all the pits easier to deal with, and oh yes, I see that it's God's love that will get me through it all!

Well, right now, I don't feel so graceful, angel-like, spirited, or able to lift anyone up. What a pathetic, hopeless romantic I am. Where has it ever gotten me?

Make something of the hope you have planted in my soul, but which is still so fragile. Let me see in the darkness what only you can see. *Let me dream your dreams for me* and measure my soul by the depth of your love for what you find in me. (emphasis added)

—John Kirvan, *Raw Faith*

Hope refined in the darkest of times sustains us
by sharpening our focus on what's eternal.

—Gerald Reed, *C. S. Lewis Explores Vice and Virtue*

July 6, 2003

Oh so many pages of my ego self.
With each letter and each word and each sentence, the flowing of my spiritual self is ever-present, and *all will be well*, for God flows through me.
Jesus lives with me.
The Spirit reminds me.
For thine is the kingdom, the power, the glory. Amen.

Help me to live in hope of what never changes.

—John Kirvan, *Raw Faith*

July 23, 2003

I haven't written in a while but have thought of doing so more than once every day. What to write about? That two Thursdays ago, how I cried and cried, feeling again for Peter, that "ever so seems to be right" feeling. Feeling hopeful. Maybe the spaceship landed for him again. It was so there!

Since that day, I see him as my very own memory again. No one will know, and that's okay. But, Lord, does he know? Will he ever realize?

Christine was right. One thing I have learned, I am able to love passionately, devotedly, and unconditionally again. God bless you, Peter.

The value of material things lies not in itself but
in the higher reality which it reflects.

—Plato

and mine too!

The work issue again. Do I give up hours for the girls? We all have needs. There is no issue. Is it my ego that makes it an issue?

Stay with me Lord. I will assume that each breath, each step is your will.

New awesome revelation (to me): God is sovereign over my life! Thank God (no pun intended).

(I drew a rectangle around these sentences.)

If we are going to live as disciples of Jesus, we have to remember that all noble things are difficult. The Christian life is gloriously difficult, but the difficulty of it does not make us faint and cave in, it rouses us to overcome. Do we appreciate the marvelous salvation of Jesus that we are doing our utmost for His highest?

—Oswald Chambers, *My Utmost for His Highest* (Quoted in Gerald Reed, *C. S. Lewis on Vice and Virtue*)

Dare I start writing of another man?

His name is Chris. We met at the Westlake Recreation Center. He runs. I don't.

First the friendly "hi" exchanged, mostly on the trail.

Second, Chris starts the conversation, full of many topics. It was easy and enjoyable.

Third, I stop and join him on the grass.

Phenomenal, intriguing, curious, uplifting.

Talk of families, song, *soul*, eyes, smiles.

Open, honest, journeys, jobs.

Chris made reference how great to see more and more people looking for a meaning.

Turns out we read the same authors of late.

Interesting fact #1: We underline our books with different color ink.

Interesting fact #2: We love to give books as gifts.

Interesting fact #3: He wants to call me Marie and doesn't know why.

I told him God will give us all new names anyway, so Marie is okay. He wondered of his new name. I later realized…*Christ*-opher. His mom knew what she was doing.

Ace and his cat, Louie, have a date at the park, soon I hope.

Last part of our conversation:

> Chris (C): Wow! I have to think about all this tomorrow.
> Me (M): I think it's called synchronicity or that other word.
> C: Serendipity
> M: Synchronicity is from *The Celestine Prophecy.*
> C: That's one of my favorite books

> If you abide in Me and My words abide in you, you will ask what you desire, and it shall be done for you. By This my Father is glorified, that you bear much fruit.
>
> —John 15:7–8 NKJV

Somewhere, more than once, I have written that if there is someone else for me here on earth that he'll have to be on his own journey too. Mmm.

So dare I write again—of what? For what?

Once again, I dream of scenarios, stop myself, and pray over and over again…

and mine too!

Dear Lord, please help to keep me from wasting time and thought on my selfishness when I should be doing your will. Is this his will?

> Your word is a lamp to my feet, a light for my path.
>
> —Psalm 119:105 NAB

I would like to ask Chris to Ron's wedding, but I may not have the opportunity.
Well, I have found the answer to the work dilemma.

> The pleasures of abiding—and the extraordinary benefits—have redefined the scope and impact of God's work through me. I see fruit everywhere I turn.
>
> —Bruce Wilkinson, *Secrets of the Vine*

July 26, 2003

> *As I bide time waiting for him*
> *I will abide in You!*
> *Someday I will not need to bide my time.*
> *All my days I will abide in You!*
> *Me*

> As the deer pants for the water brooks, so pants my soul for You, O God.
>
> —Psalm 42:1 NASB

July 27, 2003

Should I no longer follow my heart and instead follow my soul?

Most of us probably travel somewhere in between these two worlds, having known enough love to believe it's there to be found, yet needing assurance that we won't grow old without it.

—Stormie Omartian, *That's What Love Is For*

How do I push my dreams, hopes, and expectations out of my mind? Or at least out of the forefront? It seems so selfish. I should be doing more, praying more. There's too much me. I've known this, but I need more guidance away from me, I guess. How or what to pray for to make it right?

> If your instruction had not been my delight,
> I would have died in my affliction.
>
> —Psalm 119:92 CSB

> He restores my soul; He leads me in paths of righteousness for His name's sake.
>
> —Psalm 23:3 NKJV

> You cannot plumb the depths of the human heart or grasp the workings of the human mind; how than can you fathom God, who has made all these things, discern his mind, and understand his plan.
>
> —Judith 8:14 NCB

and mine too!

If you have trust in and an expectation of your own solitude, everything that you need to know will be revealed to you.

—J. O'Donohue, *Anam Cara*

Never miss a chance to love when it is offered.
What you get back will sustain you forever.

—C. Reeves

Your decrees are forever just, give me discernment that I may live.

—Psalm 119:144 NAB

A genuine experience of God emerging from the very heart of your existence.

—John Kirvan, Raw Faith

To experience, and the sharing of God with and through others *is the best.*
The Holy Spirit is sent from the Father in the name of Jesus.
The Spirit teaches me and reminds me of everything Jesus said and makes it live in me.
Spirit of the Father and Jesus never leave me for a moment, be with me forever. Amen.

Let Christ be faithful to us.

—Thomas Merton
(emphasis added)

That was the Lord's way of appearing. Sometimes He ignores our prayer request, but appears with special grace to sustain us.

—R. T. Kendall, *When God Shows Up*

August 13, 2003

I don't know how to live (11:00 p.m.).

August 14, 2003, 1:30 a.m.

> Most of us despair of ever doing what He urges.
> How can anyone live like this? That's what He wants
> us to discover. On our own, we never will.
>
> —*C. S. Lewis Explores Vice and Virtue*

> The Spirit helps us in our weakness. We do not know
> what we ought to pray for, but the Spirit himself intercedes
> for us with groans that words cannot express.
>
> —Romans 8:26 NIV

> The only reason we should judge is to uphold the truth.
> We must judge prayerfully. Prayer leads to clarity,
> and clarity to charity in judgment.
> All that mattered was that I was blessed and could bless.
>
> —Wayne Butler Yates

August 17, 2003

For the record, a day still does not go by without thoughts of Peter. He declined the spaceship.

> Do not grieve, for the joy of the Lord is your strength.
>
> —Nehemiah 8:10 CSB

I can only believe that all my days hold your will my Lord. I want for nothing more. Why would I?

and mine too!

Would love to talk with Chris again. I see him as we pass on the path, but our times are not synced like they were. Tonight, I thought of "controlling" an encounter when I realized it's not mine to control, so I gave it to God.

A prayer I thought up last week:

Dear God,

Whatever!
Amen.

I have much more to say to you, more than you can now bear.

—John 16:12 NIV

I've got many things I'd like you to do, but you're not ready yet.

—R. T. Kendall, *When God Shows Up*

I told Nick today that I can't get Peter out of my mind or heart. He doesn't know why. "But at least you're at peace with it." He is so wise and inspirational. God bless Nick.

Matt sounds confounded. Money needed, law school in his plans, etc. But I hope I shed some light on *priceless* times, like all of us together in Pittsburgh for Labor Day with Lance and his family. Jess will be with us too. Sounds like a good investment to me. He holds so much promise. God bless Matt.

Angela, *once again,* finally called. She and John heard the baby's heartbeat. They sound very happy. I still worry when she doesn't call when she says she will. God bless Ang and John and their baby!

For Pete's Sake

> The purposes of a person's heart are deep waters,
> but one who has insight draws them out.
>
> —Proverbs 20:5 NIV

> You have begun to live a new life, in which you are being
> made new and becoming like the One who made you.
>
> —Colossians 3:10 NCV

Whenever I read or hear what others have written or what they have to say and see myself sharing their path or feeling what they felt or praying with like words, I am exhilarated—literally.

Today, on tape, the words of St. Teresa of Avila said our spousal relationship with God has its ups and downs. We cannot stay on a constant plane, and if we say we are, we are living a fantasy.

Thank God, for I would be concerned with my God-lulls, fearing I was doing something wrong, or nothing at all.

> Man's steps are from the Lord; how, then,
> can a man understand his way?
>
> —Proverbs 20:24 ESV

So far, the tape has concentrated on the bridal/spousal relationship with God. I will go back and find the words that I have lived, the words that I have felt for so long.

God and *our* love manifested in Peter (I drew a triangle).

This is why he is always in my heart.

Dare I confess, I read "Of Angels and Spaceships" from *Enchanted Love* last night. And I cried and cried so—those tears, not of loneliness or sadness or madness, were tears of overwhelmingness.

Books and tapes are my tools right now that reinforce me, guide me, challenge me, and keep me on the path—my path. I am spiritual. I am mystical. I am empowered. I am loved. I am guided. God

and mine too!

cares enough not to leave me for a moment. He takes his eyes never off me, no matter how slow my steps.

> If we're forever unsure, we fail to find God's
> plan for us. When we're paralyzed by doubt, we
> don't taste the good life God has for us.

—Gerard Reed, *C. S. Lewis on Vice and Virtue*

Arrogant as it sounds, I want to share this, to tell others it's worth the time and the pain and the frustration. Nothing else will do. There is nowhere else I want to be but in the will of my Lord.

Amen.

I'm going to start a journal for my grandbaby now! For already, this life is touching its family-in-waiting.

> Though slay me, yet I will hope in Him.

—Job 13:15 NIV

> We proclaim Him, admonishing and teaching with all wisdom,
> so that we present everyone perfect in Christ. To this end I labor,
> struggling with all His energy, which so powerfully works me.

—Colossians 1:28–29 BSB

I read this the night after Chris and I talked for a while. He said, "You have a good soul" and "That's amazing." I responded with something like, "By the Grace of God go *we*." This is my gift of the day. I am an instrument of his peace. I am disciplining. The Spirit uses me as his vessel.

Well, my "good soul" may not get me a date, but it will get me to heaven—bottom line.

With thanks and love! Amen.

> For we are saved by hope: but hope that is seen is not hope: for what a man sees, why doth he yet hope for? But if we hope for what we see not, then do we with patience.
>
> —Romans 8:24–25 KJV

Been running into this guy in the apartment building. He's been here four years, and he "wonders what it means" now that we keep meeting.

First encounter: "You look mighty cute. Do you have a date? Come by and see me."

Second encounter: "Wow, you're beautiful."

He's respectful in my "unsureness" about getting together and hopes I'll change my mind. His name is Pete, and he's Black.

And the message: the Lord showing me a chance to look beyond race (personally) and ego-self? Is this another demon to be exorcised? Or is the devil once again using a child of God to lead me to temptation? Hell if I know. Or is it a "God setup?" I'll keep you posted.

> You have sown so much but harvested so little.
>
> —Haggai 1:6 ESV, Old Testament

> Everything that happens to you is an act of sowing a seed of experience. It is equally important to be able to harvest that experience.
>
> —J. O'Donohue, *Anam Cara*

and mine too!

Always:

- praying, wishing, hoping, dreaming for that deepest desire of my heart.
- my human heart longing to share with another.
- another "of my own."
- looking, searching, listening, reading for an answer, a message.

Today, September 4

I read the chapter in *When God Shows Up* (R. T. Kendall) called "The Prophetic Word," the next chapter called "A New Person in Your Life?" Mmm?

Those God loves He has already chosen, and when we let God love us, we dignify His choice of us, however unworthy we feel.

—R. T. Kendall, *When God Shows Up*

In the 1st degree God enters into the soul and she turns inward into herself. In the 2nd she ascends above herself and is lifted up to God. In the 3rd, lifted up to God, pass over completely into him. In the 4th the soul goes forth on God's behalf and descends below herself.

—Richard of St. Victor, Adapted from the translation of Clare Kirchberger from A. Harvey, *Teachings of the Christian Mystics*

Two beautiful Mother Mary prayers in this book too.

For Pete's Sake

Seek ye first the kingdom of God, and his righteousness.

—Matthew 6:33 KJV

September 7, 2003

> Every human heart seeks meaning; for it is meaning that
> our deepest shelter lies. Meaning is sister of experience,
> and to discern the meaning of what has happened to you is
> one of the essential ways of finding your inner belongings
> and discover the sheltering presence of your soul.

—J. O'Donohue, *Anam Cara*

Dare I write of my beloved—still?
Why?
How?
His words echo in my heart. How big is my heart that it echoes over and over and over like it was yesterday? My heart, or at least that part of him, is timeless. And breathless.
Yet not tearless.

> The Lord will indeed give what is good.

—Psalm 85:12 NIV

I can't leave this place. Is it because if I do, I will be alone? I don't think so because my Lord was left behind, and despite the humanness of all these emotions, I will never be alone.

More lyrics from *He Couldn't Love You More* (*Perhaps Love*) by Plácido Domingo with John Denver (emphasis added):

> I can't believe it happened
> I never dreamed you'd leave me
> We were so good together

and mine too!

> I thought we'd share forever
> The love we had before
> Is there an explanation to
> ease my sorrow
> Is it infatuation and will it
> fade tomorrow
> *Until you let me know my love*
> *won't let you go,*
> *My heart won't close the door*
> And while you make your mind up
> I beg you to remember
> Although his arms may hold you
> I don't know what he told you
> But he couldn't love you more.

The function of grace is not to do, but to behold.

—Matthew Fox, *Prayer: A Radical Response to Life*

Not a day goes by!

Does he ever think of me?

Does he even remember the words, the laughter, the plans, the touch, the sound of my voice, the words I wrote, the warmth, the sincerity, the longing to be with each other, the sharing?

Doesn't he want to feel uplifted and cared for and loved unconditionally, like he so truly mattered?

> True hope attains God by leaning on His help in order to obtain the hoped for good. Such good, is eternal life, which consists in the enjoyment of God Himself. For we should hope for Him for nothing less than Himself, since His goodness by which He imparts good things to His creature, is no less than His essence. Therefore the proper and principle, object of hope is eternal happiness.
>
> —Thomas Aquinas

Why did he choose fear over love?
Why did he choose ego-self over spiritual self?
Why did he choose being kept over being loved?
Lord, open his heart, his eyes, his lips, his arms. Amen.
Again, I so selfishly pray.

Who is this man?
Does he have any idea?
It is your presence, Lord. What else could it be? That part of him—all of him—the vessel *you* chose to use so this humble servant would *finally* see you in all glory and yearning and love.

I desire, in all my human weakness, my taste of heaven back. Do I ask too much? It must not be time. Show me the way. Show me your will, for what more do I need do?

Do not let me idle away my prayers and thoughts and dreams. I don't think I am, though. Does Satan laugh at this? Did he keep Peter in my head to keep me from growth and doing your will? I say no, but what do I know?

I know that my beloved changed me forever.

Thoughts of him and of being with him nourish me daily.

The tears I shed somehow comfort me, grace me, bless me.

And naïve me, hopeful me, faithful me, romantic me has the same heart—the heart that skips a beat and stops my breath each time the phone rings. Yep, it's true.

My miracle, my blessing, my joy to hear him say, "Hey, how ya doin', babe?"

Silly girl.

and mine too!

He's a memory no more!

> That is the Christian scheme of things, salvation history is not merely an idea; rather the stuff of creation is transformed by Grace into the instruments of redemption, right before our eyes.
>
> —George Weigel, Quoted in Gerard Reed's
> *C.S. Lewis Explores Vice and Virtue*

The vision that is beyond all these words I have written is when Peter walks down the hallway of the apartment building and I to him. I touch his right cheek with my left hand, and his right cheek becomes the cheek of Jesus Christ, and my left hand remains my left hand, and I am home. Is Peter's work done?

No, Lord, please, I want him back. Let me love him. Let him see he was loving me.

Amen.

September 8, 2003

What a difference a day makes!

Everything I wrote yesterday, so passionately, has not carried over into today—almost at all.

Was it a cleansing cry that I needed?

Was it a sort of therapy?

Don't know. Oh, the wonder of it all.

My ambitions, plans, and wishes at His feet in ashes lay.

> —An old hymn quoted in R. T. Kendall's *When God Shows Up*

My Lord is using me. I am his vessel. I've let him at the clay; the Potter is at work. Thank you. May I never let you down.

Chris seems to be the "target." He's so open and nice and pleasant. God, through me, is giving him "food for thought." It's wonderful being part of it, seeing Chris's eyes shine and the knowing nod of his head.

And God spoke through him, to me, "You're a neat lady, that aura around you."

"Is that what you call it?" was my response.

(I gave him my copy of *God Hunger* by Kirvan.)

My Lord and my God,

Thank you for these affirmations; it's so good for humanness. I trust you completely. I love you eternally.
Mary
Amen!

Dear God, I am willing to see this differently.

—A Course in Miracles

What a difference another day makes.

I am alone, don't like it that well. I want to share me, if that's okay to say.

I *trust* God *completely*.

Then why do I find myself waiting:

- for the phone to ring,
- for the words, "Would you like to…"
- for someone going just a little out of their way for me,
- Me, me, me, me—I'm tired of it!

Why do I think he's the missing piece, the remedy, the fix?
Thy will be done.

and mine too!

Goodnight!

> Humility isn't thinking less of one's self
> it is thinking of one's self less
>
> —C. S. Lewis, *Mere Christianity.*

You can know many things, even facts about yourself, but it is the truths that you realize yourself that move deeply in you. Wisdom, then, is a deeper way of knowing. Wisdom is the art of living in rhythm with your soul, your life, and the divine. Wisdom is the way you learn to decipher the unknown; and the unknown is our closet companion. So, wisdom is the art of being courageous and generous with the unknown, of being able to decipher and recognize its treasurers.

> —John O'Donohue, *Anam Cara*

In John Kirvan's books, God is the unknown, the unknowable.

> Saul got up from the ground and opened
> his eyes, but could not see a thing.
>
> —Acts 9:8 GNT

Herein is love, not that we have loved God, but that He loved us.

> —1 John 4:10 KJB

For Pete's Sake

I've got pieces April
I keep them in a memory bouquet
I've got pieces of April
but it's a morning in May.

—*Pieces of April* by Three Dog
Night, *Three Dog Night*

God speaks to the soul.

And God said to the soul:

I desired you before world began
I desire you now
As you desire me.
And where the desires of two come together
There love is perfected.

How the soul speaks to God:

Lord you are my lover,
My longing
My flowing stream
My Sun
And my reflection.

How God answers the soul:

It is my nature that makes me love you often,
For I am love itself.
It is my longing that makes me love you intensely.
For I yearn to be loved from the heart.

and mine too!

> It is my eternity that makes me love you long,
> For I have no end.
>
> —Mechthild of Magdeburg

> By prayer man renders himself capable of receiving.
>
> —Thomas Aquinas

September 12, 2003

Another day of Peter, so there. Echoes.

How and why do I "live in the past?" I never considered myself that type.

Still following my heart and, dare I say, "my soul." It feels okay. Have I become stale? Will I? No, for daily, I pray that my "day" is another day of God's will.

I have been meaning to write this down over and over and over all summer long.

The evening sky has been spectacular! Go, God!

I begin to mourn the passing of summer. This summer was so worldly beautiful, so personally blessed. Thanks again. Amen.

God is light.

> We cannot see light, though by light we see things.
>
> —C. S. Lewis, *The Four Loves*

> There is no excess of goodness. You cannot
> go to far in the right direction.
>
> —C. S. Lewis, *The Pilgrim's Regress*

How selfish of me, these moments of human loneliness. If they mirror what I did to God when I didn't call on him, when I didn't seem interested, when I thought I didn't need to see him—I'm sorry I hurt you, my loved Lord.

Remember "Of Spaceships and Angels" from *Enchanted Love* (Marianne Williamson)? And I thought it was Peter who refused to go on the spaceship, but I, too, have refused the ride, all the times Jesus, the Captain, stopped by and offered and left and offered and left and returned again. But no more. My hesitations are far and few between. And the length of those hesitations are shorter and shorter.

I still want to share the ride.

As for my Peter, the analogy fits so well. And, yes, I am the angel on his Spaceship.

> Fear has been turned to fortitude. Anguish has become joy without somehow ceasing to be anguish and we triumph over suffering not by escaping it but by completely accepting it. This is the only triumph, because there is no victory in evasion.
>
> —Thomas Merton, *Bread in the Wilderness*

As I sit here and think of all I wrote over two years, I fell in love with God (Peter should've too). All the love words are perfectly parallel (in human sense) between God and Peter. Peter is not here. Our God is eternal. Amen.

I've mentioned what I call the "God Rush," that tingly goosebump feeling. And my tears, the ones I could not label (not sad, not heartbroken, not mad, etc.), I now label them "God tears."

and mine too!

> All that was true love in them was, even on earth, far more His than ours, and ours only because of His.
>
> —C. S. Lewis, *The Four Loves*

Michael Buble sang, on TV today, *Nothing Compares to the Memory of You.*

In so much, obviously, I see Peter.
I feel him.
I search for him.
I wonder of him.
So what of the heartstrings? Where do they lead?
Where is the end?
How long are they?
Are there two ends? Peter at one end and Lord at the at the other?
Am I holding on to Peter's heart by a thread?
What is it made of?
Something incredibly strong—of this, I am sure.
A heartstring, gently touched, resounds with one single note—the note of love that continues to echo. Does it only echo for me?
Peter, look, I continue to write a love story. Ours? Or mine alone?

> I in them, and you in me; that they may be made perfect in one, and that the worlds may know that You have sent Me, and have loved them as You loved me.
>
> —John 17:23 NKJV

Eventually, the impact of this writing will somehow subside for an unknown amount of time. Then something new and alive will take me here again. It is good to be here, tears and all.
The parallel with me and God is always there.

The emotional and spiritual ups and downs in our relationship are ever-present, not down in a negative way, though. The view at the top is the best, and I never want to lose it. Yet, I must journey to the bottom of the mountain to maintain perspective and hope as I gladly make my way back to the top, no matter how long it takes. To the top where my Lord nods and smiles. Where the "God tears" fall and the "God rush" runs through me. The trek back down is even uplifting for my soul, and it is peaceful.

How long does it take? There is no pattern. I hope it's eternal. It must be because there is no time in eternity.

Goodnight.

September 23, 2003

P.S. Chris—I want to know him better. I think we can sincerely share. I don't know why we connect here and now, but in him, my humanness finds potential, hope, and promise.

What a difference a day makes. It was one of those emotionally frustrating days, one of those days where the enlightened journey has brought about a weariness, a weariness in the waiting. This will never go away. It will subside but will return—the downside of this mountain journey.

Ignorance is bliss. It was so much easier when my ego-self was put before my spiritual self. Now my commitments, my responses, my words, and my actions demand a whole new kind of responsibility.

I was incredibly responsible in my ego world. I tried to let no one down, was dutiful and gracious, and strived to do the right thing. I loved it there and wouldn't change a thing, for it brought me to this new spiritual me, and I love it here.

and mine too!

The grace of God guided me, and all that learning and trying to absorb are daily gifts, like grace, coming from God through all my encounters in nature, in human interactions, in all he created.

Through the Spirit, I trust in eternal guidance, no matter how many times my humanness gets in the way. The humanness is not eternal. My heart will go on.

Yet I wait daily for my miracle—the ego miracle—the human miracle, and this is okay because God created me. He is my need—love. And every day, I give thanks for his gift of love.

My miracle.

> The very goodness of love guarantees its depths as well as it heights. If we love, we will suffer.
>
> —C. S. Lewis

> Our human loves can be glorious images of Divine love. No less than that: but also no more.
>
> —Gerard Reed, *C. S. Lewis Explores Vice and Virtue*

> Mary becomes the prototype of what God intends to do for all humanity. This is why she can sing that every generation will call her blessed.
>
> —Leonardo Boff

> The entire physical world is a ladder for ascending to God.
>
> —St. Bonaventure

For Pete's Sake

> Hence the paradox that unselfish love cannot rest perfectly
> except in a love that is perfectly reciprocated: because
> it knows that the only true peace is found in selfless
> love. Selfless love consents to be loved selflessly for the
> sake of the beloved. In doing so, it perfects itself.
>
> —Thomas Merton, *No Man is an Island*

> But love is a daring dance of surrender. A dance of courage.
> Love is a labored waltz. The speckled trumpets of the
> foxglove sound revelry to hearts waiting to dance.
>
> —Tonia Triebwasser, *The Color of Grace*[2]

> The Holy Spirit's temple is not a body, but a relationship.
>
> —Marianne Williamson, *A Return to Love*

September 29, 2003

Chuck's having bypass surgery soon. His kidneys are at 20 percent, dialysis inevitable. Lance is going to see him. Nick called to let me know. How I cried. How I sobbed. How dare he put the kids through this!

Lots of good reading and praying.
From *No Man Is an Island* (Thomas Merton):

> Supernatural hope is the virtue that strips us of all things in order to give us possession of all things. We do not hope for what we have. Therefore, to live in hope is to live in poverty, having nothing. And yet, if we abandon ourselves

---

[2] Foxglove—the same heart healing medicine found in the leaves of the foxglove can also be used to cause a heart to fail.

to economy of Divine Providence, we have everything we hope for. By faith we know God without seeing Him. By hope we possess God without feeling His presence.

If we hope in God, by hope we already possess Him, since hope is a confidence which he creates in our souls as secret evidence that He has taken possession of us. So, the soul that hopes in God already belongs to Him, and to belong to Him is the same as to possess Him, since He gives Himself completely to those who give themselves to Him. The only thing faith and hope do not give us is the clear vision of Him Whom we possess. We are united to Him in darkness, because we have to hope.

Hope deprives us of everything that is not God, in order that all things may serve their true purpose as means to bring us to God.

Hope is proportionate to detachment. It brings our soul into the state of the most perfect detachment. In doing so, it restores all values by setting them in their right order. *Hope empties our hands in order that we may work with them.* It shows us that we have something to work for, and teaches us how to work for it.

Without hope, our faith only gives us an acquaintance with God. Without love and hope, faith only knows Him as a stranger. For hope casts us into the arms of His mercy and of His providence. If we hope in Him, we will not only come to know that He is merciful but we will experience His mercy in our own lives. (emphasis added)

It is lawful to love all things and to seek them, once they become means to love God. There is nothing we cannot ask Him if we desire it in order that He may be more loved by ourselves or by other men.

—Thomas Merton, *No Man is an Island*

What I have in God is greater than what I don't have in life. (adapted from Psalm 23:1)

—Max Lucado, *Travelling Light*

October 6, 2003

Dear Peter,

Just a note to let you know you are still with me, and you haven't missed a day.

If you have any idea why, please let me know somehow, someway.

A part of me, a lot of me, will always be waiting and wondering.

Love,
Mary

Who is this man?
Does he even know?
You're him, aren't you?
I must still be in my advent phase.

and mine too!

The safest place in the whole wide world
is in the center of God's will.

—Thelma Wells, *What's Going on Lord?*

Just ten minutes after crying over the previous, I read;

The golden moments in the past, which are so tormenting, if
we erect them into a norm, are entirely nourishing, wholesome
and enchanting if we are content to accept them for what
they are, for memories. Properly bedded down in a past
which we do not miserably try to conjure back, they will send
up exquisite growths. Leave the bulbs alone, and the new
flowers will come up. Grub them up hope, by fondling and
sniffing, to get last year's blooms, and you will get nothing.

—C. S. Lewis, *The Joyful Christian*

Did Peter plant a seed? And now must I realize that this seed needs to die...to grow anew? Help me, Lord, to do this if it is your will.

Am I strong enough? What am I afraid of?

Then every act of hope will open the door to
contemplation, for such hope is its own fulfillment.

—Thomas Merton, *No Man Is an Island*

Whether you turn to the right or to the left, your ears will hear
a voice behind you, saying, "This is the way; walk in it."

—Isaiah 30:21 NIV

For Pete's Sake

From *The Education of the Heart* edited by Thomas Moore:

> For Spirit is first of all power, the power that drives the human spirit above itself toward what it cannot obtain by itself. The love that is greater than all other gifts, the truth in which the depths of being opens itself to us, the Holy that is the manifestation of the presence of the Ultimate.
>
> You may say again, "I do not know this power," "I have never had such an experience," "I am not religious," or at least not Christian," and "certainly not the bearer of the Spirit."
>
> To this I answer, "Certainly the spiritual power can thrust some people into an ecstasy that most of us never experienced. It can drive some to a kind of self-sacrifice of which most of us are not capable. It can inspire some into the insights into the depths of being that remain unapproachable to most of us. But this does not justify our denial that the Spirit is always working in us. Without doubt, wherever it works, there is an element, possibly very small, of self-surrender. And an element, however weak, of ecstasy. And an element, perhaps fleeting, of awareness of the mystery of existence. Yet, these small effects of the spiritual power are enough to prove its presence. What I hear from you sounds like ecstasy, and I want to stay sober. It sounds like mystery, and I try to illuminate what is dark. It sounds like self-sacrifice, and I want to fulfill my human possibilities." (Paul Tillich)

and mine too!

Do not neglect hospitality, for through it some
have unknowingly entertained angels.

—Hebrews 13:2 NAB

Hope seeks not only God in Himself, not only the
means to reach Him, but it seeks, finally and beyond
all else, God's glory revealed in ourselves.

Hope is the gateway to contemplation, because
contemplation is an experience of divine things and we
cannot experience what we do not in some way possess.

—Thomas Merton, *No Man Is an Island*

God is faithful to me. How can I not be faithful to him?

All
Most (xx-ed out)
Some (xx-ed out) days I feel sheepish.
Me *October 13, 2003*

A message that has popped up more than twice in my current pile of books: when God doesn't respond to our prayers in the way or time we had hoped, he gives us peace, and to this, I am a humble witness.

For Pete's Sake

And do not be conformed to this world, but be transformed
by the renewing of your mind, that you may prove what
is that good and acceptable and perfect will of God.

—Romans 12:2 NKJV

"Kissing a Fool"

You are far,
When I could have been your star,
You listened to people,
Who scared you to death, and from my heart,
Strange that you were strong enough,
To even make a start,
But you'll never find
Peace of mind,
Till you listen to your heart.
People,
You can never change the way they feel,
Better let them do what they will,
For they will,
If you let them
Steal your heart from you.
People,
Will always make a lover a fool
But you knew I loved you,
We could have shown them all
We should have seen love through.
Fooled me with the tears in your eyes.

and mine too!

Covered me with kisses and lies,
So goodbye,
But please don't take my heart.
You are far,
I'm never gonna be your star.
I'll pick up the pieces
And mend my heart,
Maybe I'll be strong enough,
I don't know where to start,
But I'll never
Peace of mind,
While I listen to my heart.
People,
You can never change the way they feel,
Better let them do just what they will,
For they will
If you let them
Steal heart.
And people,
Will always make a lover feel a fool,
But you knew I loved you,
We could have shown them all
But remember this,
Every other kiss
That you ever give
Long as we both live
When you need the hand of another man,
One you can really surrender with,
I will wait for you
Like I always do.
There's something there,
That can't compete with any other.
You are far,

For Pete's Sake

> When I could have been your star,
> You listened to people,
> Who scared you to death, and from my heart?
> Strange that I was wrong enough
> To think you'd love me too
> I guess you were kissing a fool,
> You must have been kissing a fool.
>
> —George Michael, *Ladies and Gentlemen: The Best of George Michael*

> Those who are to meet will meet, because together
> they have the potential for a holy relationship.
>
> —Marianne Williamson, *A Return to Love*

> A dream takes its first breath from the heart.
>
> —Tonia Triebwasser, *The Color of Grace*

Where is the man who took my breath away? who transformed me into such a dreamer? who still lives in and enlivens my heart? And the two are one.

> But we, with unveiled face reflecting as a mirror, the
> glory of the Lord, are transformed into the image from
> glory to glory, even as from the Lord the Spirit.
>
> —2 Corinthians 3:18 ERV)

October 20, 2003

    Of Peter, again and still...
    All last week and before, just a thought away.
    My beloved, I asked nothing of you, yet you gifted me with so much. And the gifts that I treasure most and forever—faith, hope, and love—the greatest of these is love! How obviously and instantly our Lord makes his presence known. And those tears flow so freely, again and still.
    My beloved, do realize God has chosen you, no one else would do! He has chosen you to get to me, chosen you to reflect his Son, to get to my heart, to every deep untouched corner. And his Spirit keeps you with me. I pray you know of what I write.
    Today, I prayed aloud, "Please let me be to Peter all that he is to me." Open his heart and eyes and arms and let me fill them with my love forever. Let me heal wounds in your name.
    Let me be his shelter as he is a shelter to me (even in his absence). May we laugh and dance together forever in your light, for how could we not, knowing you have always been with us and realizing how true you are to your Word and that what you have planned for us is much better than we can imagine?
    And, once again, I add that part of my prayer for Peter from almost two years ago that said, "Here on earth where we will a life reflecting love and thanks to our everlasting Father, an example to all whose lives we touch and those who touch us."
    I just read over what I just wrote and see how God is giving to me more than I could ever imagined. What I thought was in my future is my present. Humbly, I have no words now.
    Went dancing with Anthony. Fun, yet a lesson learned. Dancing isn't everything. One must be with the right partner. Peter *swayed me in his arms* when I asked, "Will you dance with me?" Both of us knowing I spoke of our future not just of that moment on that spring night on John's patio.

Continuing to "see" Anthony is self-serving (ego; I love to dance), and I know that is not right. Spirit, let the timing and words be yours if and when the time comes. Thy will be done.

For if I am to love truly and freely, I must be able to give something that is truly my own to another. If my heart does not first belong to me, how can I give it to another? It is not mine to give.

—Thomas Merton, *No Man Is an Island*

So get rid of your old self, which made you live as you used to—the old self that was being destroyed by its deceitful desires. Your hearts and minds must be made completely new and you must put on the new self, which is created in God's likeness and reveals Itself in the true life that is upright and holy.

—Ephesians 4:22–24 GNT

On the last page of this diary, I write:

A holy relationship… Each one has looked within and seen no lack. Accepting his completion, he would extend it by joining with another, whole as himself.

—*A Course in Miracles*

Tucked in this diary, on a yellow legal page, I drew a large heart with a large cross going through it. In it, I wrote "Un grand amore Pietro Maria Dio."

and mine too!

This is Diary #6, the one with the bling

> The secret of happiness in life is to love and
> the essence of love is to serve.
>
> —Father Carrol Abbing

It's been about a week—recap of thoughts.

How do I and how can I; why do I and why can I have such powerful prayerful Peter day(s), and then the next day(s), subtle "hint-full" days of this man? No answer but a knowing that I have read of this in a book or two with the mystery being like our relationship with God. The veil—some days so thick and tangible and other days barely a trace of a veil—revealing light and love and power and hunger.

I'm glad it's a mystery, and I'm not surprised of the parallel, again, between my Lord and my Peter. I guess it helps my heart to "get it."

> I believe He knows whom to trust with certain circumstances.
>
> —Thelma Wells, *What's Going on Lord?*

> I rejoice in God's faithfulness to my children
> and trust what He is doing in their lives.
>
> —Thelma Wells, *What's Going on Lord?*

I've prayed (pleaded) aloud, "Peter, save me."

Save me from being put into a position that might compromise myself and the other person.

Anthony is the other person. We talk and share well. Honesty is evident. Spirituality is respected. We make each other laugh, and we dance great together.

The prayer doesn't seem necessary. Friday was another nice evening.

The fear was from myself, knowing my weakness and my ego's need for attention.

Thank you, Lord, for doing what you do. Your everything is everything to me! Amen.

Come with me now. My love is the key to your prison door.

—Marianne Williamson, "Of Spaceships and Angels," *Enchanted Love*

October 27, 2003

Well, here it is, less than twenty-four hours later. I am having a Peter day, and oh how I cry. Somehow at the end of my Italian class, we got "spiritual," and I told them the nutshell version of God's manifestation through Peter.

The first song as I get into the car is *Now and Forever (The Living Room Tour)* by Carole King, and oh how I cry.

> Now and forever, you are a part of me
> And the memory cuts like a knife.
> Didn't we find the ecstasy, didn't we share
> the daylight
> When you walked into my life
> Now and forever, I will remember
> All the promises still unbroken
> And think about all the words between us
> That never needed to be spoken."
>
> We had a moment, just one moment
> That will last beyond the dream, beyond a
> lifetime.
> We are the lucky ones.
> Some people never get to do all we got to do.
> Now and forever, I will always think of you.
> Didn't we come together, didn't we live

and mine too!

together
Didn't we cry together
Didn't we play together, didn't we love
together
And together we lit up the world.
I miss the tears, I miss the laughter.
I miss the day we met and all that followed
after
Sometimes I wish I could always be with you
The way we used to do.
Now and forever, I will always think of you.
Now and forever, I will always be with you

I will send him these lyrics. He needs to know…

Whom God hath brought together, the ego cannot put asunder.

—A Course in Miracles

For I know the plans I have for you declares the Lord "plans to prosper you and not harm you, plans to give you hope and a future."

—Jeremiah 29:11 NIT

Dear Lord,

Ease his burdens. Free him for me. Let me try again to help him heal his wounds with your ever-present grace. Please let him see me as I see him—as a manifestation of your Holy Self—loving and caring and waiting and forgiving and forever.

Open that part of his heart that he let me into. If I am so worthy, than so is he.

I so want to be his angel again and still.

Does he know this deep in his heart? Please take away his fears. I'm different from all the rest— he told me so. Refresh his memory and his spirit.

Let us ride the spaceship together again to him. Is it time yet?

Lord, if it is not to be me, I still pray that you lift him up to all your goodness and keep him safe and happy and peaceful.

And once again I ask for your help in taking him from my heart, for I do not have the strength or the desire to do so, if this is your will.

Two friends told me this weekend that if Peter is still in my heart, then that's where he is supposed to be for now. Were they messengers? Thank you.

If this is an obsession, forgive me.

I will never be the same, and I thank you.

With love,
Me

You have put gladness in my heart.

—Psalm 4:7 KJB

Trust in the Lord with all your heart, and lean not on your own understanding; in all your ways acknowledge Him, and He shall direct your paths.

—Proverbs 3:5–6 NKJV

and mine too!

Has not the seed lain dormant long enough?

I wait patiently, achingly, knowingly—knowing that the rebirth and growth and blossoming and nurturing of the love you planted between us will be glorious beyond words, and your handiwork will be evident to all around us.

Humbly, we will stay rooted in you, for you are kind and merciful. And angels will sing, and your people will be hopeful and faith will be renewed.

Would this be too good to be true? Is it not of this Earth? Do we not need to be uplifted? What's wrong with a little bit of heaven on earth?

I wait in your mystery. I will try to be silent. Amen.

I'll probably go read *Of Spaceship and Angels* (*Enchanted Love* by Marianne Williamson) now, again. Goodnight.

It must still be advent, my advent—our advent.

Lord, thank you for being so here.
Amen.

This is the confidence we have in approaching God: that
if we ask anything according to His will, he hears us.

—1 John 5:14 NIV

As you perceive the holy companions who travel with you, you
will realize that there is no journey, but only an awakening.

—*A Course in Miracles*

The perfect love of God's will, is a union so close that God Himself both utters and fulfills His will at the same instant in the depths of my own soul. Pure intention, in this highest sense, is a secret and spiritual word of God which not only commands my will to act, or solicits my cooperation, but fulfills what He says in me. The action is at once perfectly mine and perfectly His. But its substance comes entirely from Him. In me, it is entirely received: only to be offered back to Him in the silent ovation of His own expressible love.

—Thomas Merton, *No Man Is an Island*

In the same way, the Spirit helps us in our weakness. We do not know what we ought to pray for, but the Spirit himself intercedes for us through wordless groans.

—Romans 8:26 NIV

It's Halloween, and this morning, I'm thinking, *Spooky*, then *Mystery*, and it segues into "Peter is my mystery," and instantly, my God parallel is there! *Wow!*

Have I ever prayed for anything this long? This fervently? Nope, not in my memory. *Wow!*

Spent four wonderful days with my Matt in Chicago. We summed it up in two sentences as we hugged each other at the airport.

Mom: "We were made for each other."
Matt: "Somebody was thinking."

Thank you, Lord, so very much!

What, after all, is more personal than suffering? The awful futility of our attempts to convey the reality of our suffering to other people and the tragic inadequacy of human sympathy— both prove how incommunicable a thing suffering really is.

and mine too!

> When a man suffers, he must alone. Therefore, it is suffering that we are most tested as persons. How can we face the awful interior questioning? What shall we answer when we come to be examined by pain? Without God, we are no longer persons. We lose our manhood and our dignity. We become dumb animals under pain, happy, if we can behave at least like quiet animals and die without too much commotion.
>
> —Thomas Merton, *No Man Is an Island*

And I realize Peter was in thought, but it is when I draw nearer to God in thought and prayer is when Peter's presence is stronger, and my need and longing is greater. This is when I breathe deeper, and this is when I wonder so much of this "connection." And this is when my tears fall so easily. And I wonder. Yes, it is a gift that comforts me.

Do I need these tears?

Do I have a problem?

This connection is not my creation. Is it not yours, Lord? I have a good imagination, but my time line is different than yours. So this triangle (*drawn*) of yours that lives and rests in my heart is where it should be, in Your hands, and in my heart and somewhere in Peter's heart waiting to be rediscovered, reopened, reborn. Instead of going on and on, Lord, in my little words, I will crawl into bed and go to that place where words disappear, and I let go and go into the darkness of your mystery, not in fear but in contentment of not knowing.

See, I'm already on my way because the words are becoming without direction or overloaded with repetition.

> The secret of simple intention is that it is content to seek
> God and does not insist on finding Him right away,
> knowing that in seeking Him it has already found Him.
>
> —Thomas Merton, *No Man Is an Island*

There is a God/Peter parallel here. It is profound, and I don't think *I* can put the right words to describe it, and this is okay and good. Really. A mystery.

November 5, 2003

Peter needs to know how important he is.

I sent Peter the lyrics of *Now and Forever*. My handwriting was quite lovely. My tears fell on my shirt, not my stationery.

My heart is my God's. I trust it, to no one else. Amen.

(Drew another triangle.)

"I request that you come back" (from the movie, *Cold Mountain*).

If anyone ever reads this and all its volumes, *please* do not be sad for me. I am not sad. This has been a wonderful journey I've been on, full of hope, anticipation, unexpected depths of love and trust. It has inspired me, uplifted me, sustained me, and blessed me. I would change nothing.

It is my path, and my Lord and my Shepherd has never abandoned me as he is also with Peter.

And if our paths should cross, we cross them, knowing that our journey was our preparation for this moment. And we shall become one in our Lord, finishing our journey on our path, side by side, hand in hand, and there will be no words. There will just be "knowing."

> Be formed and perfected by tribulations.
>
> —Thomas Merton, *No Man Is an Island*

and mine too!

I'm at that "abandoned" place yet never alone; it lasts but a moment, the place where no words fit, where no questions are answered.

I am confused.

I continue to wait.

I will try not to let my Father down.

Money issues again. I hate this "place."

Will mail Peter's stuff tomorrow. I took the time to find *Now and Forever* and "burned" it for him. And I will continue waiting, wondering, wishing—living!

Praying and dreaming, I think of him as I say aloud *as I raise my hands* "Oh to lift my arms up to you." And there it is again, my God/Peter parallel.

I'm a terrible waiter.

> *Always be ready to give an explanation to anyone who asks you for a reason for your hope. But do it with gentleness and reverence,* keeping your conscience clear, so that, when you are maligned, those who defame your good conduct in Christ may themselves be put to shame."
>
> —1 Peter 3:15–16 NABRE (emphasis added)

And of Anthony, we have a good time together. He is my "ego,"– the attention I think I need or deserve or both. He is the "confuser," leading my thoughts to the temporary. Is "evil" using him to weaken me? This doesn't mean Anthony is evil, just a "look" at myself reacting to what's going on.

If Anthony has a sixth sense, like he says he does, can he "see" that I am "waiting?"

For Pete's Sake

And with all my God/Peter parallels, if God is unknowing and darkness and a forever mystery and not of this realm, is it to mean that so is my Peter?

Is Peter really the man of my dreams?

> As for me, being on the way, the Lord led me.
>
> —Genesis 24:27 KJV

Anthony and I had a fun time at the zoo, holding hands and everything. That was five days ago. Haven't heard from him. I arrogantly ask myself, "Why wouldn't he want to be with me?" What sort of puzzle piece is/was this? Did he sense Peter in my heart?

I was able to share my Lord with Jackie C. last night and she with me. It was great bringing hope and peace and sharing miracles. I told her of Peter and that when she meets him, she will see firsthand the work of God (the love of God), and she said, "I'm sure I'll meet him." My gift; and to think I didn't give much thought to going out with the Ed's gang last night and hoped Anthony would call and fill my ego. Aah, but God filled my heart and soul.

Thank you again!
Amen.

> Wrapped up mysteriously like an Enigma,
> in is His NO lies a hidden YES.
>
> —Gunter Grass

I mailed *Now and Forever* (Carole King) to Peter yesterday, the written lyrics and the burned CD for him. Sealed with a kiss, *he* should receive it Tuesday or Wednesday. How exciting!

Dear Lord,

When our Peter reads and listens of my heart please let this melt the wall he has built, even if it is

and mine too!

just a little. He must know we wait for him on the other side.

I so long to be his angel and do Your work, Your will to bring him home. He deserves to:

- *know he is loved forever.*
- *know he is never alone.*
- *know it is time.*

Please, my Lord, I pray again, use me to be the humanness to Peter that he was to me in bringing me to you so we can walk together—all of us.

Love you,
Mary

I pray that the eyes of your heart may be enlightened in order that you may know the hope to which he has called you.

—Ephesians 1:18 NIV

I have much to write to you, but I do not want to use paper and ink. Instead, I hope to visit you and talk with you face to face, so that your joy may be complete.

—3 John 1:12 NIV

There is so much to share, my love!

January 4, 2004

A new year has begun.
I have not written in weeks. No reason.
I just read over the pages of this book, and my cheeks sting.
Random update: Anthony e-mailed me to end the relationship. Whoopie *(sarcasm)*!

And the same old, same old. Not a day goes by—*I love you, Peter!*

I have much more to say to you, more than you can bear now.

—John 16:12 NIV

Temptation was on the phone yesterday. The guy down the hall; a fun, flirty conversation. It was the attention, the compliments, etc. Once again, Satan uses a child of God to lure me away, even if temporarily, from what is right.

So I prayed for the strength and words from the Spirit to put things right. He didn't call or stop over.

My God and Savior! Strength, patience, understanding, and unconditional love. You are too good, and I am worthy of your abundance and I thank you! I pray this for everyone to know this.

Oh, the wonder of you!

> But put on the Lord Jesus Christ and make no provisions for the desires of the flesh.
>
> —Romans 13:14 ESV

The night before Satan was on the phone, Nick and I talked openly of "my journey."

He wanted to know why I read like I do. It affirms my journey. It gives words to my emotions, words I want to share with everyone (enlarges my territory). It nourishes. It makes me strive. It makes me hunger for more.

Then I talked of Peter. I read the prayer I wrote and the story of the landscaper. He listened with his heart, and between my words and my tears, he glimpsed what overflows in my heart and said he, too, would pray for Peter; not for Peter and me, but for him, the man he longs to be, the child of God, knowing his mother waits for this man. Amen.

and mine too!

Experiences of God can never be planned or achieved. They are spontaneous moments of grace. They are accidents… ("Rabbi, why do we work so hard doing all these spiritual practices if religious experiences are just accidents?") To be as accident-prone as possible.

—Bo Lozoff, Shlomo Carlebach
from *Deep and Simple*

My dear Peter,

I feel you are closer to me, to us. My faith leaps, my heart leaps. In love songs, I hear you singing to me, especially today at Gale's—words with a beautiful tune enter my heart…

"I will love you for the rest of my life, just give me time…" That's all I heard. It must have been the refrain, for I heard it twice. That was gift number two for this day. Number one was the intervention of God earlier today.

When I got home, gift number three was on the page of the first book I picked up called Tea Time with God.

"For whatever is born of God overcomes the world: and this is the victory that has overcome the world—our faith" (1 John 5:4).

As you know love, I believe our love is of God, for who else could create something so strong and everlasting and enduring? And together, yet separate journeys, through him, we will overcome the world and the walls that keep us physically apart. I have a healthy and growing faith! And this faith, through you, my darling, that God has blessed most generously.

And what of you, my love? My Peter? Do you know you are my prayer, and I pray for you, like I've never prayed for another, that you find your

way, that you open your heart, that you ask for help, that you hear and see the answers to your every prayer, that you know the wonders of emotions that have no words, that you know the relief of giving to God all he asks of you and that you realize what he gives you in return—abundance, joy, and peace. God bless you!
  We love you!

Mary

P.S. *No one could love you more!*

For whatever is born of God overcomes the world: and this is the victory that has overcome the world—our faith.

—1 John 5:4 NKJV

Let us rejoice and be glad and give Him glory, for the wedding day of Lamb has come, for His bride has made herself ready. She was allowed to wear a bright, clean, linen garment.

—Revelations 19:7–8 NIV

Dear God,

  I selfishly request that we love each other here on Earth, for this, too, is your creation.
  Humbly and gratefully with all my love,

Your child, Mary

(I drew a triangle.)

and mine too!

The next batch of songs are compiled on the Rod Stewart CD *The Complete Great American* Songbook, Volumes I, II, III, IV, and V. Excellent listening!

"You Go to My Head"

You go to my head and you linger like a haunting refrain
And I find you spinning 'round in my brain
Like bubbles in a glass of champagne…
The thrill of the thought that you might give a thought to my plea
Cast a spell over me
Still I say to myself get a hold of yourself…

—J. Fred Coots

"That Old Feeling"

My heart stood still
once again I seem to feel that old yearning
And I knew the spark of love was still burning.
There'll be no new romance for me
It's foolish to start
For that old, old feeling is still in my heart…still in my heart…

—Lew Brown and Sammy Fain

For Pete's Sake

> But by the Grace of God I am what I am, and
> His grace toward me was not in vain
>
> —1 Corinthians 15:10 ESV

My Treasure

I don't need to follow any rainbows
Search the world to find my dream come true
And I don't need a lucky star to guide me
I found my treasure in you.
I don't need to climb another mountain
Set my sail across the seven seas
The paradise that I was longing for
Was found when you loved me.
And now my greatest joy is loving you
The hope lost was found and made anew
Now my lonely days are finally through
I have found my life in loving you.
I don't need to pray a prayer unanswered
Make a wish that will never, never come true
For I have found my every answer
My every wish in you.

And now my greatest joy is loving you
The hope I lost was found and made anew
Now my lonely days are fin'ly through
I have found my life in loving you.
I don't need to follow any rainbows
Search the world to find my dream come true
I don't need a lucky star to guide me
I found my treasure in you.

—Scott Wesley Brown

and mine too!

"Oh, that you would only grant me the right to hold you ever so tight and to feel in the night" (*The Nearness of You* written by Hoagy Carmichael and Ned Washington).

When God gives you a vision and darkness follows, wait, God will bring the vision He has given you to reality in your life if you will wait on His timing. Years of silence, but in those years all of his self-sufficiency was destroyed. He (Abraham) grew past the point of relying on his common sense. Those years of silence were a time of discipline, not a period of God's displeasure.

—Oswald Chambers, *My Utmost for His Highest,* January 19th

"It Had to be You"

Why do I sigh, why don't I try to forget.
It must have been something lovers call fate
Kept me saying "I have to wait"
I saw them all, just couldn't fall till we met.
It had to be you, it had to be you.
I wandered around and finally found the
somebody who
Could make me be true, could make me be
blue
And even be glad, just to be sad thinking of
You.
For nobody else, gave me a thrill with all

For Pete's Sake

your faults, I love you still.
It had to be you, wonderful you.
It had to be you

—Written by Gus Kahn
and Isham Jones

"I'll be Seeing You"

In every lovely summer's day
In everything that's light and gay
I'll always think of you that way
I'll find you in the morning sun
And when the night is new
I'll be looking at the moon
But I'll be seeing you.

—Written by Sammy Fain
and Irving Kahal

"These Foolish Things"

And still my heart still has wings
These foolish things remind me of you
A tinkling piano in the next apartment
Those stumbling words that told you what my
heart mean
A fairground's painted swings

and mine too!

> These foolish things remind me of you.
> You came, you saw, you conquered me
> When you did that to me
> I knew somehow this had to be.
> A telephone that rings, but who's to answer?
> Oh, how the ghost of you clings
> These foolish things remind me of you…
> How strange, how sweet to find you still.
> These things are dear to me.
> They seem to bring you so near to me…

—Written by Eric Maschwitz
and Jack Strachey

"Heavenly songs seem to come from everywhere" (from *Moonglow*).

"The Very Thought of You"

> The very thought of you
> And I forget to do
> The little ordinary things
> That everyone ought to do.
> I'm living a kind of daydream
> I'm happy as a king and foolish
> Though it may seem to me
> That's everything
> The mere idea of you
> The longing here for you
> You'll never know

For Pete's Sake

How slow the moments go
Till I'm near to you...
It's just the thought of you, the very thought of you, my love.

—Written by Ray Noble

To everything there is a season, a time for
every purpose under heaven.

—Ecclesiastes 3:1 NKJV

"We'll Be Together Again"

No tears
No fears
Remember there's always tomorrow
So, what if we have to part
We'll be together again
Your kiss
Your smile
Our memories I'll treasure forever
So try thinking with your heart
We'll be together again
Time's when I know you'll be lonesome
Times when I know you'll be sad
Don't let temptation surround you
Don't let the blues make you bad.
Someday

and mine too!

> Someway
> We'll both have a lifetime before us
> For parting is not goodbye
> We'll be together again.
>
> —Written by Carl T. Fisher
> and Frankie Laine

> Faith in Christ is the only thing to save you…and out of that Faith in Him good actions must inevitably come.
>
> —C. S. Lewis

Did she make you a better offer my love?
Have you realized *yet* that it was temporary?
For here I sit, unconditionally, wondering if you will be keeping me warm *this* winter.
The guy down the hall has not called. Satan left him. I told Satan in the car yesterday, "Sure, you can try, but you're wasting your time." I am not alone, and because of this realization, I am stronger.
Now, for two days, I can only say *wow* aloud and repeatedly.
The guy down the hall has his reasons, but as for me and my heart, we once again live the miracles of the love of God. *Amen!*

> Now there are a good many things not worth bothering about if I were going to live only 70 years, but which I had better bother about very seriously if I am going to live forever.
>
> —C. S. Lewis, *Mere Christianity*

January 7, 2004

    Do you have any sense of me, darling?
    How could you do the things you do to me and not have any sense of me?
    My emotions are so real and strong. When will I penetrate the wall?
    Or do I need to go over it?
    Or around it?
    Which way? Left or right?
    Should I barge through it?
    Or start digging under it?
    My love, tell me what to do.
    Will it be my lifetime before I sense heaven again?
    Must I spend my lifetime longing for you, when I could be with you, ever so lovingly?
    Come quickly, my love.

    Dear Lord,

    Please send out the spaceship again.

Thank you,
Mary

    Seek the Kingdom of God above all else, and
    he will give you everything you need.

—Luke 12:31 NLT

    I see his blue eyes!
    So much words, emotions, tears, love.
    Trying not to feel low about another quiet birthday, and then I read of Jesus's birthday and how I've neglected him on his day. How many times he has felt this, and I am sorry, sweet Jesus.
    The kids sent me a lovely bouquet of fresh flowers.

and mine too!

They "can't wait to see me" and they love me (written twice)!

He seems to ask so much, and I must remember he will give me what I need, when I need it. Thank you, Lord.

For where your treasure is, there also will your heart be.

—Matthew 6:21 NAB

"She hoped…" (Mel Gibson speaking of his wife during his wild times; from an interview with Diane Sawyer.)

And of my Peter—the tears every day for most of the week. Why? I cry aloud and I pray aloud. Does he sense me?

After all this time, I still feel he is the one to be "heaven on earth" for each other.

Till we fill the gap or time, till eternity begins for us.

And it is that ever-present God-parallel that makes this seem so right in my simple mind and humble heart.

It's been two years since we met. It was the first weekend in January. I took Nick back to school and went to the Browns/Steelers game—we lost.

Your silent prayer uttered on tear stained pillows were heard before they were said… And you direst need, your need for a Savior, was met before you ever sinned.

—Max Lucado, *God Came Near*

A revelation for me.

Outside factors do not tempt me. The temptation is mine and mine alone; the choices are mine and mine alone; and with the grace of God, I am strengthened and with these words: I declare I am not alone.

Not four days later, I read of this exact same thing in *What a Man Thinketh* by James Allen.

And I say, "*A-ha!*" over and over.

And I dance, and a new song echoes.

January 12, 2004

On this I must pray and ponder and meditate, for I am on to something.

> Trust in the Lord with all your heart; don't rely on your own intelligence. Know him in all your paths, and he will keep your ways straight.
>
> —Proverbs 3:5–6 CEB

I had the best birthday of my life.

The kids were not here, but I received the most beautiful hand-picked cards from them.

My heart *(I drew a heart)* overflows with love and tears. I am blessed; let the circle of life spiral ever upward to you, dear God! Amen!

January 19, 2004

Before Nick went back to Pittsburgh, I shared some journal stuff with him. I read my landscaper story to him, tearfully. He said it was beautiful. And I told him how Peter said I should publish it.

And today, just driving along, he planted a seed in my heart (not many, just one), and I thought of our story. Does he know? Does he hope that God has blessed it? And keeps watch over it? Protects it? Will he be pleased? Surprised? Grateful? Is he looking forward to

and mine too!

being the human hand and heart to care for this blossom on God's earth? Does he know that he is capable and qualified? Does he know there is hope of the blossom? Does he know the blossom dreams? And prays?

    Is it not yet time to share, my Lord?
    Is it not yet time to share, my Lord?
    I ask again. Amen.

    Tears. Those tiny drops of humanity. Those round, wet balls of fluid that tumble from our eyes, creep down our cheeks, and splash the floor of our hearts. They were there that day. They are always present at such times. They should be, that's their job. They are miniature messengers; on call 24 hours a day to substitute for crippled words. They drip, drop and pour from the corner of our souls, carrying with them the deepest emotions we possess. They tumble down our faces with announcements that range from the *most blissful joy* to darkest despair. The principle's simple; when words are most empty, words are most apt. (emphasis added)

—Max Lucado, *No Wonder
They Call Him the Savior*

January 22, 2004

Dear God, Lord, Spirit,

How am I doing? Pretty good, I think. Be patient with me.
Thanks, again and again.

All my love,
Mary

P.S. Sorry I took so long.

Angela is twenty-five today, but you knew that.

The sunlight of a lesson learned illuminates my understanding.

—Max Lucado, *No Wonder They Call Him the Savior*

That is why the Warrior only risks his
heart for something worthwhile.

—Paulo Coelho, *Warrior of the Light*

January 26, 2004

My dear Peter,

I keep giving you to God, and He keeps giving you back to me, if only in my heart, and this is good. As for my longing to be near you, to share with you, to live with you, to love you—this is the deepest desire of my heart, still.

and mine too!

Thinking of you.

With love,
Mary

P.S. Still, when my phone rings, I wonder if it is you.

I have appeared to you for this purpose.

—Acts 26:16 ESV

Even so, the Warrior persists. He spends
all day long talking to his heart.

—Paulo Coelho, *Warrior of the Light*

What a Lord is our Lord. The wonder of it all. He hears my tears fall and gives them consideration, even in the midst of tears of pain, in the midst of tears of hunger and thirst, in the midst of tears of loss and loneliness.

To you I give thanks all the days of my life. Amen.

Does he know he gave me love?

Will you point this out to him, please!

I always seem closest to God, my Lord, when my heart is of Peter. All I think, feel, and desire continues to parallel, and I am in awe.

Am I a hint of heaven to him?

May I be his angel?

Because I wait in love and not in impatience, you will surely ask me truly. I will come in response to a single unequivocal call.

—*A Course in Miracles*

Keep your life so constantly in touch with God that His surprising power can break through at any point. Live in a constant state of expectancy, and leave room for God to come in as He decides.

—Oswald Chambers, *My Utmost for His Highest*

February 1, 2004

> Listen to my words, O Lord, and hear my sighs.
>
> —Psalm 5:1 GNT

One person whom Christ commended…a woman…who clutched onto her hunch that He could and her hope that He would.

—Max Lucado, *He Still Moves Stones*

> Without the sovereign hand of God Himself,
> nothing touches our loves.
>
> —Oswald Chambers, *My Utmost for His Highest*

> Daughter, your faith has made you well. Go in
> peace, and be healed of your affliction.
>
> —Mark 5:34 NKJV

A friend of mine (Del) left me a book with a note that said, "Here is your next reading assignment: *The Alchemist*" (Paulo Coelho). A

and mine too!

wonderful easy read—one day—full of metaphors, and I searched for parallels in my life and mostly in my heart.

On the next few pages, I'll write quotes from *The Alchemist* (Paulo Coelho) that touched me and emphasize the words that literally match my words written throughout my journaling.

"When you want *something with all your heart*, that's when you are closest to the Soul of the World. It's always a positive force."

"One idea that seemed to repeat itself throughout all the books: all things are the *manifestation* of one thing only."

"The language that everyone on earth was capable of understanding in their heart. It was *love*."

"She smiles, and that was certainly an omen—the omen he had been awaiting, without even knowing he was, for all his life."

"With *no need for words,* she recognized the same thing."

"Because, when you know the language, it's easy to understand that someone in the world awaits you, whether it's in the middle of the desert or in some great city. And when two such people encounter each other, and their eyes meet, *the past and the future become unimportant.* There is only that moment and the certainty that everything under the sun has been *written by one hand only.* It is the hand that evokes love, and creates a twin soul for every person in the world. *Without such love, one's dreams would have no meaning."*

"When you want something, all the universe
conspires in helping you achieve it.
It's the possibility of having a dream come
true that makes life interesting."

"Remember that wherever your heart is, there you will
find your treasurer. You've got to find the treasure, so that
everything you have learned along the way can make sense."

and mine too!

"She knows that men have to go away in order to return. And she already has her treasure, it's you. Now she expects that you will find what it is you're looking for."

("I don't want to take away your freedom. I want to be part of it," I told my Peter, and he replied, "That's the idea, babe.")

"I'm going away," he said, "and I want you to know I'm coming back. I love you because—"

"Don't say anything," Fatima interrupted. "One is loved because one is loved. No reason is needed for loving."
"So, I love you because the entire universe conspired to help me find you."

"The wise men understood that this natural world is only an image and a copy of paradise. The existence of this world is simply a guarantee that there exists a world that is perfect. God created a world so that, through its visible objects, men could understand his spirited teachings and the marvel of his wisdom."

"She would have to send her kisses on the wind, hoping that the wind would touch the boy's face, and would tell him that she was alive. That she was waiting for him, a woman awaiting a courageous

For Pete's Sake

man in search of his treasure. From that day on, the desert would only represent one thing to her: the hope for his return."

(On reading this, I sent my kisses on the wind, a cold night, the last day of January 2004)

"Listen to your heart. it knows all things, because it came from the Soul of the World, and it will one day return there."

"If what one finds is made of pure matter, it will never spoil. And one can always come back."

"In earlier times, his heart had always been ready to tell its story, but lately that wasn't true."

"But his heart was never quiet."

(My journal speaks for my heart.)

"Why do we have to listen to the heart?" the boy asked, when they made camp that day.
"Because, wherever your heart is, that is where you will find your treasure."
"But my heart is agitated," the boy said. "It has its dreams, it gets emotional, and it keeps me from sleeping many nights, when I'm thinking about her."
"Well, that's good. Your heart is alive, keep listening to what it has to say."

and mine too!

"The boy and his heart had become friends, and neither was capable now of betraying the other."

"Well, then, why should I listen to my heart?"
"Because you will never again be able to keep it quiet. Even if you pretend not to have heard what it tells you, it will always be there inside you, repeating to you what you are thinking about life and about the world. Because you'll know its dreams and wishes and will know how to deal with them."

"You'll never be able to escape from your heart. So, it is better to listen to what it has to say. That way, you'll never have to fear an unanticipated blow."

(Repeatably, my heart says, "Peter knows you are waiting for him." No lie, no imagination.)

"Even though I complain sometimes, it said 'It's because I'm the heart of a person, and people's hearts are that way. People are afraid to pursue their most important dreams, because they *feel they don't deserve them*, or that they'll be unable to achieve them.'" (emphasis added)

"And that no heart has ever suffered when it goes in search of its dreams, because every second of the search is a second's encounter with God and with eternity."

This page was folded in half in my journal, must be significant.

"When I have been truly searching for my treasures, every day has been luminous, because I've known that every hour was part of the dream that I would find it. When I've been truly searching for my treasure, I've discovered things along the way that I never would have seen had I not the courage to try things that seemed impossible. From then on, the boy understood his heart. He asked it, please, never stop speaking to him. Continue to pay heed to the omens. Your heart is still capable of showing you where the treasure is."

"When you possess great treasures within you, and try to tell others of them, seldom are you believed."

"What you still need to know is this: before a dream is realized, the Soul of the World tests everything that was learned along the way. It does this not because it is evil, but so that we can, in addition to realizing our dreams, master the lessons we've learned as we've moved toward the dream."

Wow!

and mine too!

"Does a man's heart always help him?" the boy asked the alchemist. "Mostly just the hearts of those who are trying to realize their Personal Legends."

(Drew a heart)

"It spoke of journeys, discoveries, books, and change."

"The boy fell to his knees and wept. He thanked God for making him believe in his personal legend, and for leading him to meet a king… And above all for having met a woman of the desert who told him that love would never keep a man from his personal legend. Instead, it brought a scent of a perfume he knew well, and the touch of a kiss—a kiss that came from far away, slowly, slowly, until it rested on his lips. The boy smiled. It was the first time she had done that."

"He thought of the many roads he had travelled and of the strange way God had chosen to show him his treasure."

—Paulo Coelho, *The Alchemist*

So *who is this man*?
Is he my personal legend?
Was this book an omen from an unknowing friend? To give me continued hope that my heart is where it should be?

The boy found his treasure. His journey has an uncanny parallel to mine (and probably many others). Dare I see it as an omen that my treasure is very near? That my personal legend and Peter's will come together? Soon? Is the conspiracy of the universe near its climax?

Be still, my heart!

Be still and know that I am God.

—Psalm 46:10 NIV

Take my yoke upon you and learn from Me, for I am gentle and lowly in heart, and you will find rest for your souls.

—Matthew 11:29 ESV

Serene will be our days and bright, and happy will our nature be, when love is an unerring light, and joy its own security. –

—Wordsworth

Always has no direction (p. 237).

—*A Course in Miracles*

His entire creation points to Him and the glorious plan He has for you as his child.

—*Tea Time with God*

and mine too!

Fragility

Love can be as fragile
as a butterfly or a flower,
but a flower will hold
its blossoms safely in its roots
while buried
in the icy heart of winter.
With a faith
that can't be overcome
by frost,
it reaches past reason
all the way to April.
And a migrating butterfly
will wing its way
Through a thousand miles
Of impossibilities
Until it finds its flower

—John Engle

If You're Not the One

If you're not the one then why does my soul feel glad today?
If you're not the one then why does my hand fit yours this way?
If you are not mine then why does your heart return my call
If you are not mine would I have the strength to stand at all
I never know what the future brings
But I know you are here with me now
We'll make it through
And I hope you are the one I share my life with
I don't want to run away but I can't take it, I don't understand

For Pete's Sake

If I'm not made for you then why does my heart tell me that I am?
Is there any way I can stay in your arms?
If I don't need you then why am I crying in my bed?
If I don't need you then why does your name resound in my head?
If you're not for me then why does this distance maim my life?
If you're not for me then why do I dream of you as my wife?
I don't know why you are so far away
But I know that this much is true
We'll make it through
And I hope you are the one I can share my life with
And I wish that you could be the one I die with
And I pray that you are the one I can build my home with
I hope I love you all my life
I don't want to run away but I can't take it, I don't understand
If I'm not made for you then why does my heart tell me that I am
Is there any way that I can stay in your arms?
'Cause I miss you, body and soul so strong
that it takes my breath away
And I breathe you into my heart and pray
for the strength to stand today
'Cause I love you, whether it's wrong or right
And though I can't be with you tonight
And know my heart is by your side
I don't want to run away but I can't take it, I don't understand
If I'm not made for you then why does my heart tell me that I am
Is there any way I can stay in your arms?
No, that trauma you faced was not easy.
And God wept that it hurt you so;
But it also allowed you to shape your heart
So that into his Likeness you'd grow.

—Russell Kelfer

and mine too!

> I think He meant, "The only help I will give is
> help to become perfect. You may want something
> less: but I will give you nothing less."
>
> —C. S. Lewis' interpretation of our Lord's words,
> "Be ye perfect." From *Mere Christianity*

> We don't see things as they are, we see them as we are.
>
> —Anais Nin

> Reflect on what I am saying, for the Lord will give you insight.
>
> —2 Timothy 2:7 NIV

> By all means use to be alone, Salute thyself;
> see what thy soul doth wean.
>
> —George Herbert

The Spirit is forever in me. Our relationship feels new. Peter needs me.

Looking back, I've always recognized the Trinity in my life but did not realize I could be an active participant!

I'm loving the light.

Amen!

February 5, 2004

What an incredible afternoon of reading! So incredible I'm going to write it down.

They also spoke of perfection—wow.

- Chapter 12, "The Way to Remember God" from *A Course in Miracles*.
- Book 4, "Counting the Cost" from C. S. Lewis, *Mere Christianity*.
- "Standing Alone" from J. Allen, *As a Man Thinketh*.
- "Pay Attention" (page 124) from *Tea Time with God*.
- "Christian Perfection (December 2)" from Oswald Chambers, *My Utmost for His Highest*.
- "You Are Not An Accident" from Rick Warren, *A Purpose Driven Life*.

February 5

> Joan: I hear voices telling me what to do. They come from God.
> Robert: They come from your imagination.
> Joan: Of course. That is how the messages of God come to us.
>
> —George Bernard Shaw, *Saint Joan*

An evening of emotions and callings and metaphors and dreams, etc.

The words will make no sense, so I will not attempt them tonight.

and mine too!

Yes, Peter, you every day. I would have it no other way until you are with me.

And then I will write of us and dreams come true and there will be more love and light in the world. I promised God that when we are together, I will tell the world, "Behold the handiwork of the Lord."

The Lord will fill His purpose for me.

—Psalm 138:8a NIV

There is a *moment* of surrender, and there is a practice of surrender, which is moment by moment and lifelong. (emphasis added)

—Rick Warren, *A Purpose Driven Life*

Dear Peter,

All my thoughts connect to you, and it's not complicated either. You are so here, and the parallels continue.

You two are my dark knights, always at the same time. Surprised? Not me.

It gets "harder to explain."

I think I should send you The Alchemist.

Loving you,
Mary

For Pete's Sake

Surrender yourself to the Lord, and wait patiently for him.

—Psalm 37:7a GWT

For you will believe in what you manifest, and as you look out so will you see in. Two ways of looking at the world are in your mind, and your perception will reflect the guidance you have.

—*A Course in Miracles*

February 19, 2004

Hi, Lord,

You make me smile, giggle, and I love when you make me feel like dancing.

I just read "If any want to boast, they should boast that they know and understand me… These are the things that please me" (Jeremiah 9:24 TEV).

I love how you touch me!

All my love and thanks,
Mary

Dear Peter,

What are you going through while I'm also "going through?" Will you ever know that I think of you every day? Will I ever know if you ever think of me? Just wondering.

and mine too!

Hope you are well!

With love,
Mary

Draw close to God, and God will draw close to you.

—James 4:8 NLT

Love, too, is recognized by its messengers. If you make love manifest, its messengers will come to you because you invited them.

—*A Course in Miracles*, p 231

Feb. 22, 2004

A nice weekend in Pittsburgh with Ang and John. They included me in their housewarming, and it has been delightful.

Our baby countdown has begun, and if I think about it for too long, it is so much!

On Ang and John's hilltop home, I am practically in Peter's backyard, yet Saturday found him to be that "dark knight." On Sunday, I talked and cried aloud and for him, the same tears with no name to describe them. And I realize that in all I have written and described and shared, it is but the tip of the iceberg with the immense, deep, penetrating, and hidden portion in my heart and soul that no words of the earth can be written and spoken.

Oh, glorious God!

For Pete's Sake

To what will you look for help if you will not look
to that which is stronger than yourself?

—C. S. Lewis, *The Business of Heaven*

Continue praying, keeping alert, and always thanking God.

—Colossians 4:2 NCV

Between Wednesday and Friday last week, I read:

Allow Him to be the source of all your dreams, joys and delights and be careful to go and obey what He says. If you are in love with someone, you don't sit and daydream about that person all the time—you go and do something for him.

—Oswald Chambers, *My Utmost for His Highest*

And:

The future is the present, and every dream—
will have a chance to be heard.

—Paulo Coelho, *Warrior of the Light*

And:

Surrendered hearts show up best in relationships.

—Rick Warren, *The Purpose Driven Life*

The Lord looks on the heart.

—1 Samuel 16:7 NRSV

and mine too!

> Faith is the assurance of things hoped for,
> the conviction of things not seen.
>
> —Hebrews 11:1 NRSV

> That in the silence of his heart he will hear
> an order that will guide him.
>
> —Paulo Coelho, *Warrior of the Light*

He chose to forget. I chose to hope.

—Me

This I wrote the day Lena called and asked that I stop sending stuff to Pete, etc. I hung up the phone and responded, "Mmm." She said Peter would send the book (*The Alchemist*) back.

That was at least three weeks ago...

Then the Lord said, "It is not good for man to be alone."

—Genesis 2:18 ESV

Joy is sometimes a blessing, but it is often a conquest.

—Paulo Coelho, *By the River Piedra I Sat Down and Wept*

For Pete's Sake

I have a new man in my life—my grandson, my Johnny. Born February 24 at six pounds and twelve ounces and twenty inches long; with brown hair, blue eyes, and he has touched a new part of my heart. The new family is healthy and happy and loved and blessed! Thank you, God!

I go to Pittsburgh every weekend, and by Thursday, my heart yearns for my little guy.

And God will see to it that you have a number of
opportunities to prove to yourself the miracle of His grace…
and you will never cease to be the most amazed person
on earth at what God has done for you on the inside.

—Oswald Chambers, *My Utmost
for His Highest,* March 23

March 26, 2004

>He said yes
>He said yes
>He said yes
>and I wept
>Amen

My dark knight, yet still my dream!

and mine too!

Dreams disappear when light has come and you can see.

—*A Course in Miracles*

All my dreams of Peter are when I am totally awake in the light. Once, in these past two years, he was in one dream as I slept.

The universe does not judge; it conspires in favor of what we want. That is why the Warrior has the courage to look in the dark places of his soul in order to ensure that he is not asking for the wrong things.

—Paulo Coelho, *Warrior of the Light*

By the way, I lay awake, thinking of and loving Peter. I clutched one of the pillows I bought two years ago, and it "was" Peter. I stopped and prayed, "Oh, Lord, if this is not from you, please make it go away."

It did not go away.

And my horoscope that day? "Your domestic life will change in the near future."

And Mary Jean asked if I heard from Peter.

"No."

To which she responded, "He'll show up."

And I went to Pittsburgh with much anticipation.

Now it is Monday, and the dark knight of my heart once again is there. I saw a rainbow today, and I am almost sure it's been more than a year since I've seen one.

For Pete's Sake

The Holy Spirit leads me unto Christ, and where else would
I go? What need do I have but to awake in Him?

—*A Course in Miracles*

May my tears run just as far, that my love may
never know that one day I cried for him.

—Paulo Coehlo

The Bible uses the term *heart* to describe the bundle of desire,
hope, interests, ambitions, dreams, and affections you have.
Your heart represents the source of all your motivations—
what you love to do and what you care most about.
Your heart reveals the real you, what you truly are, not what
others think of you or what circumstances force you to be.
Your heart determines why you say the things you do, why
you feel the way you do and why you act the way you do.

—Rick Warren, *A Purpose Driven Life*

How I love to do your will, my God! I
keep your teachings in my heart.

—Psalm 40:8 GNT

I was there because suddenly, life presented me with life.

—Paulo Coehlo

April 29, 2004

Two pages ago, the dark knight of my heart, but not today. My God gifted me with those feelings that connect me *with only Peter,* and I cried.

and mine too!

And I thought, *How many more tears? And which tear carries all the love, devotion, and power to break the wall in my lover's heart? Is it one tear of endless magnitude? Or all the tears eroding this wall?*

I will continue to shed them, for in them, I find comfort. They are a gift from heaven because my humanness needs the tangible. They cleanse me, and I pray they flow to my love to cleanse him too!

Thank you, Lord, for only You could create such a love story. Amen.

In real life, love has to be possible. Even if it not returned right of way, love can only survive where the hope exists that you will be able to win over the person you desire. Anything else is a fantasy.

—*A Course in Miracles*

May 2, 2004

Today, like many days, thoughts of Peter make my heart beat faster (noticeably).

Thank you, Lord.

"Dreams: a key to a locked door."
Are my dreams Peter's key?

For Pete's Sake

Though it tarries, wait for it.

—Habakkuk 2:3 NKJV

May 4, 2004

Sometimes we'll sigh.
Sometimes we'll cry.
And we'll know why, just you and I
Know true love ways.

—Buddy Holly, *Buddy Holly Greatest Hits*

My dear Peter,

Where are you? Besides in my heart; besides in so many of my thoughts; besides in the tears I shed.

How can you be so with me and so not be here? I long for every part of you.

There is so much to tell you.

There is so much to share. I want you to meet my parents. They would be so happy to meet you and you will love them.

I want to grow old with you. I don't want you to be one of those Five People You Meet in Heaven (Mitch Albion).

I want to take care of you and have you take care of me. Wouldn't that be a wonderful change for both of us?

Only by the grace of God can these emotions and desires endure throughout these past two years.

I know I am not the first to wait for an answer to a prayer. So I will continue to wait in love with you, my darling, for this part of my heart is yours.

And so often these past few weeks, you are almost constant in my thought, in my heartbeat, in

and mine too!

my breath, and that I've looked into the sky and said your name aloud.

"A man's heart determines his speech" (Matthew 12:34).

And I wonder if this means you are getting closer to me, to my dreams, my eyes, my voice, my hands, my heart, my life.

All of me awaits all of you.

This is all so wondrous and beautiful. Let us thank God all our days, for our love will surely reflect God in us.

Once again, I selfishly pray that dear Jesus will send the spaceship and his angels to invite you aboard (now that I have stopped sobbing, I started to write). And I pray you say yes, and you did, my love. My heart heard it on March 26, seven pages ago. And the angels smiled.

Oh, glorious Lord and God, this love of ours we offer to you, for where else would we want to be than in the hands of the Creator of all things beautiful and timeless in your image? Creator of each of us, individually brought together by your love for us and kept together through time, for your time is eternal.

It seems odd to ask God to manifest all the dreams, hopes, desires, and love from all these pages, for I feel (truly) that he already has.

Amen! Amen! Amen!

P.S. I look forward to reading this to you soon, my love.

Goodnight!

Mary

P.S. Time to moisturize!

> Guesses, of course, only guesses. If they are
> not true, something better will be.
>
> —C. S. Lewis, *The Business of Heaven*

May 5, 2004

> My faith and my belief are centered on what I treasure… I love what only God loves with me, and because of this I treasure you beyond the value you set on yourself, even unto the worth that God has placed you. I love all that he has created, and all my faith and my belief I offer unto it. My faith in you is as strong as all the love I give my Father. My trust in you is without limit, and without fear that you will hear me not. I thank the Father for your loveliness and for the many gifts that you will let me offer to the Kingdom in honor of its wholeness that is of God.
>
> —*A Course in Miracles*

The next night, I read "After great moments of exaltation come the struggles and failures of ordinary life; but there the promise is lived out"*(Encounter with God)*. My Bible study guide.

> Whatever your reactions to the Holy Spirit's Voice may be, whatever voice you choose to listen to, whatever strange thoughts may occur to you, God's will *is* done. (emphasis added)
>
> —*A Course in Miracles*

> Be ready at all times to answer anyone that asks you to explain the hope you have in you, but do it with gentleness and respect.
>
> —1 Peter 3:15b–16 TEV

and mine too!

> Writing helps clarify what God is doing in your life.
>
> —Rick Warren, *A Purpose Driven Life*

> My wanderings you have noted; are my tears not stored in your vial, recorded in your book?
>
> —Psalm 56:9 NAB

> And even though you cannot see Him right now and cannot understand what He is doing, you know Him.
>
> —Oswald Chambers, *My Utmost for His Highest*

> You cannot keep yourself from talking about what you care about most.
>
> —Rick Warren, *A Purpose Driven Life*

May 18, 2004

(In the margin, I wrote a love letter.)
A few pages back, look up "*May 5, 2004.*"
I have spent almost two weeks in "ordinary life." Peter is but a thought here and there throughout these days, that's all. And I wonder if this is it—a letting go. Or will I again be thrown into that aura of the love triangle? I do not dwell on these thoughts but am in awe of such power which belongs to the Creator of all love. I miss him, especially when he is not so near. I hope he is well, and I wonder.

Every day is joyful. There is always a miracle, a gift for me, and I give thanks for my new eyes and new heart to see and feel my new life.

Thy will be done, Lord. Use me.
I love you. Amen!

For Pete's Sake

He'll show up.

—Mary Jean Galloway

He leadeth me and knows the way, which I know not. Yet He will never keep me from what He would have me learn. And so, I trust Him to communicate to me all that He knows for me.

—*A Course in Miracles*

Great reading: *A Course in Miracles*, chapter 14, "III The Decision of Guiltlessness."

I've been on my "desert journey."

All my words and tears and emotions have helped me to heal because today I realized this: a time for every purpose under heaven. Thank you.

Amen.

For whatever things were written before were written
for our learning, that we through the patience and
comfort of the Scriptures we might have hope.

—Romans 15:4 NKJV

Angela unknowingly gave me a Mother's Day present. She picked up and read from *Grace for the Moment* by Max Lucado.

May 20, 2004

A thought here
A thought there
Out of the blue he slips randomly

and mine too!

In and out of my heart
my mind
my breath.

May 22, 2004

My days
My nights
My love!

Our waiting is not dependent on the providence
of God, but on our own spiritual fitness.

—Oswald Chambers, *My
Utmost for His Highest*

Awesomely great weekend. Matt skipped his commencement to be with us in Minnesota. Dad said Matt's decision would be the right one. Sue and I had a ceremony for him in Minnesota, and in Papa's commencement speech, he said, "Matt's graduation is now complete because we are all together."
Perfect.
Thank you, my Lord.
Amen.

I love the hustle and activities of the day, but I so look forward to being with God in our way. I am grateful for what each day brings me, but "our" time is what I look forward to.

For Pete's Sake

> Looking at everything in relation to Him, because
> our abiding awareness of Him continually
> pushes itself to the forefront of our lives.
>
> —Oswald Chambers, *My
> Utmost for His Highest*

How do I write of Peter? He's been with me. In each undistracted moment, when I don't have to think of daily doings, he is there, and that thought instantly goes to God-thoughts. It's the triangle. And there are the other times when God thoughts connect to Peter thoughts.

This is effortless.

The only prayer that is unchanging is "thy will be done."

June 1, 2004

Tonight, I read a license plate: 2BBlessed.
Amen.
Goodnight.

June 3, 2004

My thoughts of Peter that have merely trickled in and out of my last week or so became a deluge of thoughts, and tears. I sat in the sun, thinking, praying, and listening. When I opened my eyes, tears flowed, so many, so unexpected. I knew my heart was crying, but not my eyes.

But whenever a person turns to the Lord the veil is removed. Now the Lord is the Spirit, and where the Spirit of the Lord is, there is freedom. all of us, gazing with unveiled face on

and mine too!

the glory of the Lord, are being transformed into the same image from glory to glory, as from the Lord who is Spirit.

—2 Corinthians 3:16–18 ESV

Great reading in 2 Corinthians 4 and 5.
Some thoughts from this time:

- Send a "flyer" with John and Ang's old address. "He needs a sign."
- Write a book with our love triangle in the title… Peter parallels his time with mine.
- I've been sleeping on his side of the bed…keeping it warm for him.
- We are home for each other.

It's cold tonight. And whenever I get cold like this, I recall Peter's words to me when he was cold. "You should be here with me."

Only by being a *manifestation* of His beauty, loving kindness, wisdom or goodness, has any earthly beloved existed our love. (emphasis mine)

—C. S. Lewis, *The Business of Heaven*, June 3

Last night, I was drawn to *Enchanted Love* by Marianne Williamson. I began to read the words I underlined. And they touched me again and more than ever. *Affirmation for my heart from my Lord!*

And I listened to *A Brand New Me* by Dusty Springfield. Why? Thank my Lord of love.

Amen!

P.S. From my "tanning" place, I heard Peter say to me over the phone, "You're crying. I'll come to wipe them away."

In the margin, I write "How my heart pounded and my breaths were so audible" (*June 4*).

Lyrics I heard: "It's the last night you'll be alone" (Eagles). I think I'll check it out.

I imagine sharing Peter with my parents, and oh, the happiness for all.

I continue with *Enchanted Love* (Marianne Williamson) "highlights."

June 6, 2004

My past few walks, I've listened to *Dark Knight of the Soul* by Ron Roth and *Conversations with God* by Neale Donald Walsch.

Both pointed out that we are created in God's image and likeness so he could experience himself. And in being so, we, too, can create and recreate. And through our feelings, he feels too.

So look what I have created over the past two years with words and a pen and all the unspoken words of my heart. Peter, touching my heart anew, started a wondrous work in me. Does he have any idea how vital he is? And why I desire him to join my heaven? For he is so much a part of it and that he lived here already.

I know not how to create his presence next to me so I cry unto my God the Creator of the creative to show me, to help me, to continue it all for my heart and soul, how the simple human mind sees that "how could this not come to be."

What am I missing, not getting?

And you feel what I feel because you created me? You cry with me in frustration in that people "don't get it yet" when it all seems so obvious. I pray with you and let me do what I humanly can for you, in your name, to all you've created as we walk the earth together.

and mine too!

I continue my daily prayer, my selfish prayer. Let Peter see my heart, and remember how I know his and how we each have a part of each other's heart. All those words of love that effortlessly went from loving lips to loving ears.

How could it be anything else or anyone else?

Lord, send the angels again to my beloved.
May I dare ask that they be swift and sure this time?
May these tears I cry, the tears I have not been able to label all these pages, become the perfected tears of wondrous joy and love. The tears that speak the words the lips cannot find.

After the walk, I turn on the radio to instantly hear "God Only Knows" by the Beach Boys.

Amen.

Later that afternoon, as I'm watering the flowers on the balcony, I hear, "And for this you were created"

I cried, "And he for you." I cried some more. I am blessed some more. Thanksgiving!

Amen, some more.

Today is Trinity Sunday!

I drew a triangle with a cross on top.

I have been speaking out loud lately when I'm alone, of thoughts, of feelings.

My thoughts are synonymous with my feelings.

And the words I repeat most often? *"I love you, Peter."*

- Lots of "heavy-duty stuff" these days.
- I have an inkling that he is closer.

This is where Volume #6 ends. The next seven entries were tucked in it.

For Pete's Sake

Some People

Some people come into our lives
and quickly go. Some people stay
for a while, and give us a deeper
understanding of what is truly
important in this life. They touch
our souls. We gain strength from
the footprints they have
left on our hearts, and we will
never ever be the same.

*—From a card I received from
my girlfriend, Joyce Ann*

Capricorn (December 22—January 19): "You come to a strong realization that events surrounding your domestic life will change in the near future. Do not project, just go with the flow. Tonight, let your hair down." (*My horoscope*)

Love quiz.
The loyal lover.
You're a lover you can lean on. Loyal with a heart of solid gold.

Today, I can say with utter sincerity how grateful I am
the liberation did not happen rapidly, because the lessons
learned on the way were both precious and much needed.

—P. Pradervand, *The Gentle Art of Blessing*, p. 84

And the incredible certainty that everything under the sun
has been written by one hand only. It is the hand that evokes
love and creates a twin soul for every person in the world.
Without such love, one's dream would have no meaning.

—Paulo Coelho, *The Alchemist*

and mine too!

If we desire/seek perfection, all kinds of obstacles arise. If we obey our destiny, we are free everywhere, everyone.

—*A Course in Miracles*

Perhaps Love

Perhaps love is like a resting place
A shelter from the storm
It exists to give you comfort
It is there to keep you warm
And in those times of trouble
When you are most alone
The memory of love will bring you home
Perhaps love is like a window
Perhaps an open door
It invites you to come closer
It wants to show you more
And even if you lose yourself and
don't know what to do
The memory of love will see you thru
Oh, love to some is like a cloud
To some as strong as steel
For some a way of living
For some a way to feel
And some say love is holding on
And some say letting go
And some say love is ev'rything
Some say they don't know
Perhaps love is like the ocean
Full of conflict full of pain
Like a fire when it's cold outside

For Pete's Sake

Thunder when it rains
If I should live forever
And all my dreams come true
My memories of love will be of you
And some say love is holding on
And some say letting go
And some say love is ev'rthing
Some say they don't know
Perhaps love is like the ocean
Full of conflict full of pain
Like a fire when it's cold outside
Thunder when it rains
If I should live forever
And all my dreams come true
My memories of love will be of you.

— Plácido Domingo, words and music by John Denver, *Perhaps Love*

Volume #7—the spiral bound purple and green one

On the inside cover, I write:

Providing further evidence of what every writer is bound to discover eventually: that not only language, that finest of human inventions, inherently inadequate as the tool for the expression of that which we most want and need to say, but that punctuation and grammar have their limitations too.

—D. Schoemperlen, *Our Lady of the Lost and Found*, p. 134

June 8, 2004

> I've been walking
> I'm still reading
> I've been listening
> I've been praying
> and learning
> and loving
> and growing
> and hoping.

We are *created* in God's image and likeness so we are able to *create*—*create* our way back home by the choices we make. Can I *create* Peter *with* me *here* and now? I believe in my *creative* energies and have seen results, but my Peter, what of my Peter? Is he *creating* his way to me and our God who *created* us?

I called on God. "Help me. Let us cocreate this time. I am not afraid." It's that I so want to do his will.

I created a love story on paper and a love story in my heart that contains the unwritten words. The love story that began, and Peter heard, from my lips not so long ago.

A love story inspired by God and kept alive by his grace, and I am grateful, for where would I be?

Oh, that Peter would see the wondrous God through me as I saw Jesus by loving him.

Part of me wants to call him when I get to Pittsburgh this weekend. I hesitate. Why? I do not know for sure, yet. I want to, God. I guess.

Last night, I read "Whatever you ask in my name, that I will do" (John 14:13 ESV). Is this what I've been missing? Not going through the Son? Maybe.

So, today, I walked and prayed aloud in the sunshine, and the words came freely. Time and heat meant nothing.

I prayed the way I wanted to live:

- lovingly.
- in his likeness.
- in his will, on earth as it is in heaven.

For in becoming like Christ, we do the will of God.
How can this love I have for Peter and us not be when it already is?

You will ask what you desire, and it shall be done for you.

—John 15:7 NKJV

Once the call comes to you, start going and never stop.

—Oswald Chambers, *My Utmost for His Highest*

I need him not. I desire him completely. I desire to be his soul's companion. I already am. And somewhere in his heart of hearts, he knows I have been with him. He has been in my heart and soul, no doubt, especially if you've read these many pages.

Soul mates—not a cliché this time.

When the triangle *(drawn)* becomes our circle *(drawn)* of love.

Matter is frozen fire/energy. Oh, to melt my love's heart as he has melted mine.

June 10

Where are you? Where did you go? Will you be back, like you've done before? How do you do that? What does it take? What am I missing, besides you? Are you real? Will you ever be in my reality as

and mine too!

you are in my heart and soul? Is it so wrong to want to be so right about this? Is it all ego? *No,* this love frustrates the ego! My heart knows the who, but how? When? Where?

This place unsettles me.

Goodnight.

Remember that you can never give another person what you have found, but you can cause him to have a desire for it.

—Oswald Chambers, *My Utmost for His Highest* (June 10)

And then you fall off the face of my soul, my heart. How? Why?
And I anticipate another enlightenment that feeds my heart and my soul with hope and love and patience and peace.

Hold on My Heart

Hold on my heart
Just hold on to that feeling
We both know we've been here before
We both know what can happen
Hold on my heart
Cos I'm looking over your shoulder
Ooh please don't rush this time
Don't show her how you feel
Hold on my heart
Throw me a lifeline

For Pete's Sake

I'll keep a place for you
Somewhere deep inside.
So, hold on my heart
Please tell her to be patient
Cos there has never been a time
That I have wanted something more
If I can recall this feeling
And I know there's a chance
Oh, I will be there
Yes, I will be there
Be there for you...
Whenever you want me to
Whenever you call oh I will be there
Yes I will be there
Hold on my heart
Don't let her see you crying
No matter where I go
She'll always be with me

—Genesis, *Hold on My Heart*

What is more beautiful than a bride? The bouquet of promises she carries.

—Max Lucado, *The Applause of Heaven*

There is indeed a peculiar charm, both in friendship and in Eros, about those moments when appreciative love lies, as it

and mine too!

were, curled up asleep, and the mere ease and ordinariness of the relationship (free as solitude, yet neither is alone) wraps us around. *No need to talk. No need to make love.* No need at all except perhaps to stir the fire. (emphasis mine)

—C. S. Lewis, *The Business of Heaven*

You Don't Have to Be a Star
(To Be in My Show)

You can come as you are with just your heart
And I'll take you in, though you're rejected
and hurt
To me you're worth what you have within.
Oh honey, I don't need no superstar
'Cause I'll accept you as you are
You won't be denied, 'cause I'm satisfied
With the love you can inspire…
Somebody nobody knows could steal the
tune that you want to hear
So stop your running around
'Cause now you've found what was cloudy is
clear
Oh honey, there'll be no cheering from the
clouds
Just two hearts beating out loud.
There'll be no parade, no TV, no stage only me
till your dying day…
Don't think your star has to shine for me
To find out where you're coming from…

—Marilyn McCoo and Billy Davis Jr., *I Hope We Get to Love in Time*

For Pete's Sake

Life is full of miracles, but they're not always the ones we pray for.

—Eve Arden

Happiness comes through doors you didn't know you left open.

—John Barrymore

Wrote this on a postcard with "+P" as a return address, mailed it Monday, June 21, from Pennsylvania addressed to Peter:

It is summer again;
I wish you by my side,
hope you by my side,
dream you by my side,
pray you by my side,
to walk in the sunshine,
to sit in front of sunset,
to hold me during a thunderstorm.

Immortality

So, this is who I am
And this is all I know
And I must choose to live
For all that I can give

and mine too!

The spark that makes the power grow.
But I will stand for a dream if I can
Symbol of my faith in who I am
But you are my only
And I must follow on the road that lies ahead
I won't let my heart control my head
But you are my only
And we don't say good bye
We don't say good bye
And I know what I've got to be…
Immortality
I make my journey through eternity
I keep the memory of you and me
inside.
Fulfill your destiny
It's there within the child
My storm will never end
My fate is on the wind
The king of hearts
The joker's wild
We don't say goodbye
We don't say goodbye
I'll make them all remember me.
Cause I have found the dream that must
come true
Every ounce of me must see it through
But you are my only
I'm sorry I don't have the role of love to play
Hand over my heart I'll find a way
I will make them give to me…
Immortality
There is a vision and fire in me
I keep the memory of you and me
Inside
And we don't say goodbye
We don't say goodbye

For Pete's Sake

In all my love for you
And what else we may do
We don't say goodbye.

—Bee Gees, *Their Greatest Hits: The Record*

When I called out, you answered me; you strengthened me.

—Psalm 138:3 ISV

The routine of life is actually God's way of saving us between our times of great inspiration which come from Him.

—Oswald Chambers, *My Utmost for His Highest*

June 16, 2004

I know nothing, so thy will be done, dear Lord.

To remember always that God is here, in the middle of the relationship, and what your beloved cannot give you today, God gives you always.

—Marianne Williamson, *Enchanted Love*

and mine too!

June 19, 2004

    I read (again).

There is such a stillness here in this place, where there is only you and I, with the knowledge that this has been going on forever. We paused in conversation, for what—a thousand years? Speak to me again for you voice is coded with the music I have longed to hear. I will join you in this dialogue, I will speak my word and sing my part. The silence lasted long enough, and it is time to begin again.

—Marianne Williamson, *Enchanted Love*

When I first read this in 2003, I double underlined the last sentence and wrote, "Please—something" at the end.

A woman's feelings aren't necessarily rational, they're just feelings.

—Marianne Williamson, *Enchanted Love*

The story of a love is not important—what is
important is that one is capable of love. It's perhaps
the only glimpse we are permitted of eternity.

—Helen Hayes

My Heart

June 24, 2004

    It was not so long ago as I rubbed my beloved shoulders and arms and commented on how strong he is. He commented back, "Babe, you should have seen me before."
    Well, my love, you are wondrously strong, for you have lifted my heart to unheard of heights and have held it there unwaveringly

since the beginning. And if I recall, my heart was very heavy then. Thank you, dear!

I walked and thought I was falling in love with my Peter with the heart of a forty-seven-year-old me.

Since then, my heart has grown and revealed more and more of God, our Creator, the creator in me.

And through each layer or step into my heart, I have loved him. As much growing and learning and changing and questioning and understanding, the highs and lows, the joys, and the longings, I have loved him. He has fit in everywhere, one way or another, effortlessly, and he is mine.

Fly away, little angels, and whisper of such love that awaits him. Have him call me that I might read these words of love to his hungry heart. I am ready.

> For every tear in anyone's eye, there is someone out there to kiss it away.
>
> —Marianne Williamson, *Enchanted Love*

> Only one thing will bear the strain, and that is a personal relationship with Jesus Christ Himself—a relationship that has to be examined, purified, and tested until only one purpose remains and I can truly say, "I am here for God to send me where He will."
>
> —Oswald Chambers, *My Utmost for His Highest*

and mine too!

Another gift, a message today, a book or so ago, I wrote of how I, as Peter's angel, had only one wing, and he had one wing and that only together, we could fly. This came, also from *Enchanted Love*. I thought for sure and maybe even wrote that our rings would be shaped as one wing, each, well, today in an Avon catalogue were two wings (silver) that are ear cuffs.

And I smiled throughout the day:

- a message of hope
- a sign of nearness
- the nod of knowing

Amen.

He put a new song in my mouth, a song of praise to our God.

—Psalm 40:3 ESV

What can be more joyous than to perceive
we are deprived of nothing?

—*A Course in Miracles*

June 27, 2004

Through all this time
Through all these pages and every
Unwritten thought and hope and dream
If it's about Peter, it leads to prayer.
Thank you, dear God.

July 1, 2004

And then the haze makes the clarity of previous days threatened.

And I question the when, the why, the how, but never the who.

And the answer is "Mary" (with a sigh), but who answers? My heart? My dream? My wish? My God?

And do I continue these *thoughts* because I *think* I should? What compels this feeling of love? What sustains these feelings of love and peace?

So many questions. I know the answers and I have all along, in my heart of hearts, the part of my heart that is part of Peter's.

So why have I gone on and on for over two years and many pens and pages:

    a)   for my book?
    b)   to sustain my hopes?
    c)   to make the wait more bearable?
    d)   to read back to my beloved some day?
    e)   all of the above

> The power of love, which is its meaning, lies in the
> strength of God that hovers over it and blesses it silently
> by enveloping it in healing *wings*. Let this be and do
> not try to substitute your "miracle" for this.
>
> —*A Course in Miracles*

Dear Lord,

That part of my heart, which is part of Peter's heart, longs to free and become his heart of hearts. I believe. Create with me, for I need you. Your touch,

and mine too!

reassurance, your word, and guidance, your unconditional love for both of us and all your children – may we re-gift you the same – how easy and how beautiful.
   I sign off now in a pinball game of thoughts.

Love you,
M

Is something better than nothing?
You have nothing?

July 2, 2004

I recall the words of my beloved. "Maria, you know my heart."

- He believed it or he wouldn't have spoken it.
- I believed him—what an honor.
- I still believe it—what a treasure.
- My heart knows this—for it has never been the same.

Oh, Lord, that he would remember and know he believed it, and it is real. Later that afternoon, "Let's do it!"

N: Would this be against their will?
G: No, I would arrange it so that everyone you wish to share the experience of love with in this way, also wishes to do so with you.

—Neale Donald Walsh,
Conversations with God

July 4, 2004

Only you!
And you call me and say, "Do you know who this is?"
And I say, "Yes, it is, my beloved."
It's only you!
Anthony and I have spent time together: it's fun and casual, but only you could make me feel like your lady, make me want to touch more than your hand, make me feel this is where I belong, etc.
I love you.
In the margin I write; I ask God for a sign, and he asks, "Aren't your tears enough?" Thank you.

Dear Peter,

I want to be your everything. Why do I feel I can be everything to you? Everything you need? Where does this sureness come from? Is it arrogance? Or maybe a confidence of my heart, opened for you (for us) by the loving hand of God our Father.
I must know. I do know.
I must wait. I will wait for a love like never before.

M

Commit your way to the Lord, trust also in
Him, and He shall bring it to pass.

—Psalm 37:5 NKJV

and mine too!

> For love asks only that you be happy, and will give you everything that makes for happiness.
>
> —*A Course in Miracles*

July 6 in *My Utmost for His Highest* (Chambers), titled "Vision Becoming Reality"

> God gives us vision and then He takes us down in the valley to better us into the shape of that vision. Every God given vision will become real if we only have patience.

Until we get to the point where He can trust us with the reality of the vision. Ever since God gave us the vision, He has been at work.

—Max Lucado, *Grace for the Moment*, July 7, titled "Closer Than You Think"

P.S. Life is joyful.
My children are all doing wonderful.
We are blessed with the presence of my parents.
We are blessed and grateful, dear God. Amen.

> Just for you, just for you
> And my arms they are open
> Just for you, just for you.
> And these tears I am crying
> Are just for you, just for you.

—Lionel Ritchie, *Just for You (Tuskegee)*

For Pete's Sake

July 9, 2004

Dear God,

I know it seems I put Peter first, yet we know he wouldn't be part of my life if it were not for your divine and eternal love for all your children. I have been gifted with so much since you gifted me with him, not so long ago.

I've read you are a "jealous God," and in your all-knowingness, you know I love you, never want to let you down, and doing your will is the bottom line.

Always and forever with love.

*From your child,
Mary*

One week later I read; over and over again God has to remove our friends to put Himself in their place. July 13 in *My Utmost for His Highest* (Chambers). *Wow.*

Sometimes I stare into space
Tears all over my face
I can't explain it, don't understand it
I ain't never felt like this before
Don't pass up this chance
this time it's true romance

—Linda Ronstadt, *Heat Wave*,
Linda Ronstadt Greatest Hits

and mine too!

Here's something beautiful from *A Course in Miracles*, Chapter 16, IV:

> To your most Holy Self all praise is do for what you are, and for what He is Who created you as you are. Sooner or later most everyone bridges the gap he imagines exists between his selves. Each one builds the bridge, which carries him across the gap as soon as he is willing to expend some little effort on behalf of bridging it. His little efforts are powerfully supplemented by the strength of Heaven, and by the united will of all who make heaven what it is, being joined within it. And so, the one who would cross over is literally transported there.
> Your bridge is built stronger than you think, and your foot is firmly planted on it.
> Have no fear that the attraction of those who stand on the other side and wait for you
> Will not draw you safely across. For you would come where you would be, and where your Self awaits you.[3]

There's somebody I'm longing to see, I hope that he turns out to be *someone to watch over me.*

—George Gershwin

---

[3] I read this twice, and when I wrote it, I had such a visual of me and you know who.

For Pete's Sake

Then He Kissed Me

Well, he walked up to me and he asked me if
I wanted to dance.
He looked kinda nice and so I said I might
take a chance
When we danced he held me tight
And when he walked me home that night
All the stars were shining bright
And then he kissed me.
Each time I saw him I couldn't wait to see
him again.
I wanted to let him know he was more
than a friend.
I didn't know just what to do
So, I whispered I love you
And he said that he loved me too
And then he kissed me.
He kissed me in a way that I've never been
kissed before.
He kissed me in a way that I wanna be
kissed forever more
I knew that he was mine so I gave him all the
love that I had…

—The Crystals, *Da Doo Ron Ron:*
The Very Best of the Crystals

July 8, 2004

How many times have I heard this over two years? And just yesterday, the first eight lines became the song in my heart as if the writer was there the night Peter and I met in January and as if the lyrics lingered in my heart through the months that followed. *Wow.*

and mine too!

"Single"

Like crystal beads spilled on a
jeweler's cloth
The stars are set before me through
the skylight
an engaging sight;
yet no one has chosen me
to string along.
Clasp, me Lord
against this loneliness;
kiss me with sweet dreams.
Give me patience to believe
that my star
is waiting in Your wings.

—Gail McCoig Blanton

To have faith is to be sure of the things we hope for,
to be certain of the things we cannot see.

—Hebrews 11:1 GNT

"Calling All Angels"

I need a sign to let me know you are here
All of these lines are being crossed over the
atmosphere.

For Pete's Sake

> I need to know that things are gonna lookup
> 'Cause I feel us drowning in a sea spilled
> from a cup…
> And I'm calling all angels
> And I'm calling all angels
>
> I want a reason for the way things have to be.
> I need a hand to build up some kind of
> hope inside of me.
> I won't give up if you don't give up.
>
> —Train, *My Private Nation*

> It's the sign of the times that your love for
> Me is getting so much stronger.
> It's the sign of the times and I know that I won't
> Have to wait much longer.
> Maybe my lucky star at last decided to shine.
> Maybe somebody knows how long
> I've waited to make you mine.
>
> —Petula Clark, *It's a Sign of the
> Times, Ultimate Petula Clark*

and mine too!

Time, like beauty, is in the eye of the beholder.

—Diane Schoemperlen, *Our Lady of the Lost and Found*

"He Couldn't Love You More"

I can't believe it happened
I never dreamed you leave me
We were so good together
I thought we'd share forever
The love we had before.
Is there an explanation to
ease my sorrow?
Is it infatuation, and will it
fade tomorrow?
Until you let me know my love
won't let you go.
My heart won't close the door.
And while you make your mind up
I beg you to remember
Although his (her) arms may hold you,
I don't know what he (she) told you,
But he (she) couldn't love you more.

—Plácido Domingo, *Perhaps Love*

Living Pages

Let me leave margins of silence
Around the activities of day,
Letting You write down there
Whatever it is you would say.
Then looking backward, I find,
No matter how much I revise,
It is in your footnotes
That the heart of my life lies.

—Elizabeth Searle Lamb, *Bedside Prayers*

Interesting in how my taste in and love for music has sent me endless messages; at least that's what I think.

July 8, 2004/July 9, 2004

Spent Thursday on an eternal cloud, a walk at the rec center, music through the headphones, and waves and waves of tear-shedding—the nameless ones, of course. I was lifted and gifted and blessed. I spoke of Peter to two friends at the ISDA and could not stop smiling, especially my eyes.

Then Friday knocked down a few notches. Why? What for? What did I do? To what end?

By the night, I cry those overwhelming tears again. Where is he? How can I feel like this and he not appear? Does it take more angels? Am I so wrong? Can I be so far off track? I don't know how to let it go. Is it fear? Is it my shield?

And, yes, *each* time the phone rings, "Dear God, let it please be him, it must be him."

And, yes, each trip to the mailbox, I wonder if today is the day.

and mine too!

Goodnight.

> When I cry out from my heart, you are there.
>
> —Betty J. Eadie, *Embraced by the Light*

He is the tide.
I the shore that waits.
He comes to me in waves
and I wait and wonder which wave will touch me today.
The wave that teases my toes and recedes simply. Or,
The wave that covers my feet and sends a chill through me
and slips away leaving my footprint. Or,
The wave at low tide that I lovingly walk out to meet,
for how could I go day without his touch? Or,
The wave at high tide, when he is so very close
to me, when he hesitates not. Or,
The wave of a storm that rushes in, catches me
off guard and takes my breath away.
Wave after wave of emotion.
My tears become a part of his ebbing and flowing
ways. No pattern. Unpredictable, yet daily.
How do I continue to wait? Even that wave that
teases me is better than no wave at all.
Does he sense that with each ebbing the grains of
sand he takes with him are parts of me?
And there is nowhere else the grains would
rather be, and they are endless.

P.S. I always take a dress to Pittsburgh; he likes women in dresses.

> The beloved's heartbeat and the sky have always been there. These moments are simply waiting our arrival.
>
> —Donna Farhi, *Yoga, Mind, Body, & Spirit: A Return to Wholeness*

July 12, 2004

Does love not take two hearts?
So what then am I doing?
This has nothing to do with ego.
There's a new song out by Los Lonely Boys. Beautiful sound, it's called *How Far Is Heaven?*
Me: About 120 miles east.

July 13, 2004

I've been taking notes on *Conversations with God*.
Part of today's notes:
My life will take off when I become very clear about my life... what I want to be, what I want to do, what I want to have:

- then think of this often till I am very clear about it.
- then think about nothing else, no other possibilities, put all negative thought away.
- when clear and steadfast begin to speak them as truths— *out loud.*

Interesting, and the out loud part, oh, just ask the sky and the air that hovers when I walk and the blades of grass and the leaves on and off the trees, the pond and puddles of water, the deer, bunnies, gulls, mallards—my part of the world has heard me.

> Say his name aloud,
> search for him aloud,
> cry for him aloud,
> ask for him aloud,
> proclaim my love for him aloud,
> and so, I wait.

> I will make you my promised bride forever, I will be good and fair: I will show you my love and mercy.
>
> —Hosea 2:19 NCV

> We do not obtain the most precious gifts by going in search of them, but by waiting for them.
>
> —Simone Weil

July 14, 2004

Today, the sky was magnificent. Throughout the day, every possible shape a cloud could be, it was. They came and went, blew over, exposed the blue sky, ballooned, and shrank all day long. Not only that, but the colors they contained and reflected and refracted were breathtaking. So many shades of each color of the spectrum were well represented.

From 8:00 a.m. till 9:40 p.m., and all my comings and goings throughout this day, I was dazzled.

It was memorable.

It is a gift.

For Pete's Sake

Oh to share it.
Is it a sign?
All good things come from God. Amen.

Lord, you take my breath away. And He smiled.
Love, M.

God established His relationship with you to make you happy, and nothing you do that does not share His purpose can be real.

—*A Course in Miracles*

I read this on a day (July 15), when Peter was barely a thought. As the day went on, and I "heard" his laugh and smiled. And this night, before bed, I read this verse (interesting).

Praying with expectant faith.

—*The Word Among Us* (A Daily Catholic Bible Study)

July 17, 2004

And I wake up to: I am for you, because the Holy Spirit has been with me since you "left" me.
P.S. I cried.
Within half an hour, I read:
"The Miracle of Belief," the title for July 17 from *My Utmost for His Highest* (Oswald Chambers).
P.S. I did not cry.
I am begotten.

July 18–19, 2004

Read 1 John 5 NAB.

My dear Peter,

I have just gotten home from an evening with my dear, fun and forever friends. We drank, danced, had a few shots. Anthony was there, not that it meant anything. Some flirting, as always, because it is safe. One of the guys confided that his wife is taking care of herself but not taking care of him.

And as I drive home, I know I can and do love you with all my heart, mind, soul, and body. Why would any woman deprive her man of all of her? And I fight back the tears tonight fearing it is the alcohol that exaggerates my emotions.

Tomorrow I drive my parents and my brother to Pittsburgh. Oh, if you were to call soon and then you could meet these good people that I call Dad and Mom and Mike.

Is my longing not enough to reach you? And your heart? And your needs? And your wants? And your happiness?

Loving you,
Mary

And I, when lifted up from the earth, will draw people to myself

—John 12:32 NIV

Dear God,

How much more sincerity do you want? Do I need? Do you need?
Just asking, with all my love.

Mary

On *July 18, 2004*, the Gospel reading: "The Lord said to her in reply, 'Martha, Martha, you are anxious and worried about many things. There is need of only one thing. Mary has chosen the better part *and it will not be taken from her*'" (Luke 10:41–42 NRSV; emphasis added).

Oh, the God rush at Mass, and to hold back my tears that I now shed seven hours later. They also played "Lord of the Dance," to which I could not sing lest those around me hear the tremble in my voice.

My God is beautiful, and I love him.

I picked up the ear cuffs that I had ordered, the ones shaped as wings. They are perfect and sweet. I wear one on my right ear, the other sits in view on my bookshelf.

So far, it seems that at a thought of Peter, I reach to my earlobe and run my finger down the wing.

And as I write this, I realize I have now something tangible. Oh my God, is it a hint that he is closer and will be in my touch soon?

and mine too!

My breaths are deeper—I am not a silly, infatuated schoolgirl!

 Some common terms for this experience are self-realization, the Universal Body, or God consciousness, all describe a state where separateness has disappeared and guidance for your life is supplied from within. *The state is often described as two lovers joining ecstatically after enduring a long search for each other.* (emphasis added)

—Alice Christensen, *Yoga of the Heart*

Some interesting words from *A Course in Miracles*. I read tonight:

> The Holy Spirit would not deprive you your special relationships, but would transform them. And all that is meant by that is that He will restore them the function given them by God.
>
> The holy relationship shares God's purpose, rather than aiming to make a substitute for it." *(Me: we did it! Did we do it? Are we doing it?)*
>
> The gift with which God blessed it, and by His blessing enabled it to be healed. This blessing holds within itself the truth about everything. And the truth is that the Holy Spirit is in close relationship with you because in Him is your relationship with God restored to you.

> And through Him have all your holy relationships been carefully preserved, to serve God's purpose for you.

Wow.

> You have begun a new life, in which you are being made new and are becoming like the One who made you.
>
> —Colossians 3:10 NCV

> The real challenge is not to simply survive. Hell, anyone can do that. It's to survive as yourself, undiminished.
>
> —Elia Kazan, Director

July 21, 2004

My baby turned twenty-one today.

July 22, 2004

Peter has been in that "cloudy" area throughout the past day or so, and I thought, *Oh, well, it's happened before*, shrugged it off, a feeling of *I don't get it.*

And I read my books, as usual, and the sections of "The Herald," "Relationship," "Setting the Goal," "The Call for Faith," and "The Conditions of Peace" from *The Course in Miracles* penetrated my heart and soul and mind and eyes. I read and cried and read aloud and underlined word after word and shed tear after tear. Profound is an understatement multiplied a hundred times.

It wrote of me and he and we and thee. Words I have used in the same way in my writings leapt out at me from the pages. I almost tore the pages out to insert in this book. But when I have recovered

and mine too!

my readings, I will write in my book with my pen all those words that caught me off guard.

I suppose it won't impact me the way it did when I first read it, but I look forward to doing it just the same.

My Lord, my miracle, my thanks, my love.

A domani!

Turn around, look at me.

—*The Vogues, Greatest Hits*

My dearest Peter,

I hope you are well! I think of you so often in so many ways and I await us, "like the bride waiting for her bridegroom."

Know that I am waiting and will be ready, for the Lord is my shepherd.

Goodnight again, my love.

M

He is my soul mate,
my heart mate,
my mind mate—forever.
And one very sacred day he will be
my body-mate, for as long as we both shall live.

For Pete's Sake

The following are lines from *A Course in Miracles* that I wrote of a page ago:

> Offering the relationship to the Holy Spirit, to use for His purpose.
>
> At once His goal replaces yours. This is accomplished very rapidly, but it makes the relationship seem disturbed...even distressing. In its unholy condition *your* goal was all that seemed to give it meaning.
>
> Many relationships have been broken off at this point, and the pursuit of the old goal reestablished in another relationship. For once, the unholy relationship has accepted *the goal holiness;*, it can never again be what it was. Yet now the goal will not be changed. Set firmly in the unholy relationship, *there is no course except to change the relationship to fit the goal.* A relationship, undertaken by two individuals for their unholy purposes, *suddenly has holiness for its goal. This is the time for faith.* You let this goal be set for you. That was an act of faith. Do not abandon faith, now that the rewards of faith are being introduced. Have faith in your brother in what may seem to be a trying time. *The goal is set.*

And think not that you can direct the course of love, for love, if it finds you worthy, directs your course.

—Kahlil Gibran, *The Prophet*

and mine too!

But if you love and must needs have desires; let these be your desires: To melt and be like a running brook that sings its melody to the night *To know the pain of too much tenderness. To be wound by your own understanding of love; and to bleed willingly and joyfully.* To wake at dawn with a winged heart and give thanks for another day of loving; To rest at the noon hour and meditate love's ecstasy; To return home at eventide with gratitude; *And then sleep with a prayer for the beloved in your heart* and a song of praise on your lips. (emphasis added)

—Kahlil Gibran, *The Prophet*

If you think about it, every experience is worth having.

—Henry Ford

Time

Time is
Too Slow for those who Wait,
Too Swift for those who Fear,
Too Long for those who Grieve,
Too Short for those who Rejoice;
But for those who Love
Time is not.

—Henry Van Dyke

Excellent page.
Now the ego counsels thus; substitute for *(her)* this another relationship to which your former goal was quite appropriate.

For Pete's Sake

Have faith in Him who answered you. *He heard.* Has He not been very explicit in His answer? Can you deny that He has given you a most explicit statement?

—*A Course in Miracles*

July 23, 2004

Mine.
Phenomenally, today, throughout, this statement entered and echoed all day long.
It is exactly like this…
"There is no substitute."
And I smile with each repetition.

Now He asks for faith a little longer, even in bewilderment. For this will go, and you will see the justification for your faith emerge, *to bring you shining conviction.* Abandon Him not now, nor your brother. *This relationship has been reborn as holy.*

—A Course in Miracles
(emphasis added)

and mine too!

Here I am standing at your door. I've always been standing at your door. Now who's going to save you?

—Mary Jane to Peter Parker, *Spiderman 2*

If you have to make a mistake, it's better to make a mistake of action than one of inaction. If I had the opportunity again; I would take chances.

—Federico Fellini

The next fourteen quotes are from *A Course in Miracles* (emphasis is mine)

"Accept with gladness what you do not understand."

"A sense of aimlessness will come to haunt you and to remind you of all the ways you once sought for satisfaction and thought you found it."

"For your relationship has not been disrupted. It has been saved." (I drew the love triangle)

"In your *newness*, remember that you and your brother have started again, *together*."

"And take his hand, to walk together along a road far more familiar than you now believe."

"For you have chosen but the goal of God from which your true intent was never absent."

"You have joined with many in the holy instant, and they have joined with you."

"Think not your choice will leave you comfortless, for God Himself has blessed your holy relationship."

"Join in His blessing, and withhold not yours upon it. For all it needs now is your blessing, that you may see that in it rests *salvation*."

"Condemn *salvation* not, for it has come to you."

"And welcome it together, for it has come to join you and your brother in a relationship in which all the Sonship is together blessed."

"You undertook together, to invite the Holy Spirit into your relationship. He could not have entered otherwise."

"Although you have many mistakes since then, you have also made enormous efforts to help Him do His work."

"And He has not been lacking in appreciation for all you have done for Him."

The ultimate reunion with God is through
the communion of your two souls.

—Neale Donald Walsh,
Conversations with God

and mine too!

> You have granted him his heart's desire; you
> did not refuse the prayer of his lips.
>
> —Psalm 21:3; God's Word

> Ask, and ye shall receive, that your joy may be full.
>
> —John 16:24 KJB

> The experience of an instant, however compelling it may be, is easily forgotten if you allow time to close over it. It must be kept shining and gracious in your awareness of time, but not concealed within it. *The instant remains.* To give thanks to your brother is to appreciate the holy instant, and thus enable its results to be accepted and shared. You have received the holy instant, but you may have established a condition in which you cannot use it. As a result, you do not realize that it is with you still. And by cutting yourself off from its expression, you have denied yourself its benefit. And it is impossible to deny yourself, and to recognize what has been given and received by you. You and your brother stand together in the holy presence of truth itself. Here is the goal, together with you. Think you not the goal itself will gladly arrange the means for its accomplishment?
>
> —*A Course in Miracles*, (emphasis added)

> And beauty is not a need but an ecstasy…a
> heart enflamed and a soul enchanted.
>
> —Kahlil Gibran, *The Prophet*

When you are in the dark, listen, and God will give you a very special message for someone else once you are back in the light.

—Oswald Chambers, *My Utmost for His Highest*

The means as they stand now which seems to make you suffer, but which makes heaven glad. If heaven were outside you, you could not share in its gladness. Yet because it is within, the gladness, too, is yours. You are joined in purpose, but remain still separate and divided on the means. Yet the goal is fixed, firm and unalterable, and the means will surely fall in place because the goal is sure. And you will share the gladness of the Sonship that it is so. As you begin to recognize and accept the gifts you have so freely given to your brother, you will also accept the effects of the holy instant and use them to correct all your mistakes and free you from their results.

—*A Course in Miracles*

God's purpose for me? To depend on Him and on His power *now*. (emphasis added)

—Oswald Chambers, *My Utmost for His Highest*

You will have also learned how to release all the Sonship and offer it in gladness and thanksgiving to Him Who gave you your release and Who would extend it through you. There are specific guidelines He provides for any situation, but remember that you do not yet realize their universal application. In any situation, in which you are uncertain, the first thing to consider, very simply, is "What do I want to come of this? What is it for?" The clarification of the goal belongs at the beginning, for it is this which will determine the outcome. The value of deciding in advance what you want to happen is simply that you will perceive the situation as a means to make it happen. You will therefore make every

and mine too!

effort to overlook what interferes with the accomplishment of your objective and concentrate on everything that helps you meet it.

—*A Course in Miracles*

Enjoy serving the Lord, and He will give you what you want.

—Psalm 37:4 NCV

It is quite noticeable that this approach has brought you closer to the Holy Spirit's sorting out of truth and falsity. The situation now has meaning, but only because the goal has made it meaningful.

—*A Course in Miracles*

July 26, 2004

And the conversation I had tonight was my voice, aloud, speaking the words of my heart, my imagination.
We stand before each other.

> M: I love you! I never stopped loving you!
> P (*smiles*): How do you think I got here?
> M: I don't know what else to do but love you. I don't know how to do anything else but love you. I don't want to do anything else but love you.
> P: Anything?
> M: If I can love you, I can do anything!

Peter smiles, embraces. The scene fades to tears.

For Pete's Sake

> In a nonviolent love relationship, you bring your own
> reserves of happiness and strength to the relationship,
> meeting your lover half-way to complete the union.
>
> —A. Christensen, *Yoga of the Heart*

Have I not cried a river?
Does it not flow to his heart?
Has it not reached him yet?
Just follow this stream that lies before you, my love…
I know he knows.
I know his heart—he told me so.
If I hold the key, shouldn't he be here by now?
Am I so shallow?
so naïve?
so simple?
so selfish?

This is a terrible case of being a hopeless romantic!

In the margin, I write, "And all this emotion passes, and it's "business as usual?"

The other day, on a walk, I heard, "We have to buy a house." It was God.

And then?
And then?
And then?

> The longings of your heart, then, are not incidental: they are critical
> messages. The desires of your heart are not to be ignored; they
> are to be consulted…so God uses your passion to turn your life.
>
> —Max Lucado, *Just Like Jesus*

and mine too!

A customer died, thirty-eight years old, of melanoma. A few days prior, her grandmother died. So the mother/daughter buried her mother and her daughter in the same week. And I cry for what?

July 27, 2004

In listening to *Conversations with God*, Neal Donald Walsch:

> We have brought ourselves to the relative world so that we might have the tools with which to know and experience who we really are, who we create ourselves to be in relationship to all the rest of it.
>
> *Personal relationships are the most important elements in this process—this is Holy Ground!* (emphasis added)

Wow!

Now I spoke of this to my kids, and I might have written it down in one of these books; and it goes something like this: "When Peter and I meet together again, wherever it is will be *holy ground*."

In the margin, I write "Not reunited, because we've never been separated."

July 28, 2004, 12:30 a.m.

Pulled out the card from Jesus I received almost two years ago to share with a hospice patient. The picture of the roses fell out, and for the first time, I *noticed* there were *three!* Wow.

For Pete's Sake

The work of the soul is to wake yourself up. The work of God is to wake everybody else.

—Neale Donald Walsch,
Conversations with God

July 28, 2004, 7:16 a.m.

Immediately following, I read:

The Voice Within

I took a little walk today
To listen to God's word, and when I stopped to rest awhile
This is what I heard;
"Dear one there's someone waiting
To hear from you today,
Someone who needs your loving heart
To spread joy in its own way;
Never turn away my child
I bid you to press on.
Let you light forever shine
To reach this precious one.
Who knows what happiness can,
Come from loving thought so true,
Go forth and spread your sunshine
Only good can come to you."
And as I left my quiet place
I felt such peace within,
Because I knew what I should do
To love and honor Him.

— Jan Edwards
from *Bedside Prayers* (June Cotner)

and mine too!

July 28, 2004, 7:15 a.m. I read:

Hold Fast Your Dreams

Hold fast your dreams!
Within your heart
Keep one still, secret spot
Where dreams may go,
And, sheltered so,
May thrive and grow
Where doubt and fear are not.
O keep a place apart,
Within your heart,
For little dreams to go!

—Louise Driscoll
from *Bedside Prayers* (June Cotner)

"Someone's waiting to hear from you today."

—from my daily horoscope

Do I take this literally?
Is it my beloved who is waiting?

Dear God, Father of mine,

I give this to you. If it is your will, guide me to pick up the phone and call him. If it is your will, it will be Peter.

In the meantime, I have sent my angels to him, and when they arrive to my beloved, he will know they are me! Grant him strength and peace.

I will press on. And how can my light not forever shine when it's your light? Thank you for using me as a vessel of your everlasting light.

Father, is he getting closer? All the emotions of this past week have been so powerful and beautiful and overwhelming that I feel they would act like a magnet drawing us together again.

Calm the racing of my heart and still my breath in the knowledge that all that is good comes from you, my Lord.

Thank you, again,

Lovingly,
M.

I woke up early today. Now I know why!

Blessed is he who is not offended because of me.

—Matthew 11:6 NKJV

I have had dreams and I have had nightmares. I overcame the nightmares because of my dreams.

—Jonas Salk

Bedside Prayers (June Cotner) was given to me by Father Ray. Part of what he wrote on the inside cover reads "I have a feeling that there may be one or two prayers in here that God wants you to discover."

FYI, the two poems/prayers I wrote down today were "discovered" on my second read through.

Later, that same morning, ego made manifest in me in the mutual flirtations, compliments, and sexual innuendos between a

and mine too!

guy who will remain nameless and me (don't worry, it's someone I've known). And besides that, Mary Jean Galloway suggested I meet her daughter's brother-in-law.

Needless to say, the ego is lifted and being noticed by me finally.

The ego's side is once again a tug-of-war for me. Throughout the day, I ask myself, will any of these possible pursuits serve my "highest self," which is my spirit?

The obvious answer is *no*. My spirit is my heart, and my heart is for my beloved.

Then I am challenged with how can instant (more or less) gratification hurt? Pursue it and get over it! It would not be that easy. I am sure of this. I would anguish over it. It definitely would be a setback of sorts.

> David's immediate response was to go and sit in God's presence, thanking Him, and acknowledging his unworthiness.
>
> —*The Word Among Us* (daily readings)

This is easy to write about, but the strength of the ego's lure is much harder to shake off than in other times past.

So by the grace of God, I gain my strength to turn away again and again and again, knowing that one of these turns will slam the door. Slam it forever? Probably not.

And with heavy breaths and a beating heart, I pray for the day when the compliments and the flirting and the sexy teasing will be from the lips and touch of my beloved.

God be with us.

July 29, 2004

And today, again, I hear his voice. The words are new. They are not the words we shared in the past nor were they the words my heart has put together for when we are together.

It is simple and quiet, and the words are his: "Wait for me, Mary."

Oh, how these words echo, and I imagine it will not let up anytime soon! Sounds crazy, I know. I cannot run away from myself.

> Wait on the Lord.
>
> —Psalm 37:34 NKJV

> Wait patiently for Him.
>
> —Psalm 37:7 NKJV

July 30, 2004

Spirit vs. ego—spirit wins, ego is disappointed.
I am safe, angsty, but safe.
In the margin, I write "Behold the Grace of God. There needs to be gaps along the way or there would be no path." Heard on a tape.

July 31, 2004

> My spirit has proven itself again,
> stronger than my ego.
> And today I wonder why it is not
> strong enough (yet) to bring my beloved
> to me!

I wait, knowing the spirit of my beloved is "breaking through," passing his ego. And the "chance" his ego spoke of will be the miracle of his spirit and the soul mates will be one, an absolute in this relative world?

Or is Peter my ego? Sometimes I wonder, but I have always followed my heart, and Peter is of my heart! Amen.

and mine too!

> Seek not to understand that you may believe,
> but believe that you may understand.
>
> —St. Augustine of Hippo

> A wonderful thing about God's silence is that His stillness is contagious – it gets into you causing you to become perfectly confident so that you can honestly say, "I know that God has heard me."
>
> —Oswald Chambers, *My Utmost for His Highest*

August 2, 2004

Had a nice weekend in Pittsburgh. Johnny is a sweetheart, and his mom and dad are doing well too!

Nick is home, school is done, it is amazing and wonderful!

Once again, I left Pittsburgh. This time with more of waiting for Peter than longing for him. Usually leaving there and knowing we were so close would have me with heavy heart.

> To accomplish great things, we must not only act but also dream, not only plan but also believe.
>
> —Anatole France
> from *Our Lady of the Lost and Found* (Diane Schoemperlen)

For Pete's Sake

"I Have Nothing"

Share my life, take me for what I am
Cause I'll never change all my colors for you
Take my love, I'll never ask for too much
Just all that you are and everything that you do
I don't really need to look very much farther
I don't want to have to go where you don't follow
I won't hold it back again this passion inside
Can't run from myself
There's nowhere to hide.
Well, don't make me close one more door
I don't wanna hurt anymore
Stay in my arms if you dare
Must I imagine you there
Don't walk away from me...
I have nothing, nothing, nothing
If I don't have you.
You see through, right to the heart of me
You break down my walls with the strength of your love
I never knew love like I've known it's with you
Will a memory survive, one I can hold on to
I don't really need to look very much farther
I don't want to go where you won't follow
I won't hold it back again, this passion inside
I can't run from myself
There's nowhere to hide
You're love I'll remember forever.

and mine too!

—Whitney Houston (from *The Body Guard*), *The Bodyguard: Original Soundtrack Album*

August 5, 2004, 12:30 a.m.

> Two hours ago, my beloved called me
> he called me
> he called me Maria
> he laughed
> he made love to me
> he said it was good to hear my voice
> he thought of me
> he kept my number.
> Oh, gracious hand of our Father
> all that is good goes back to you
> and He smiles
> and the angels sing.

And my ego-self interrupts, "Now that you got what you want do you really want it?" and I told it to go to hell!

My beloved, I raised my hands to the heavens and my heart has not stopped racing. I tremble, I cry, I hesitate mid-thought. I am in awe. Part of me can't believe it. I am at a loss with everything.
I will call my Peter at 4:15 to awake *with* him.
"My God."
"I know," he replies.

I have always known that writing is an act of faith, the one which has always been my own salvation.

—Diane Schoemperlen, *Our Lady of the Lost and Found*

Here are a few quotes from *Grace for the Moment* (Max Lucado).

- August 4 is titled "You Have Captured God's Heart"
- August 5 is titled "God's Plans"
- "Enjoy serving the Lord, and he will give you what you want" (Psalm 37:4 NCV).
- "The longings of your heart, then, are not incidental; they are critical messages. The desires of your heart are not to be ignored; they are to be consulted."
- "God is too gracious to ask you to do something you hate."

I am humbled to the bottom of my heart.
We are worthy.
We are blessed.
It is.
He had the "Happiness is…" postcard in his hand.

and mine too!

1:30 a.m.

>my heart beats differently
>he said, "Amore, aspetto, fa sabato."
>"Love, I'm waiting, come quickly."
>AMEN (so be it)
>AMEN

When I call him later, I'm going to read to him.
So many unwritten words. Look out, paper.

2:40 a.m.

My heart feels bigger.

>Patience produces character and character produces
>hope. And this hope will never disappoint us.
>
>—Romans 5:4–6 NCV

>It's a funny thing about life; if you refuse to accept
>anything but the best, you very often get it.
>
>—W. Somerset Maugham

>When I asked for all things, so that I might enjoy life,
>I was given life, so that I might enjoy all things.
>
>—unknown Confederate soldier

For Pete's Sake

5:00 a.m.

He didn't sleep much either.

I called Peter. I knew I would wake him up. He didn't seem to mind too much. He wasn't feeling right. *We'll see each other.*
My day. My heart was trying to get out of my chest, all day, a kind of aching along with my whole upper body.

my heart has a new beat
it feels like my metabolism shot way up
it feels like I lost 5 lbs.
and my mouth is so dry, and water is so temporary
beautiful sunset

August 6, 2004

Thinking back to how my beloved was feeling and the way I was and am, could we be lovesick?
He takes my breath away.
I think so many thoughts, and all that comes to mind and pen is "Oh my God," and I bring my hand to my mouth to stifle the sighs, but I cannot hold back the tears (thank goodness for sunglasses).

All day long, at work
driving,
walking, running.
So much,
so very much.
How does he feel? What is my Peter thinking?
I breathe so deeply.

When I drove this morning, I prayed to God, "What if—"
And he interrupted with, "We've gotten this far, haven't we?"
I cry.
Love songs on the radio.

and mine too!

I cry.
How Far is Heaven? (Los Lonely Boys)
I really cry.
I was chosen to be the one for Peter to create in him what he created in me.
Crying again.
I called Bettina and told her my beloved called. She couldn't talk just then, and she told me to "hold that thought." We hung up, and I thought, *I've been holding it for over two years.*
Crying still.

> Your ears shall hear a word behind you,
> saying, "This *is* the way, walk in it."
>
> —Isaiah 30:21 NKJV

> While we wait for God to show that we are his children.
>
> —Romans 8:23 CEV

I get giddy.
I feel like I wear a new smile.
My stomach hurts.
I want him to call tonight, but I'm beginning to realize my ego wants him to call.
Aah, but the spirit is calm. Amen.

Julie said she couldn't believe it, and then said she can believe it because of how I believed it and my faith.
Oh, Lord, your work is being done, and together, the three of us will do our part to light the world.

So much; if it's not on paper, you can find it in my heart!
Goodnight
He knows. He knows. He knows I love him.
And the Spirit of my Lord is with me, so my every thought, word, and deed will heal and love.

> Jesus said to her, "Did I not say to you that if you would believe you would see the glory of God?"
>
> —John 11:40 NIV

> But the fruit of the Spirit is love, joy, peace, long-suffering, kindness, goodness, faithfulness, gentleness, self-control; against such there is no law.
>
> —Galatians 5:22–23 NKJV

> Allowing love to take its own course.
>
> —*A Course in Miracles*

August 8, 2004

I cannot force the words.
Nor find them in any order to make sense.

August 10, 2004

Another day of racing heartbeats, deep short breaths, and that strain in my heart. Be still my heart.

and mine too!

I am thrilled when Peter calls me. We laugh and talk about our day, reminisce, and fill in some blanks from the past two years (it is interesting, yet irrelevant).

I seem to be waking between 4:00 and 5:00 a.m. Is this because my beloved thinks of me when he gets ready for work?

August 11, 2004

Aah! What a day!

For a week, my happy thoughts have blended with my daily routine.

Not today, beside myself with—I don't know what, but it is true and it is real.

And I say his name aloud throughout my days.

August 8

> Our reuniting.
> *I expected* the ground and the heavens to open up and
> the tears to fall like rain.
> *I got* a kiss, a warm embrace or 2 or 3 or 40, dinner, city
> lights and gentle touches.
> *it was perfect.*

And he hath put a new song in my mouth, even praise unto our God; many shall see it and fear, and shall trust in the Lord.

—Psalm 40:3 KJB

I wonder how he feels? Yet I know his heart holds the words, and I hold his heart. Does any of this make any sense?

He wants to read my "journals." I told him it will take years. "My journals." "Our love story."

Things are different now.

I share my words, thoughts, and heart with him.

Ink has been replaced with a dream come true, a prayer answered, a new happiness.

The love songs I hear now are a different kind of love song.

Not the forlorn, hopeful, bittersweet ones, but the present and forever kind.

August 12

The Spirit will let my heart know when it is time to tell my beloved that *I love him*.

If it can be dreamed, it can be done.

—Walt Disney

All the things that you can change
There's a meaning in everything
And you will find all you need
There's so much to understand.

—Phil Collins, *Look Through My Eyes* from Disney's *Brother Bear*

and mine too!

Choose well: Your choice is brief and yet endless.

—Ella Winter

August 13, 2004

Had the best time on the phone tonight. I was on the beach on the phone with my beloved.

I tell him virtually everything.

I spill my guts.

I hold nothing back.

I actually told him I would go to the ends of the earth for him. And I would.

Peter even agrees he can't believe all he tells me, but all is good: the honesty, the fun—it's safe; it's real.

Then as I tell others that he is back in my life, they seem surprised and skeptical and throw doubt my way—how the ego loves that. And my God speaks to me.

"Has your heart not gotten you this far? Why would you not follow it now?"

This is it!

August 14, 2004: We are together again and I am delighted and delightful. It is hard to say goodnight. The Jacuzzi awaits us!

August 15, 2004, 8:30 p.m.: Calls to take me for ice cream. How sweet is that? I told my beloved I fell in love with him. He said, "I know, babe."

August 16, 2004: I cry on the drive home. I didn't expect leaving Pittsburgh would be so lonely and heart-aching.

The details are unnecessary on paper. Just know that each and every one of them is etched on my heart and obvious in my smile and in the smile of my eyes.

For Pete's Sake

Dear Lord,

Let Your love shine through me and he and we. We are your servants.
Amen.

The doubt that gets cast is not a good feeling. So it is not of love, *and I choose love.*

August 16, 2004, Morning

I cannot believe how I am feeling! What an onslaught of emotion.

Evening.

I am joyous (drew a heart)!
He needs to hear it *(drew a heart)!*
Affirmation.
And this I do with all my heart.
All is well, so well.
The days are fine, not without a problem or two, yet fine.
But, oh, how I look forward to talking with my beloved and then to wish him a goodnight, and knowing my last thought of the day is of him and us. And that my first thought for tomorrow will be the same.
Thank you, Lord.
Again and again, so very much.

All the way to heaven is heaven.

—Catherine of Sienna

and mine too!

The Lord will always lead you.

—Isaiah 58:11 CSB

His goal is not to get you what you want,
it is to get you what you need.

—Max Lucado, *A Gentle Thunder*

August 21, 2004

My beloved was with me, here. How have I prayed for this moment and could not sleep, for sleep would keep me away from him.

There is a kind of silence between us, a silence to be broken by the words of our restless hearts. With me, there is so much in my heart. Where to begin? When to begin? And I pray to my Spirit, finding and knowing that the time and the words will come from our Creator—another gift.

When Peter's heart is truly ready, my heart shall truly speak.

This sense of silence may be a part of knowing we must part ways for another week—the unavoidable. He is stronger. I avoid and I linger.

And, today, I am sad to tears and eventually sleep. Peter called when he got home and said it was sad there too (oh wow), and it's gonna have to be that way for now.

Nobody could possibly understand this. I ramble on and on trying to put sense to it with words. But for one thing I am sure, this is real, this is absolute, this is of heaven (3:00 p.m.).

Will Peter ever feel like this?

"Yes, in time" (God 6:30 p.m.).

He left his toothbrush next to mine!

With our reunion, I thought my tears would subside, but at least now I can give them a name—sadness.

The "new" love songs bring me to tears as much as the old ones—didn't plan on that either.

For Pete's Sake

August 24, 2004

I am like a teenager! I think of him all the time and try not to bring his name up in conversation too much (I love him).

August 30, 2004

Nick, Ang, John, Johnny and I been in California for six days now.

From Santa Cruz on the first day, I told my beloved I did not want to be anywhere without him.

Our daily conversations (sometimes more than once a day) have been good company.

As usual, we have fun, we flirt, we play, and oh how I tell him everything.

> What is your will for me, O God? I await your plan. I want to live only for you.
>
> —St. Jane Frances de Chantal

Easy for a saint to say? This saint, a passionate woman with strong desires had to keep revising her understanding of God's plan for her.

—*The Word Among Us*

Peter is glad I am having fun and tells me to enjoy myself—how sweet and how unselfish.

In a phone call from Yosemite (*August 29*), as I tell my beloved "Goodnight," somehow, he tells me he heard me almost say "I—"

But I didn't finish. I deny it. He must hear the voice of my heart.

So we laugh and tease about it and say goodbye.

Within ten minutes, I call my Peter back and tell him, "I love you," and we are both laughing and smiling and teasing about this wonderful moment. No mush; no tears; no physical contact; so unplanned; so unexpected; so perfect; so gifted.

I felt myself turn red, turn warm, blushing.

I told him "What a relief"—an extraordinary relief.

Is it possible to hear someone smile? Smile with love?

And that is that (drew a heart)*!*

Grow old with me, the best is yet to be.

—Robert Browning

I am no stranger to putting my own life into words.

—Diane Schoemperlen, *Our Lady of the Lost and Found*

September 1, 2004

Beautiful, quiet morning. Started reading, turned into praying, ended up meditating.

Wine country, Napa, was wonderful at Sterling Vineyards. I missed and longed for Peter, to tears.

"He loves me," my heart hears.

Back home, back to Pittsburgh to my beloved.

Our Saturday night, the Italian Festival.

I met Peter's brother, Jack, his wife, Nancy, their son, Eric, and his wife, Marie, and their friends, Toni and Frank; and some other friends—delightful.

In the margin, I write "And we danced."

Walked along the river and danced alone on the walk as the band played "Goodnight, Sweetheart"—enchanting!

Enjoyed Ang and John's hot tub—hot.

Went for coffee and conversation of our future together—exciting.

For Pete's Sake

Laid under the stars and treetops—a perfect ending to the day.

How we spend our days is, of course, how we spend our lives.

—Annie Dillard

Your heart will be where your treasure is.

—Matthew 6:21 GW

But as it is written, "What no eye has seen, nor ear heard, nor the heart of man imagined, what God has prepared for those who love him."

—1 Corinthians 2:9 ESV

and mine too!

Sunday, after working 3:00–11:00, my darling wants to be with me, so we're back at Eat 'n' Park—I love him.

Monday, I spent the first half of the day longing for him and crying tears that still have no name. My prayers, even the ones I read, touch my heart to tears. We play house. I clean, he makes a yummy dinner, and we share our sleep. Content.

September 7, 2004

And, oh, how I delight to hear his voice tonight!

September 8, 2004 (circled)

And he faintly says, "I love you too" in response to my "Goodnight, I love you."
Does he know he said it?
Does he know I heard it?

In the hidden recesses of our being dwells, not an angel, not a philosophy, not a genie, but God.

—Max Lucado, *When God Whispers Your Name*

"Totus tuus." *All yours* in Polish.

—Diane Schoemperlen, *Our Lady of the Lost and Found*

For Pete's Sake

> The words "I love you" at long last fall from those much desired lips that are long last clamped onto yours.
>
> —Diane Schoemperlen, *Our Lady of the Lost and Found*

September 12, 2004

An amazing rendezvous weekend. We are very much on the same page, even in regards to what we packed for our "picnic."

Peter asked me if I thought this was just sexual, to which I replied or asked, "How could I keep you in my heart for so long for just sex?"

He agreed but was looking for my opinion; or was it his need for affirmation?

He agreed with my heart (drew a heart)!

September 13, 2004

I delight in hearing my beloved's voice.

I read from my recent journal writings and some Bible and book quotes that I wanted to share.

He reminded me that all the day and night before he called me, he asked himself, "Should I call her or leave her alone? Should I call her or leave her alone?"

Then he called me, and he's not going to leave me alone (drew a heart)!

And I delight with laughter to hear these words!

In terms of faith, what brings meaning and integration to one's experience, the facts are quite secondary. *It's the story*

and mine too!

(and not the facts) *that grips the imagination, impregnates the heart, and animates the spirit within.* (emphasis added)

—Diamond O'Murcher, "Quantum Theology," from Diane Schoemperlen, *Our Lady of the Lost and Found*

Our greatest glory is not in never falling
but in rising every time we fall.

—Confucius

It is better to be approximately right than precisely wrong.

—Warren Buffet

I did not expect sheer delight and laughter to define romance and passion.
Now I know differently.
And it is ours.
Peter seems amused when I'm at a loss for words in regards to my feelings, but after saying "Goodnight" tonight and laying in quiet darkness, I come up with *rapture*.[4]

September 14, 2004

And *bliss*.[5]
And tonight, I cry some, for I long to be with him.

---

[4] *Rapture* (rap'cher), n. (1) Ecstatic joy or delight, joyful ecstasy. (2) (often pl.) an utterance or expression of ecstatic delight. (3) The carrying of a person to another place or sphere of existence. (4) Obs. act of carrying off. <f.rapt-ure> (*American College Dictionary,* 1962).

[5] Bliss (blis), n. (1) Lightness of heart; blitheness; gladness. (2) Supreme happiness or delight. (3) Theol. The joy of heaven. (4) a cause of great joy or happiness. [ME blisse, OE bliss, bliths, der. blithe BLITHE] - Syn. 2. See happiness. – Ant. 2. despair. (American College Dictionary, 1962).

September 15, 2004

I forgot to write about an amazing "message" I viewed (this past weekend), coming out of the hotel parking lot driveway, a sign on the building across the street: *Heaven on Earth*—oh yes!

Seems it was a religious store not yet opened. That part of the storefront was blocked by a delivery truck. But all I needed to see was *Heaven on Earth!*

The greatest thing you can ever learn is to love and receive love.

—Unknown

Sometimes what looks like irony turns out to be, in fact, grace.

—Diane Schoemperlen, *Our Lady of the Lost and Found*

I mentioned this sign to Peter. He didn't see it. I told him to be aware of signs and messages—they're everywhere! And, immediately, he said, "Like that one there?"

It was a statue of a girl kneeling at the cross on the dashboard of a car in the parking lot. I answered, "Yes," and we laughed.

And tonight, before we said "Goodnight," my beloved told me to "keep your heart up, babe."

"I will, babe."

I accept.

I am honored.

And I will, with all my heart.

Dear Lord, thank you, with all my heart. Amen.

and mine too!

September 21, 2004

So much to say, to write, to share.

For now, I will keep it in my heart and replay his words, our words, his touch, our love, our togetherness, for it brings me happiness, joy, peace, and contentment. For I am sure.

> Tell all the truth but tell it slant...
> The truth must dazzle gradually
> Or everyman be blind.
>
> —Emily Dickinson

> We are not sent into this world to do anything
> into which we cannot put our hearts.
>
> —John Ruskin

For I am sure whoever reads this may be pleased and happy for these two hearts. They cannot really "get it," for words dare not go so deep, where their meaning will be dulled in the presence of the light of God growing in these two souls.

I wish this feeling for everyone, and as I have experienced in my writing, the wish is now a prayer.

Oh, how I love his laugh (drew a heart)!

So others, far-away friends, right ideas, holy and personal influences stepped into the breach, and I am so grateful. Each fragile undertone and leading of encouragement furthered my good, turned my attention toward truth; toward some authentic and essential impulse in me or some intimate communion with the qualities that comprise who I am…the Spirit of truth has guided me, that truth alone has power and that the mentor's spirit lives in anything or anyone who helps us search out truth in the hidden wisdoms of our own heart.

—Marsha Sinetar, *The Mentor's Spirit*

Message to self: "Work on humility."

January 4, 2005

Yes, a new year. Yes, I have not written. Oh, I have picked this book up, but what to write of?

- All the words we've shared?
- All the passion we've felt?
- How love has grown?
- How we feel about our apartness?
- How we can't keep our hands off each other?

And if I did:

- Who would listen/read of it?
- Who would really care?
- Who would understand this blessed event?

And:

- How do I find the words?
- Are there words?
- How would I use them to be comprehensible to hearts that have not been here and long to be here?

and mine too!

I would want the words to be prayerful and not boastful.

The greatest need we have is not to do things, but to believe things.
His silence is a sign that He is bringing you into an
even more wonderful understanding of Himself.
Time is nothing to God.
It is God's Spirit that changes the atmosphere of
our way of looking at things, and then things begin
to be possible which before were impossible.
But if this time of soaking before God is being spent getting
rooted and grounded in Him, which may appear to be impractical,
then you will remain true to Him whatever happens.

—Oswald Chambers, *My Utmost for His Highest*

Now an update

Ang and John and Johnny are well. Their home was delightful at Christmas.

Johnny is amazing, and we have a beautiful relationship. He is a delight and a joy. It would be nice to spend as much time with his mom and dad one of these days.

Nick is PA-ing in Canton with Neurocare and loves it. He and Laura are now officially engaged to be married September 24, 2005. Her ring is beautiful! In the spring, they plan to house hunt, and I know they wait for that day to be together every day with much happiness.

My Matt is back in Chicago after four months in New Jersey. He's looking into law enforcement work, and I know he will find his calling. I miss him so.

For Pete's Sake

Mom and Dad are well. Uncle is not, and I've been to four funerals since November.

My family had a surprise fiftieth birthday for me just before the holidays. What an effort! What fun! How do you say thank you enough?

My time away from my beloved is spent doing things till we are together again. He wants me there, and there is where I want to be.

But what about my business? My parents? Although they unselfishly said it was okay to move.

We've talked of three days Cleveland, four days Pittsburgh.

I need to get out of my lease.

Do I buy a home?

Do I move in with Dad and Mom?

I told Pete that God got us this far, and he won't leave us hanging.

It is odd to write "Pete." He is so much more: Babe; Sweetie; Hon; Honey; my beloved; my joy; my breath; my heart.

Random thoughts and moments:

- He asked me where I was forty years ago. I replied that I was nine and he was eighteen, and he would have been arrested. He replied, "I would have waited."
- We say grace now. "We can't eat until Maria prays." And the Lord lets me be an instrument of His peace. Thank you.

"For behold, the kingdom of God is within you" (Luke 17:21 Webster's Bible Translation).

and mine too!

Where there is great love there are always miracles.

—Willa Cather

Bidden or not, God is present.

—Carl Jung

This was tucked in my journal.

Taking You Home

I had a good life
Before you came
I had my friends and my freedom
I had my name
Still there was sorrow and emptiness
Till you made me glad
Oh, and this love
I found strength
Never knew I had
And this love
Is like nothing I have ever known
Take my hand love
I'm taking you home
Taking you home
There were days, lonely days
When the world
Wouldn't throw me a crumb
But I kept believin' that this day would come
And this love
Is like nothing I have ever known baby

For Pete's Sake

>
> Take my hand
> I'm taking you home
> I'm taking you home
> Where we can be with the ones that really
> care
> Home
> Where we can grow together
> Keep you in my heart forever
> Oh, and this love
> Is like nothing I have ever known
> Take my hand
> Taking you home
> Yes, I am
>
> —Don Henley, *Inside Job*

I met Dana and Matt first, and she thanked me for "giving me my father back." *Wow!*

They are a couple happily in love.

Then I met Eric and his wife, Kristen—another pleasure. They definitely enjoy each other's presence and company. Kristen said, "Eric is so happy that Dad is so happy."

Just met Pete and Heidi over the Holidays. They, too, are happy, and the combination of all his kids makes for sincere and relaxing fun.

I look forward to when it's yours and mine and the combination will be ours.

My beloved gifted me with a beautiful heart bracelet and earrings. The bracelet is full of little hearts, like a tennis bracelet. They are so sweet and delicate and feminine.

I love it! I love him! And some silly jammies too!

and mine too!

I pray and read daily. So many of my thoughts are of my love. I have asked the Lord to accept them as prayers. And the parallel of my Lord and my beloved continue, moment after moment.

> The whole experience of life is designed to enable us to enter into this closest relationship with Jesus Christ.
>
> —Oswald Chambers, *My Utmost for His Highest*

And when I speak of Pete to others or proclaim my love for him, I know the parallel with my relationship with God. Oh, if those who listen to those ramblings and gushings would see this as more than two people in love; to see and sense two humble hearts brought together by God, the greatest love of all, to be an everlasting light to each other and to reflect this love to those we live among so that they, too, will open themselves to such a love as this, that he longs to share with all his children.

For our love would not be if not for *His* love. Amen.

January 6, 2005

I hope I can write this next "revelation" without sounding self-indulgent.

I saw a friend of mine that I had not seen for over a year or so, and she commented that I look wonderful, my face was glowing, and this was before my, "in a nutshell," love story that I share.

Well, I've heard this from others also.

And I would think "My love for my beloved" is written all over my face. I can't hide it. I'm sure this is true to some point.

But, today, I realized this is the glow they speak of in the Bible, the glow Moses had when he came down from the mountain, and I think Elisha glowed from his encounter too.

I understood that once our prayers of desire have been
released, we need to let go of them and trust in the power
of God to answer them... Once we have asked with
sincere desire, doubting nothing, we will receive.
I am as I have grown to become. Bless me as I continue
to develop, to reach my fullest potential, that I may
become as you created and desire me to become.

—Betty J. Eadie, Embraced by the Light

I am humbled and honored that I have seen the Lord alive in me. And so I shall live in his light with strength from the Spirit. I will be there to light the path for all who touch my life and praise our God so that they will follow him and not me, an instrument of his peace.

January 18, 2005

As I leave my love this morning, the air is frigid, and three stars are in clear view above rolling hills of white clouds on twilight blue wallpaper. The sunrise chases me back home to Cleveland from

and mine too!

California Drive. That feels more and more like my home away from home, and I like it.

> The irony is that pride's desperate longings for real significance in this world and for real life in the next can be realized, but only through the destruction of our false pride when we come empty-handed to God's door.
>
> —*Encounter with God* (a daily Bible study guide)

This may be a repeat: *Lungo e il commina ma l'amore e forte* (Long and difficult is the walk, but love conquers all). And now that I write this, I realize it is a repeat. Oh well.

Also found written on my *March 2004* calendar:

"Joy is sometimes a blessing, but it is often a conquest."

"May my tears run just as far, that my love may never know that one day I cried for him."

"I was there because suddenly life presented me with life."

"In real life love has to be possible. Even if it is not returned right away, love can only survive where the hope exists that you will be able to win over the person you desire. Anything else is a fantasy."

February 10, 2005

And so I will complete the annulment papers that I refused to complete last summer. I will put my pride out of sight, answer all

For Pete's Sake

these annoying questions, and *celebrate my faith,* and *it* feels so right. How could I not?

Obviously, I do not write regularly, although I have been writing quotes from my reading.

For there are no words or not enough words to express the depth of the love my beloved and I have been blessed with. *We are inseparable*—all three of us.

I love him to pieces, and on and on and on.
We've shared so much, and on and on and on.
I delight in the goodness of our Lord!
And on and on and on.

Get into the habit of saying, "Speak, Lord,"
and life will become a romance.

—Oswald Chambers, *My Utmost for His Highest*

Thank you for allowing me to witness answers
to my prayers that have blessed me with greater
confidence in myself to ask for miracles.

—Betty J. Eadie, *Embraced by the Light*

I hold nothing back from my beloved. I tell him everything—what I do, how I feel, my feelings. I do not mince or sugarcoat my words; he need not read between lines.

Passionately, I listen to him and cling to his every word.

Passionately, I speak to him, knowing he, too, listens with his heart.

and mine too!

Passionately, I make love with him, wanting always to be near him, in his presence, always a part of my body making even the slightest contact with his.

April 24, 2005

> Happiness/bliss + sadness as we part = a new emotion.
> Part longing.
> Part contentment.
> Part thanksgiving.
> And I continue to pray...
> Stop smoking, stop smoking, stop smoking, stop smoking.

For as he thinketh in his heart, so is he.

—Proverbs 23:7 KJV

Their prayer came up to his holy dwelling place, even unto heaven.

—2 Chronicles 30:27 NKJV).

July 20, 2005

> Wow, haven't been writing, obviously.
> Have been loving, praying, caring, planning, loving, reading.
> I'll plan to catch up with my pen on the beach in Wildwood on thoughts and conversations, etc. I'm sure if the words need to be written, my heart will guide my pen.
> I write tonight because my beloved and I had a wonderful conversation that went like this...

Pete: So what's up?

For Pete's Sake

Me: Mmm, the wedding invitations went out today.
Pete: Yours and mine?
Me (laughing): No, Nick and Laura's. That's what I'll do, send you an invitation to your own wedding.
Pete: That's it. There ya' go.

> Then he denies saying, "Yours and mine."
> I requote him, and he laughs (such a tease).

Me (laughing): For someone who said he'd never get married again, you've been bringing it up a lot.
Pete: My ex is wearing a rock.
Me: I don't need a diamond. You are my rock. Doesn't Pietro mean rock?
Pete: Yeah.
Me (laughing): Well, there you go, and you get off easy.
Pete (laughing): Good for you, babe.

Then he said something in Italian that sort of translated into a blessing.
Amen!
I plan to stay in Allison Park starting *August 11*.

> I seek God daily and find Him in my heart. When
> God love is established in consciousness, it will draw
> to us all that we require to make us happy.
>
> —The Reverend Della Reese,
> *What Is this Thing Called Love?*

Over the past weekend, we talked about when we first met, and Pete said he remembers it all—that first night was "special," "caught

and mine too!

my eye," etc. And for the first time, he said he didn't pursue a relationship because he didn't think I'd ever leave Cleveland because of family, friends, business, etc., and he figured the closer we would get, the hurting would be harder and longer.

I'll be back. 11:30 p.m.

> At best, being a warrior gives us an opportunity to transcend the dream of the planet, and to change our personal dream to a dream that we call heaven.
>
> —Don Miguel Ruiz, *The Four Agreements*

> As we have a thought, and we love that thought, we can create that thought. As I love the thought (dream) that I conceive, and believe in it, I must receive it.

On the *rest* of the pages, I write:

Begin doing what you want to do now. We have only this moment, sparkling like a star in our hand—and melting like a snowflake.

—Marie Beynon Ray

> He offered her "living water" that had the power to cleanse her and make her whole. Somehow, Jesus gave her such an incredible thirst for God that she couldn't refuse. No one had to talked to her like that before. The amazing thing about drinking Jesus' water of life is that even as he *quenches* our thirst, he also mysteriously *increases* our thirst." (emphasis added)
>
> —*The Word Among Us*, "Lenten Series," 2/27

They mourned for Him, they prayed and wrestled and sought for Him day and night, and when they had found Him the finding was all the sweeter for the long seeking.

—W. Lozier, "Thought #9," *Waiting on the Lord*

God loves us the way we are, but He loves us too much to leave us that way.

—Leighton Ford

Snippets that fell out of this journal:

When the powers of love unite in our universe, miracles do happen.

From three fortune cookies:

- A refreshing change is in your future
- Your ideals are well within your reach
- Nothing in the world is accomplished without passion.

Go after your dreams. Allow yourself to dream big. Visualize yourself already having attained your goal, and feel the confidence flowing through you. Share your dreams with people who will encourage and support you.

"When you're on a path of the heart, everything works," says Alex.

All I want for Christmas is you!

A pretty card that says "Dreams come true."

On a random envelope, I wrote "Yes."

and mine too!

Not yet. I have something better in mind.

My astrological forecast—Capricorn (Dec. 22–Jan. 19):

> Check out facts and figures. Reach out for someone at a distance whom you really care about for a break. In the afternoon, you might want to discuss what you have discovered in your searching and questioning. Tonight: A must show.

Also, I heard the voice of the Lord, saying, Whom shall I send, and who will go for us? Then said I, here am I; send me.

—Isaiah 6:8 NIV; April 14

Now the God of hope fill you with all joy and peace in believing, that ye may abound in hope, through the power of the Holy Ghost.

—Romans 15:13 KJV; May 29

And Jesus answering saith unto them, Have faith in God.

—Mark 11:22 KJV; June 6

And he said to the woman, thy faith hath saved thee; go in peace.

—Luke 7:50 KJV; June 12

Watch ye and pray, lest ye enter into temptation.
The spirit truly is ready, but the flesh is weak.

—Mark 14:38 KJV

For Pete's Sake

The original daily prayer I wrote:

>Please let Peter be the strong man he wants to be—strong enough to humble himself and ask for his gift of grace so that he may be filled with a peace so long overdue in his life. Let him feel like a child of God who can go to his Father for anything. Let him see that I am his gift for the rest of his years on Earth till we get to heaven. Here on Earth, where we will live a life reflecting love and thanks to our everlasting Father, an example to all whose lives we touch and those who touch us.
>
>And for those we loved once, a prayer that their lives will be good and they will find our Lord on a daily basis and not feel forsaken.
>
>In the name of my Lord, Jesus Christ—Satan, begone!
>
>And all is right.
>
>Peace on earth.
>
>My dear Lord, please tell my dear Peter not to be afraid.
>
>Thank you for my gift of Peter, for he brought me closer to you, no matter what, only you are forever.

May 21, 2003

>We are home
>We are where we shall be forever
>Trust in me, for you know I won't
>Run away
>From today this is all that I need
>And all that I need to say
>Don't you know how you've changed me?
>Strange how I finally see
>I found home

and mine too!

You're my home
Stay with me
One passion, one dream
One thing forever true
I love you.

—*Beauty and the Beast* Soundtrack

September 2006

To my beloved, heart and soul
mind and body
My beloved, and so much more
Time disappears with passion.
To live in thanks.
Random connections (it's all connected)

Flying to MN from Pittsburgh, "the veil is lifted and there is light" from darkness to grayness to sheerness to warmness, so many veils in our lives.

Keep me aware.

I tell my beloved, "I wish you would go out of your way for me once in a while."

He does not hesitate in responding, "Why go out of my way when I'm right here?"

My ego asked.

My God answered.

And I am in awe.

March 3, 2010

Recopying random words I've saved.

When I began writing, the words that inspired me were these:

> A writer is someone who has written today. If you want to be a writer, what's stopping you?
>
> —J. A. Jance

> Which choice would set me free? Words, once they are printed have a life of their own.
>
> —Carol Bronuff

> Dreams are illustrations…from the book your soul is writing about you.
>
> —Marsha Norman

> Your novel lies in your heart; it is a book about today—a story that could only have come from you.
>
> —*Ode Magazine*, 8/2007

January 17, 2011

Me + my laptop + my words = this is where I should be (and I cry, my face in my hands).

This portion of my words could be titled "The Ego that Stayed too Long" or "The Ego that Got in the Way."

January 22, 2011

My Angela is thirty-two.

As I continue on the laptop, I realize and physically feel the burden of ego.

I am transcribing "*June 24, 2004*," and I am crying. This is my journey.

and mine too!

On "*July 7, 2004,*" I wrote we are blessed with the presence of my parents.[6] Sobbing, I sit back from the laptop and cry some more.

January 30, 2011

In my journal from *July 9, 2004*—"Where is he?"
Right downstairs. Wow.

February 5, 2014

So I've been angsty and quick to ire for a while now, maybe since our trip to Italy in October or after my trip to Chicago, which was right after the trip to Italy.

I still like going to work and the work itself.

I do not enjoy the routine of home—what is expected of me, cooking, cleaning, laundry. It's not that time-consuming, but it's always there.

Technically, I've been married twenty-seven years plus the two years with Pete, "living in sin."

So what's the beef?

Saw a YouTube video about the baby who lived ten days and how he touched so many in such a short period of time.

So what's my beef?

Thank God for my kids and grandkids. They bring joy, give me something to look forward to, and lift my energy level and spirits.

Maybe I fear (too strong a word?) the idle times.

Sure, I could be washing shears and walls and vacuuming furniture, etc., the classic "spring cleaning" at home, but then what?

---

[6] Mom said that so much, especially after Dad died. It became kind of an annoyance.

For Pete's Sake

I don't want to sit and wait for life to come to me, but Pete does not feel the same.

Heading for Florida for one and a half weeks. Do you believe it? He's retired and says one and a half weeks, and he doesn't want to go.

He scoffs at going out to eat. *He* does not like to.

He scoffs at going to the movies. *He* does not like to ("I pay for cable.").

Likes my new recipe for pasta fagioli once; now *he* doesn't like it.

He answers a question with a question, every time.

I get interrogated. *He* doesn't have to answer to me.

The double standard. He doesn't want to see it.

He does take care of my car and gave me garage space this year.

He stacks breakfast, lunch, and dinner dishes in the sink.

He does clean up after he makes bread and uses the meat slicer.

He occasionally will help clear the table.

He sits and watches TV when all the kids and grandkids come over for whatever.

He'll go to Lowe's, Home Depot, Trader Horns, but doesn't call it shopping.

He cannot give a compliment, and every question sounds like an accusation, putting me and everyone else on the defense. Nothing happy can come from that.

So where did the bliss go? Is daily life on earth supposed to shroud our bliss so we keep looking for it?

No, I think bliss is ever-present. My ego is doing a stupendous job of denying it. For bliss and ego are not of the same ilk.

In an envelope I addressed to Mr. Peter Tucciarone (in my handwriting): "Dreaming Italy" cut out of a magazine.

and mine too!

A small piece of paper that reads "Many waters cannot quench love, neither can floods drown it" (Song of Solomon 8:7 ESV).

Real love is a pilgrimage. It happens when there is no strategy but is very rare because most people are strategists.

—Anonymous

So, fall asleep love, loved by me…for I
know love, I am loved by thee.

—Robert Browning

Love is an irresistible desire to be desired irresistibly.

—Robert Frost

The photo of the three roses the angel brought to me at the moving sale. Written on the back "Three roses, my Trinity."

Another small piece of paper: "Great love involved great risk."
Love deep and passionately. You might get hurt, but it's the only way to live life completely.

Pete showed me two notes I had mailed to him before *August, 2004*. On a piece of stationery, I wrote:

Dear Peter,

I hope things are well with you. I moved back in October. My new phone #440-734-0028. Cell phone #440-655-3454 the same.

For Pete's Sake

Take care of yourself.
I think of you often!

Maria

Dear Peter,

After reading this over and over and over again, I could not not send this to you.

Boldly, bravely, and always,
M

This second note included pages 39–49 that I gently tore from *Enchanted Love* (Marianne Williamson) titled "Of Space Captains and Angels."

Pete and I were together every day and almost every night between three hospitals over two months. I told my beloved I felt that I had let God down and him down.
He responded, "No, Maria, I let you down."
He died, February 10, 2019.
I buried him with a huge part of my heart on February 14.

and mine too!

May 2020

Started to keep a mini-diary as I transcribed my diaries.

I am the product of many other lives, and to deny this would be to deny my bond with the eternal, immeasurable connections that fill me with a sense of meaning, responsibility, and destiny.

—G. Beck and K. Ablow, *The Seven Wonders that will Change Your Life*

May 12, 2020

The story of me because of the story of Pete.
Crying with my journal.
"Come back!" (out loud)
Sobbing.
Nowhere to turn for comfort
Except into myself
It used to work like that.
Into myself, my God
He doesn't stop my tears.
They must be shed
and shed,
and shed,
and shed,
oh, Honey,
and shed.
Tears of loss,
Blessings,
Love,
Sadness.
Tears floating on my readers.

My laptop is ready for the completion of my journals.
I embrace his photo to my heart.

For Pete's Sake

I want to do it all over again.
He'll never know these words.
It seems like yesterday that I wrote this.
Stinging cheeks.

New title—A Heart on a Sleeve? My Heart on My Sleeve?

- And we lose the house part of my diary—I still cry over it.
- Now the paragraph about Mom. I can barely see the screen. I never gave her enough credit, and I apologize out loud.
- Dad.
- The paragraph ended, "How God like they are."
- Sobs.
- (Reading from *Nov. 2002*)

"I long for his voice and laughter, and touch, and his lips."
Longest cry yet.

For where your treasure is, there also will be your heart.

—Luke 12:34 NIV

A heart has its reasons that reason knows not.

—Blaise Pascal

July 19, 2020

Finally, a good cry, a sobbing cry.
I've missed him.
"Where have you been? Where have you been?"

July 21, 2020

Tonight's tears brought to you by…
"I want the tall quiet man." (2003)

July 27, 2020

"He is Peter."
I now write this, and feel this as his widow!
"Let him speak"
Now I cry as his widow some more. Feeling drained again like most other nights as I copy my pages.

July 30, 2020

In transcribing my journals, I realize I wasn't just in love with Pete. I kept falling more and more in love with him with each page.

August 4, 2020

Thought of a new title: Cry Baby—funny.
When my beloved and I are together again in heaven there will be *The Applause of Heaven* (Max Lucado).

August 9, 2020

Pete: Maria, look what you can do now.
Me: But I love you most! (*October 29, 2020 tears again*)

August 11, 2020

The Three of Us—new title?

August 12, 2020

"The rest of my life waiting for heaven?"

Now as a widow in love!

August 13, 2020

Home front?
Stay the course.

August 14, 2020

I only notice the deep silence when I totally stop thinking.

August 15, 2020

Saving my journals keeps me close to my beloved.
He's less gone.

August 18, 2020

Delight yourself in the Lord, and he will
give you the desires of your heart.

—Psalm 37:4 ESV

Remember when it was you and Peter, Lord?
Kids (July 31).

Rather than scolding yourself for your humanness, remind
yourself that I am both with you and within you.

—Sarah Young, *Jesus Calling*.

and mine too!

September 3, 2020

Now as his widow I read from my...
Journal *June 27, 2003*: I think of Peter every day, but it feels like he is becoming a memory.

September 5, 2020

As I reread *September 12, 2003 – September 23, 2003*.
I can only believe.
I have to stop, because I can't stop, crying.

September 20, 2020

Tears and crippled words.
My beloved's funeral. I didn't know it would hurt so much.
I cried today about Italy. Two years ago, we were there together. I miss there.
I will never forget that morning when Pete died, when his brother Mario called me from Italy. He cried in Italian and I cried in English. And this memory usually brings me to tears.

September 30, 2020

Title? When the Triangle (drawn) Becomes Our Circle of Love.
My knight in rusted armor. I coined this phrase after reading from *February 5, 2014*.

October 2, 2020

Crying again—a lot.
My heart.

> Only one thing will bear the strain, and that is a personal relationship with Jesus Christ Himself, a relationship that has to be examined, purified, and tested until only one purpose remains. I can truly say, "I am here for God to send me where He will."
>
> —Oswald Chambers, *My Utmost for His Highest*

I put the Kleenex box on the desk.
And I fell in love with Jesus too.
This is like reading a wonderful book you don't want to put down.
Will I miss this time?
Oh yes!

October 20, 2020

I realized I cried more than I remembered.
As I cry now.

October 23, 2020

Summer was beautiful. The fall has been outstanding. The trees are on fire with color. It's like they're competing for top prize. In all my memory, I've never seen such beautiful panoramas! Amen to our Creator.

This week, two customers who became dear friends told me I looked wonderful; I feel changed too. Without trying to sound smug, I feel I've moved up another level on the celestial plane, whatever that may be. Thank you to our Creator.

October 24, 2020, 6:30 a.m.

I penned the dedication to my book:

and mine too!

To my beloved, who unknowingly reintroduced me to God, the Father, Son, and Holy Spirit.

"For your relationship has not been disrupted. It has been saved"(from *A Course in Miracles*).
Oh my (sobbing).
This stands true for today.
Passion
I fall apart again and some more as I read *July 26, 2004*.
My beloved, a man of few words!
Just to See Her (Smokey Robinson, *My World [The Definitive Collection]*) is playing.
August 4, 2004 – He called me.
August 4, *Grace for the Moment* (Lucado) You have captured God's heart.
Heaven on earth. I'm a wreck. Read a few pages ahead—tears and tears. Typing brings more tears over the same words.
I don't want to feel any other way.
Can we do it again, Honey?
Three of his photos surround me in the office.
I don't want to go to bed. I haven't cried myself to sleep in quite a while.
Those damn tears that still don't have a name.
My chest and heart hurts.
You are My Special Angel (Vogues)
"Through eternity"—but, Honey…
It's 12:47; still crying.
I want to hold this book in my arms tonight. And I shall.

> Perhaps, indeed, the better gift we pray for, the more time is necessary for its arrival. To give us the spiritual gift we desire, God may have to begin far back in our spirit, in regions unknown to us, and do much work that we can be aware of only in results.
>
> — C. S. Lewis, *Why We Must Wait*

October 25, 2020

Today I am crying and typing the words I read last night when I was crying.

This reminds me of how I felt when he died; such the heart-wrenching depths that I loved him *(choked up again)*. And, obviously, I still do. I wasn't done.

Still crying.

I want to talk to my mom.

And we will dance.

I wonder if he ever cried.

This aloneness, as I transcribe my journals, is like writing these words eighteen years ago.

I'm re-reading, re-living *August 16* and *21, 2004* and the Kleenex is piling up.

It Must Be Him (Vikki Carr, *The Best of Vikki Carr*) is playing from my playlist.

I don't want to write the word *cry* again.

I clutch his picture and clench my teeth. Such drama.

He left me. Then I kissed him.

I can't put the picture down (the one from Enrico's wedding). He's so handsome.

How can I?

Such a moment. Such a long moment.

You left me *(sighing and tearing)*.

I set the picture down.

He's not becoming a memory!

My tears are back as I reread *August 29, 2004* from Yosemite.

If You Could Read My Mind by Gordon Lightfoot plays.

and mine too!

You've Made Me So Very Happy by Blood, Sweat & Tears.

Still *October 25, 2020*. After a few hours away from this, I'm back at transcribing, choking up, and crying.

He left me alone.

September 21, 2004—I'm living the dream.

He left me alone.

Now tears for my parents.

Three hours later, I decide to call it a night. It's like reading a book you can't put down.

I don't want to cry myself to sleep again.

I'm in mourning, yet thankful.

Pietro Tucciarone
1946–2019
My Beloved
2002–

It's not even a sad story.

October 26, 2020

And I Love You So by Perry Como.

October 28, 2020

Still transcribing.
Still crying.
I'm getting close to finishing this and am crying at the thought of it—Ooh, sweetie.

For Pete's Sake

He was my echo. Everything I do is quieter now.

—Fredrik Backman, *Anxious People*

That's the power of literature, you know, it can act like little love letters between people who can only explain their feelings by pointing at other people's.

—Fredrik Backman, *Anxious People*

I just finished rereading *Our Lady of the Lost and Found* by Diane Schoemperlen.
Lots of dog-eared pages.
For example:

"I've always known that writing is an act of faith, the one which has always been my own salvation."

"Time like beauty, is in the eye of the beholder."

"In the act of looking back, the past is inevitably colored by everything that has happened between then and now."

"Times change, Mary said. Or should I say: Time changes how we look at things."

and mine too!

This is not irony so much as grace, that in learning to be faithful to his vow of celibacy, the monk developed his talent for relationship.

—Kathleen Norris, *The Cloister Walk*

November 20, 2020

Started to "proofread" my printed diaries.
I cry over the words and pages again. I am somewhat surprised and very overcome, again.

November 23, 2020

He is my heaven still.
I wish I could draw emojis!

November 24, 2020

If not for my Fitzy's close by, I would not have love in Pittsburgh.
I love my friends here, and they love me. Yet, it's not the love that you can cling to and reach out to and hug and count on, on a daily basis.

November 27, 2020

Opened the lease agreement a few hours ago.
I feel I've lost part of my will, not my will to live, just something. Maybe it's just the wind sucked out of my sails or whatever the hell that saying is.
Crying yet not quite hyperventilating…trying to take deep breaths to keep the sails up.
Is Jesus crying with me like he did in *2002*? My constant companion.
I don't want to cry myself to sleep.
I know it's not over. The tears are from my disheartened heart!

November 29, 2020

    Proofreading some of my book up to page 92 today.
    Tears ebb and flow.
    Page 113, *Of Space Captains and Angels* brings me to tears every time (from *Enchanted Love*, Marianne Williamson).

December 1, 2020

    So loving is like being a Eucharistic minister. I get more out of giving then receiving.
    Tears of loneliness? Or holiness?

December 2, 2020

    Tears still ebbing and flowing as another sixty-five count tissue box gets emptied.
    The Alchemist (Paulo Coelho) portion of my journals.

December 4, 2020

    "My God."
    "I know." he replies.
    Yes, crying.
    I wish he would have treated me/us a little better. I should assume he was doing the best he could, but then again, not.

All the following words were penned in 2021

January 23, 2021

    New book title: *For Pete's Sake (And Mine Too)*

and mine too!

January 24, 2021 (traveling to Cleveland for a funeral)

This weekend, I realized that the night I met Pete, the first thing he spoke was, "Do you want to dance?"

And if you know me, what could be more perfect?

His first touch was his hand on my waist on the crowded dance floor. For the past year or so, I have physically felt his large hand resting on my waist, comforting and reassuring. He misses me.

I like being aware of how much I miss him. It brings him closer. Sounds odd, I know.

In the similar fashion of my two and a half years of roundtrip drives between Cleveland and Pittsburgh, I cry. It doesn't help that I play Italian songs from my playlist.

January 26, 2021

> Lady, I have had a feeling of compulsion
> to tell my own story once again.
> I do not know what it was laid on my heart to tell it right now.
> I do not need to know.
> Nor do I need to offer any apology for doing so, for
> did not Christ say, "Go home and tell thy friends
> what great things the Lord hath done for thee."

In my story, Peter Marshall is not glorified, but the Lord.

—Catherine Marshall, *Mr. Jones, Meet the Master*

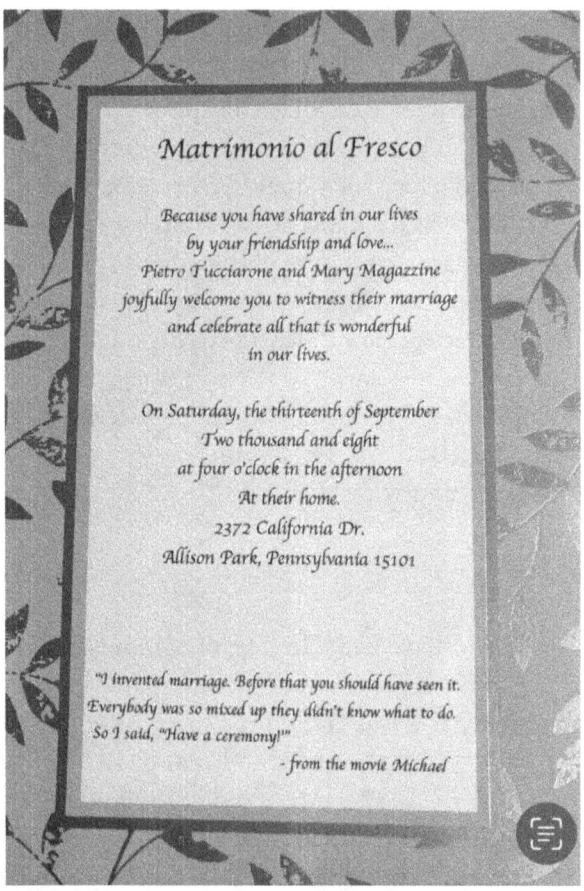

and mine too!

Should I write off our Wedding Day, *September 13, 2008*. One hundred and twenty-five beautiful friends and family blessed us with their presence, in our lovely backyard, under the chestnut tree, the one with the two trunks shaped like a heart.

Should I write of my "heart attack?"

Should I write of our sixty-six days in the hospitals?

Should I write of his death and funeral?

I miss all the Italian in my life:

- My Italian husband.
- Italian conversations and my pretty good attempts at it.
- Our weeks-long trips to our apartment in Italy with all that was wonderful.
- Our friends stopping over per café e dolce.
- Sunday morning cappuccinos down in the Strip District followed by groceries from Pennsylvania Macaroni Co.
- Shuffleboard Friday nights at the Spigno Club that overflowed with Italian.

Marina di Minturno, Italy 2017

Perugia, Italy 2018

View of the Mar Tirreno from our apartment in Tufo di Minturno, Italy

and mine too!

February 1, 2021

Do you like when I passionately miss you?
I'm having "writer's block" on what to do with the last portion of my journals. It's choppy.

February 5, 2021

The elusive cardinal arrived, singing. I heard him before I saw him, so red and bold and strong, perched in our back forty!
Just you!

February 16, 2021

Less than two weeks later, I'm still tweaking my book the best that I can. *Midsummer 2002*, I read "And so often, I feel his hand resting on my waist. Is it for support? Reassurance? Comfort? Hope? Desire? Yes, yes, yes, yes, and yes."
He has me waiting for him again!
A miracle.
A message.
A gift.
Overwhelmed and crying and with an exploding heart.
Another miracle.
Another message.
Another gift.
Reading through *For Pete's Sake* again.
It's been two years since he was buried

We all carry burdens. Perception is key. Last night, the words and thoughts came for me so I could verbalize it.
When family and friends ask how I do it (facing all the snags/crap through my life) so well, my confident go-to response is by the grace of God.

My burdens have become less burdensome because Jesus helps me always. He's been through it all with me like he said he would. It is his yoke. He is so strong.

February 27, 2021

I love missing him.

March 21, 2021

Another good sob.

March 22, 2021

He's not here again.

March 24, 2021

I recognize my tears. They're the ones I couldn't name throughout my journals.

March 28, 2021

In the margin of *My Utmost for His Highest* (Oswald Chambers), on this date, I write in the margin "*Write the book!*"

May 2, 2021

> But death is given no power over love. Love is stronger. It creates something new out of destruction caused by death; it bears everything and overcomes everything.
>
> —Paul Tillich

and mine too!

July 31, 2021

> Rather than scolding yourself for your humanness, remind yourself that I am both with you and within you.
>
> —Sarah Young, *Jesus Calling*

August 12, 2021

So while I'm in my heart, it all makes sense:
January 2002—God gets my attention with the tall Italian guy.
May 2002—God removes the object of my attention.
May 2002–August 2004—I get closer to God while loving Pete.
I have been a good servant and child, so God grants me the deepest desires of my heart.
August 4, 2004, Pete calls.
I live my love with and for Pete.
February 10, 2019, God removes the object of my attention and affection.
From this day forward, I get closer to God while missing Pete.
The end.
The beginning.

Living Pages

Let me leave margins of silence
around the activities of day,
letting You write down there
whatever it is You would say.
Then looking backward, I find,
no matter how much I revise,
it is in your footnotes
that the heart of my life lies.

—Elizabeth Searle Lamb

For Pete's Sake

October 2, 2021

Revised title: *For Pete's Sake (And the Heart on My Sleeve)*

October 4, 2021

Sitting down to tweak the end of my love story. But there is no end to love. Thank goodness.

In reading just the last two pages, I once again cry, immediately.

Find your delight in the Lord who will give you your heart's desire.

—Psalm 37:4 NAB

God brings us into particular circumstances to
educate our faith, because the nature of faith is to
make the object of our faith very real to us.

—Oswald Chambers, *My Utmost
for His Highest*, October 30

She learned to be comfortable in her own company.

—Matthew Kelly, *Resisting Happiness*

January 22, 2022

My heart on my sleeve, wet with tears again.

My journal is now in book format. I began to edit the publisher's first edit.

February 21, 2022

Wendy said we cry because it is so special. And this is so very, very special.

March 26, 2022

Thank you for the love and loss of Pete Tucciarone.

March 27, 2022

I face each problem with a prayerful heart and willingness to grow.

— Betty J. Eadie, *Embraced by the Light Devotional*

Keep believing.
"Am I my brother's keeper?" (Genesis 4:9 NAB).
I can be, by my prayers for the world.

March 28, 2022

He is having mercy on us!

March 30, 2022

God has given me more than a family.
I do not feel worthy today.
I feel very, very shallow.

March 31, 2022

>The world is a mess, but
>the world is still His.

April 1, 2022

>We ask too much.
>God: Keep asking.

April 2, 2022

>I know the Lord is doing a work in me.
>I do not know the depths of His work in me!

April 4, 2022

>Lord, Your presence brings all in my thoughts back to You.

April 7, 2022

>We are where we are because of His mercy on us, individually and universally.
>I must be worthy because You keep asking…

April 8, 2022

>So if I will do whatever God asks me to do but I don't "hear" His requests…
>Our relationship must be in a very good place. He abides in me by His grace.
>Amen for faith.
>
>My human mind minds that I cannot stay in the mind of my heart when I pray.

and mine too!

Lord, I need more of you to follow you!

April 9, 2022

Does God not want to share me again?
He took Pete out of my life twice, and all I was left with was Him.
By His grace, go I.
And God says, "Ssshh."

April 10, 2022

> The aroma of Christ to God among those who are being saved and among those who are perishing.
>
> —2 Corinthians 2:15 ESV

> My spirit truly thrills to the fragrance of your spirit and to the life you created for me.
>
> —Betty J. Eadie, *Embraced by the Light Devotional*

So for over a month, I have sensed a scent randomly. It's a little musky, a little woody, a little espresso, a little bitter, and a little sweet. Is this my new God rush?

God: You will have no questions because our hearts are one.

April 11, 2022

So I asked the cardinal this morning out loud: "What are you going to do with me?"

April 13, 2022

Could We Start Again, Please?
from *Jesus Christ Superstar* (Andrew Lloyd Webber and Tim Rice)

April 14, 2022

He loved my humanness!

April 15, 2022

Faith.

April 16, 2022

God, aren't you tired of being sad?

April 17, 2022

Trust in Jesus. He knows you won't do it perfectly, but do it faithfully and he will answer you.

—Joshua Cooley, *The One Year Devotions with Jesus*

So while doing the Divine Mercy Chaplet during Lent, I wrote down many of my thoughts. I had a lot of thoughts. I was frustrated that I struggled with staying focused on the Chaplet. My thoughts seem like gifts now, given by God to reward my good intentions. Thank you!

April 23, 2022

> Let the children know of heroes.
>
> —C. S. Lewis, *The Business of Heaven*

Me: I'm feeling lonely.
God: I know.
Me: I'm not the only one feeling lonely.
God: You're all that matters.

April 24, 2022

    I adopted Lou into my heart. Within minutes and without hesitation, his whole family too. This was followed by those special tears. Thank you.

June 13, 2022

    Mystery is God's story.

June 15, 2022

    Love consists not in feeling that we love, but in wanting to love.

> —René Voillaume

March 4, 2023

    Reflecting. We were good together.

The Bible is the only book where the author is in love with the reader.

Some of the Bible quotes I used are as varied as the authors and books I read them in. For others, I was guided to my own Bible (NAB) from daily devotionals and other sources.

For your reference:

- AMP (The Amplified Bible)
- CEV (Contemporary English Version)
- GWT (God's Word Translation)
- KJV (King James Version)
- MSG (The Message)
- NAB (New American Bible)
- NASB (New American Standard Bible)
- NCV (New Century Version)
- NIV (New International Version)
- NLT (New Living Translation)
- NRSV (New Revised Standard Version)
- BSB (Berean Standard Bible)
- TEV (Today's English Version)

For Pete's Sake

**Here are the other books; in
the order they appear...**

_____	Siddhartha	Herman Hesse
_____	The Rhythm of Life	Matthew Kelly
_____	The Book of Jabez Devotional	Bruce Wilkinson
_____	The Prophet	Kahlil Gibran
_____	The Screwtape Letters	C. S. Lewis
_____	The Gift for All People	Max Lucado
_____	Grace for the Moment	Max Lucado
_____	He Still Moves Stones	Max Lucado
_____	A Gentle Thunder	Max Lucado
_____	In the Grip of Grace	Max Lucado
_____	Lift Up Your Heart	Fulton J. Sheen
_____	The Hymn of the Conquered	Fulton J. Sheen
_____	The Power of a Praying Woman	Stormie Omartian
_____	God Hunger	John Kirvan
_____	Everyday Grace	Marianne Williamson
_____	The Applause of Heaven	Max Lucado
_____	Praying God's Will for Your Life	Stormie Omartian
_____	Just Like Jesus	Max Lucado
_____	Enchanted Love	Marianne Williamson
_____	The Cloud of Unknowing	
_____	Silent Hope	John Kirvan
_____	Illuminata	Marianne Williamson
_____	When God Shows Up	R. T. Kendall
_____	A Woman's Worth	Marianne Williamson
_____	Heart of the Soul	Gary Zukav
_____	Anam Cara: A Book of Celtic Wisdom	John O'Donohue
_____	The Luminous Mind Workshop (audio)	Marianne Williamson
_____	Prayer: A Radical Response to Life	Matthew Fox
_____	Raw Faith	John Kirvan
_____	The Springs of Contemplation	Thomas Merton
_____	The Great House of God	Max Lucado
_____	How Much Joy Can You Stand?	Suzanne Falter-Barns
_____	C. S. Lewis Explores Vice and Virtue	Gerard A. Reed

and mine too!

_____	On Faith	C. S. Lewis
_____	That's What Love is For	Stormie Omartian
_____	A Course in Miracles	
_____	The Four Loves	C. S. Lewis
_____	The Pilgrim's Regress	C. S. Lewis
_____	Bread in the Wilderness	Thomas Merton
_____	No Man is an Island	Thomas Merton
_____	A Return to Love	Marianne Williamson
_____	The Color of Grace: Thoughts from Garden in a Dry Land	Tonia Triebwasser
_____	Traveling Light	Max Lucado
_____	What's Going on Lord?	Thelma Wells
_____	The Joyful Christian	C. S. Lewis
_____	Education of the Heart	Thomas Moore
_____	Deep & Simple	Bo Lozoff
_____	My Utmost for His Highest	Oswald Chambers
_____	Mere Christianity	C. S. Lewis
_____	God Came Near	Max Lucado
_____	What a Man Thinketh	James Allen
_____	No Wonder They Call Him the Savior	Max Lucado
_____	Warrior of the Light	Paulo Coelho
_____	The Alchemist	Paulo Coelho
_____	Tea Time with God	
_____	The Purpose Driven Life	Rick Warren
_____	The Business of Heaven	C. S. Lewis
_____	The Dark Knight of the Soul: A Sacred Journey to Joy and Enlightenment (audio)	Ron Roth
_____	Conversations with God (audio)	Neale Donald Walsch
_____	The Gentle Art of Blessing	Pierre Pradervand
_____	Our Lady of the Lost and Found	Diane Schoemperlen
_____	Bedside Prayers	Elizabeth Searle Lamb
_____	Embraced by the Light	Betty J. Eadie
	Yoga, Mind, Body, & Spirit:	
_____	A Return to Wholeness	Donna Farhi
_____	Yoga of the Heart	Alice Christensen

For Pete's Sake

_____	When God Whispers Your Name	Max Lucado
_____	The Mentor's Spirit: Life Lessons on Leadership and the Art of Encouragement	Marsha Sinetar
_____	What Is This Thing Called Love?	Della Reese
_____	The Four Agreements: A Practical Guide to Personal Freedom	Don Miguel Ruiz
_____	The Seven Wonders That Will Change Your Life	Glen Beck & Dr. Keith Ablow
_____	Anxious People	Fredrik Backman
_____	Mr. Jones Meet the Master!	Peter Marshall
_____	Jesus Calling	Sarah Young
_____	Resisting Happiness	Matthew Kelly
_____	Embraced by the Light Devotional	Betty J. Eadie
_____	The One Year Devotions With Jesus	Joshua Cooley

MY SOUNDTRACK

"Quando Quando Quando"	Engelbert Humperdinck	*Engelbert Humperdinck 50*
"It Must be Him"	Vikki Carr	*The Best of Vikki Carr*
"Return to Me"	Dean Martin	*The Capitol Years*
"Brand New Me"	Dusty Springfield	*A Brand New Me*
"You'll Never Find Another Love Like Mine"	Lou Rawls	*All Things in Time*
"Two Less Lonely People in the World"	Air Supply	*Playlist: The Very Best of Air Supply*
"My Love"	Petula Clark	*The PYE Anthology*
"Strangers in the Night"	Frank Sinatra	*Ultimate Sinatra*
"The River Is Wide"	The Grass Roots	*The Best of the Grass Roots, The Millennium Collection*
"Non Dimenticar" (Don't Forget)	Dean Martin	*Italian Love Songs*
"Tu Sel La Mia Vita"	We Three	*Con Amore*
"Il Mondo" (My World)	Patrizio Buanne	*The Italian*
"I Could Be Happy with You"	West End Orchestra and Singers	*The Boyfriend Soundtrack*
"(Your Love Has Lifted Me) Higher and Higher"	Rita Coolidge	*The Best of Rita Coolidge, The Millennium Collection*
"Swearin' to God"	Frankie Valli and the Four Seasons	*The Very Best of Frankie Valli and the Four Seasons*

"Someday We'll Be Together"	Diana Ross and the Supremes	*The Best of Diana Ross and the Supremes, The Millennium Collection*
"I Believe You"	Carpenters	*The Singles: 1969–1981*
"Let It Be Me"	Petula Clark	*Don't Sleep in the Subway—Her Greatest Hits*
"Happy Heart"	Petula Clark	*Don't Sleep in the Subway—Her Greatest Hits*
"Show and Tell"	Al Wilson	*Show and Tell: The Best of Al Wilson*
"Just to See Her"	Smokey Robinson	*My World (The Definitive Collection)*
"You'll Be in My Heart"	Phil Collins	*Tarzan (Original Motion Picture Soundtrack)*
"Now and Forever"	Carole King	*The Living Room Tour*
"Two Hearts"	Phil Collins	*The Singles*
"The Long and Winding Road"	The Beatles	*The Beatles 1967–1970*
"Hello"	Lionel Richie	*Can't Slow Down*
"He Couldn't Love You More"	Plácido Domingo	*Perhaps Love*
"Pieces of April"	Three Dog Night	*Three Dog Night*
"Kissing a Fool"	George Michael	*Ladies and Gentlemen: The Best of George Michael*
"You Go to My Head"	Rod Stewart	*The Best Of… The Great American Songbook*
"My Treasure"	Plácido Domingo	*Perhaps Love*
"It Had to Be You"	Frank Sinatra	*Ultimate Sinatra*
"The Very Thought of You"	Rod Stewart	*The Best Of… The Great American Songbook*
"Perhaps Love"	John Denver and Plácido Domingo	*Perhaps Love*

and mine too!

"You Don't Have to Be a Star (To Be in My Show)"	Marilyn McCoo and Billy Davis Jr.	*I Hope We Get to Love in Time*
"Immortality"	Bee Gees	*Their Greatest Hits: The Record*
"Just for You" (featuring Billy Currington)	Lionel Richie	*Tuskegee*
"Heat Wave"	Linda Ronstadt	*Linda Ronstadt Greatest Hits*
"Someone to Watch over Me"	Sheena Easton	*No Strings*
"Then He Kissed Me"	The Crystals	*Da Doo Ron Ron: The Very Best of the Crystals*
"Hold on My Heart"	Genesis	*Turn It On Again: The Hits*
"Calling All Angels"	Train	*My Private Nation*
"A Sign of the Times"	Petula Clark	*Don't Sleep in the Subway—Her Greatest Hits*
"Heaven"	Los Lonely Boys	*Los Lonely Boys*
"I Have Nothing"	Whitney Houston	*The Bodyguard: Original Soundtrack Album*
"Taking You Home"	Don Henley	*Inside Job*
"If You Could Read My Mind"	Gordon Lightfoot	*If You Could Read My Mind*
"You've Made Me So Very Happy"	Blood, Sweat & Tears	*Blood, Sweat & Tears Greatest Hits*
"And I Love You So"	Perry Como	*The Very Best of Perry Como*
The Best of My Love	Eagles	*On the Border*

ABOUT THE AUTHOR

Mary Tucciarone has three children and nine grandchildren. When she and Pete reunited, the word *blended* became obsolete as their families happily joined, shared, and grew in so many ways together. The total of their fourteen grandchildren were born during their years together. She resides in Pittsburgh, Pennsylvania, and is currently dabbling in semiretirement.

Printed in the USA
CPSIA information can be obtained
at www.ICGtesting.com
LVHW021753091124
795855LV00002B/3